Prizewinning Political Cartoons

Prizewinning Political Cartoons

2010 EDITION

Edited by Dean P. Turnbloom
Original illustrations by Lucas P. Turnbloom
Foreword by Steve Breen

PELICAN PUBLISHING COMPANY
GRETNA 2010

Copyright © 2010
By Dean P. Turnbloom
All rights reserved

*The word "Pelican" and the depiction of a pelican
are trademarks of Pelican Publishing Company, Inc.,
and are registered in the U.S. Patent and Trademark Office.*

ISBN: 9781589808294

Printed in Korea
Published by Pelican Publishing Company, Inc.
1000 Burmaster Street, Gretna, Louisiana 70053

Contents

Foreword 7
Acknowldgments 8
Introduction 9
The Pulitzer Prize 11
    Steve Breen 12
    Matt Wuerker 34
    Mike Thompson 54
The National Headliner Awards 67
    Steve Breen 68
    Don Asmussen 73
    Clay Bennett 76
Society of Professional Journalists' Sigma Delta Chi Award 87
    Chris Britt 88
The Overseas Press Club's Thomas Nast Award 95
    Steve Breen 96
    Kevin Kallaugher 105
The Scripps Howard National Journalism Award 112
    Mike Luckovich 113
    Don Asmussen 126
    Alexander Hunter 133
The National Cartoonist Society's Reuben Award 144
    Michael Ramirez 145
Robert F. Kennedy Journalism Award 167
    Jack Ohman 168
The John Fischetti Editorial Cartoon Competition Award 183
    Lee Judge 184
    Mike Luckovich 187
    Michael Ramirez 189

The National Press Foundation's Clifford K. and James T.
    Berryman Award 191
    Nate Beeler 192
The Herblock Prize 199
    Pat Bagley 200
The Ranan Lurie Political Cartoon Award 219
    Michael Kountouris 220
    Valeriu Kurtu 222
Index 224

Foreword

"Sic transit gloria mundi." ("Thus passes the glory of the world.")

I begin this introduction with that saying for two reasons. First, quoting an old Latin phrase always makes you sound smart. Second, when you're talking about awards, you couldn't find more appropriate words. Don't get me wrong, I'm extremely proud of the accolades I picked up this year, but you have to keep things in perspective. For one thing, there's a little bit of luck involved. Shhh! Don't tell anyone that came from me. Winners aren't supposed to acknowledge luck or divine intervention.

Plus, the more you let yourself get caught up in the praise and fanfare that awards bring ("I won? I'm awesome!"), the bigger the frustration the years you don't get anything. ("I lost? I'm a loser.") That's no way to go through life. Besides, how can any journalist think he's a loser when he has the greatest job in the world?

And then there's the reaction of others when you win something: your peers instantly despise you, your readers automatically expect more from you, and your friends are looking for reasons to start calling you a diva. ("I guess Mr. Pulitzer winner feels he's too important to return my phone call right away.") Only our families truly care . . . sorta. I mean, I showed my two-year-old daughter the Overseas Press Club Thomas Nast Award certificate, and I got no reaction. No pat on the back, no smile, nada. Just a blank stare. That's rough on the ego.

Still, despite all this, I'm sure I'll keep entering these contests. Why? Because editorial cartoonists are artists as well as journalists, and everyone knows that artists are insecure, attention-starved adolescents. (In my case I think it's because I wasn't held enough as an infant.) Anyway, I know that even though prizes ultimately don't mean anything and bring unexpected headaches, I'll still seek the validation and temporary glow of glory they provide. It's a paradox, I realize. Cartoonists are complex creatures, what can I say? Well, I'd better get going. I'm off to the post office to mail my entry for the "2010 Best Forward for a Book about Cartooning Awards Award." Wish me luck.

Steve Breen

Acknowledgments

First and always, I want to thank my wife, Nanette. More than anyone else, she has supported, encouraged, and made it possible for me to put this book together. She has spent endless nights watching as I obsessed over unanswered e-mails, late submissions, format errors, and lost files. Through it all, she has put up with a sometimes cantankerous and often sullen son of a gun, maintaining her own sanity and helping me maintain mine. She has my deepest gratitude and undying love. Thank you, Nanette.

Next, I want to correct a grievous error from my last book. My son is a wonderful artist, illustrator, cartoonist (syndicated through Universal/Uclick), and caricaturist; his original artwork graces the cover and interior pages of my first edition as well as this one. I owe much of the look of both books to his incredible talent. The grievous error was that I failed to acknowledge him. I apologize most vociferously for that error. I would have been at a great loss without his assistance. And he has never let me forget it. Just kidding; he was wonderfully good-humored about it, but I am grateful to have this chance to set the record straight.

I also want to thank each of the cartoonists who were so generous in allowing me to use their work for this book, in the order of their appearance in the book: Steve Breen, Matt Wuerker, Mike Thompson, Don Asmussen, Clay Bennett, Chris Britt, Kevin Kallaugher (KAL), Mike Luckovich, Alexander Hunter, Michael Ramirez, Jack Ohman, Lee Judge, Nate Beeler, Pat Bagley, Michael Kountouris, and Valeriu Kurtu. Without their generosity, talent, and good grace, I would have had nothing to celebrate with this book.

A special thanks to Sue Porter, vice president of programs, Scripps Howard Foundation; Marianne Sugawara of Creators Syndicate; Daryl Cagle, Cari Dawson Barkley, and Brian Davis of Cagle Cartoons, Inc.; and Doug Weaver of the *Kansas City Star* for their special assistance.

And once again, a special thanks to Ranan Lurie, whose early encouragement and kind words made me think this work might have some potential after all. His continued support and encouragement during the production of this second edition is sincerely appreciated. I count him as a friend.

Last, but certainly not least, I want to thank Pelican Publishing for giving me this opportunity. Thank you, Nina Kooij, Heather Green, and especially Dr. Milburn Calhoun for having faith in this small project.

Dean P. Turnbloom

Introduction

I wanted to take this opportunity to explain a few things about this year's edition of *Prizewinning Political Cartoons*. The astute observer will notice that some of the cartoon contests state that they are in one year, while others state a different year (e.g., the 2009 Pulitzer Prize versus the 2008 Berryman Award). This is confusing to the uninitiated (in point of fact, it's confusing to the initiated too, they just pretend it isn't). The reason for this apparent disparity, at least my understanding of the reason, is that some of the contests use the year in which the winning cartoons appeared in print as part of their award title (a la the Berryman) while others use the year in which the contest is held (Pulitzer, etc.). You can judge for yourself which methodology is the more pretentious.

I can certainly empathize with the awards and am in no position to throw stones. The first edition of my book was entitled *Prizewinning Political Cartoons: 2008 Edition*. This appeared to me to be a little odd, since the contests included in the book were held in 2007, and the awards were for cartoons that appeared in print in 2006. But since the book wasn't available until early 2008, the publisher rightly made the decision to use 2008 in its title. After all, who is going to go into a bookstore in 2008 and buy a book of cartoons with 2007 in the title. Be forewarned, the cartoons in this book were first in print in 2008, with the prizes awarded in 2009. That is, of course, with the exception of the Berryman, which was awarded in 2008 for cartoons published from late 2007 to late 2008—the Berryman is the only contest in the volume that is not held (cartoons submitted) in the first quarter of the year.

As I began this second entry in the *Prizewinning Political Cartoons* series, many things went through my mind—would my publisher be interested in a second edition (they were); would this new edition sell enough issues to continue the series (the jury is out on this one); how could I continue to impose on the good offices of the many cartoonists who've been so supportive of this effort (it would be impossible to pay them for their work, unless the book were to become a bestseller—needless to say, they weren't paid a dime); how to answer the concerns of my many critics (okay, maybe not "many" but certainly critical)—but I decided to give it another shot anyway.

If you were one of the few who had the opportunity to see the first edition, you will notice some changes in this one. First is the format. I wanted to give it a different look, so I asked the publisher to change the orientation and decrease the overall size slightly.

Another change is that I'm fortunate enough this year to have conned the Pulitzer winner into writing the book's foreword. I've decided that this should be done each year, at least the offer of the opportunity should go to the Pulitzer winner each year the series continues (editorial cartoonists rarely get a chance to editorialize in words vice cartoons).

One of the major criticisms of the 2008 edition of this book was that "many of the cartoons were repeated several times." I'm not certain this is a fair criticism when you consider that the book was intended to display the top entries for the various cartoon contests. It only stands to reason that the cartoonists would enter the same cartoons for a number of awards if they felt these were their best work, or work they believed would appeal to the judges of the various awards. Notwithstanding the unfairness of the criticism, I capitulated, being a sycophant to public opinion (perhaps I should run for political office), and in an effort to answer this criticism, I have tried to signal where the repetitions are in this volume.

Where it made sense (multiple repetitions from a cartoonist), I have had the cartoons that are repeated printed smaller than the first time they appear; where this did not make sense (a single cartoon repeated), I noted below the cartoon that it was a repetition and for what contest it was also entered. This, I believe, is the best way to handle the situation as it is my aim to display the artists' contest entries in their entirety and to completely eliminate them seems to me to be doing a disservice to the cartoonists. This I want to avoid at all costs. Thankfully this year, the repetitions are fewer than in the previous edition.

An addition to the book this year is the Reuben Award for editorial cartoons. It deserves special mention in the introduction because it probably should have been in the last volume. The Reuben is an award given by cartoonists for cartoonists—of all types—and illustrators. I was particularly happy to include it this year as the winner is my all-time favorite editorial cartoonist, Mike Ramirez.

A final change this year is the cartoonist interview. I wondered how these practiced purveyors of visual communication would react with a few simple questions for which they could not opt out with art to answer. I hope it is enjoyable to the reader, but it occurred to me that it might get monotonous to have each cartoonist answer the same question; therefore, in the interest of form, fit, function, and space, I excerpted from the questions asked what I considered each cartoonists' best answers. I hope they agree or at least do not vehemently disagree.

Finally, I wanted to say what a great privilege it is to showcase the outstanding artwork in this volume, which entertains, informs, and sometimes even enrages. Regardless your political point of view, you should agree that these cartoonists are worthy of their awards, and this book is meant to record their achievements in a single volume for posterity.

Admiringly,
Dean P. Turnbloom

The Pulitzer Prize

The Pulitzer Prize for editorial cartooning is the hallmark of any cartoonist's career. The path to the Pulitzer starts with the cartoonist selecting up to twenty of his (or her) best cartoons, or at least twenty cartoons he (she) believes will best favorably appeal to the jury and the board. After carefully making the selection of the cartoons he (she . . . you get the picture) wishes to enter, the cartoonist must put together an exhibit of the work, in scrapbook format, including the name of the newspaper or news organization and the date each cartoon was published. Although online material is eligible for submission, it must be derived from print media. To quote the eligibility rules, "Since their creation in 1917, the Pulitzer Prizes have been awarded exclusively for newspaper journalism."

In addition, the exhibit must include a biography, a picture of the cartoonist, and a cover letter demonstrating eligibility and summarizing the contents. All entries must be accompanied by fifty dollars and a completed entry form.

Each year there are twenty-one categories in which a Pulitzer is awarded; 102 judges are divided into twenty juries. Each jury is asked to screen the applicants in their respective categories and to make three nominations, which are put before the Pulitzer Board for final selection. This year the jury for the editorial cartoon category contained a newspaper editor, a former editor, two editorial page editors, and an editorial cartoonist/columnist (and previous winner in the category).

2009 Pulitzer Prize Winner
Steve Breen—*San Diego Union-Tribune*

This is the second time around for Steve Breen, winning his first Pulitzer in 1998. Steve Breen was born in Los Angeles in 1970 and attended the University of California, Riverside. Editorial cartoonist for the *San Diego Union-Tribune* since 2001, his work is nationally syndicated by Creators News Service and regularly appears in *USA Today,* the *New York Times,* and *Newsweek.* Breen also the recipient of the National Press Foundation's 2007 Berryman Award for editorial cartooning. In 2009, Breen not only took home the Pulitzer, but he was also awarded the Overseas Press Club's Thomas Nast Award and the National Headliner Award. Congratulations, Steve.

In his spare time, he writes and illustrates picture books, including the titles *Stick, Violet the Pilot,* and *The Secret of Santa's Island.*

Breen lives in San Diego with his wife and four children. He enjoys reading, running, playing the guitar and piano, and watching old movies on cable.

Steve Breen Interview

Dean: Turn-of-the-century journalist Finley Peter Dunne is quoted as saying, "The job of the newspaper is to comfort the afflicted and afflict the comfortable." What do you see as the role of the editorial cartoonists?

Steve: I see it along these lines as well. I feel duty-bound to provide a voice for the little guy. In terms of going after the comfortable, the cheaters, the liars, and the bullies . . . that's the fun part of the job. Cartoonists love a villain.

Dean: What do you feel distinguishes your work from that of your peers?

Steve: I really try to see both sides on the issues, not that my peers do NOT try to do this. But I like the way that a reader looks at my work and can't tell if I'm a liberal or a conservative. True, I tend to lean conservative, but I think I'm pretty fair in tweaking the donkey noses as well as the elephant trunks.

Dean: Although the bulk of this book is dedicated to editorial contests in the U.S., the final section of this book deals with the international Lurie Award. How do you think U.S. cartoons differ from those of other countries?

Steve: I like the way that the foreign cartoonists seem to embrace the visual. I think the best cartoons have few, if any words.

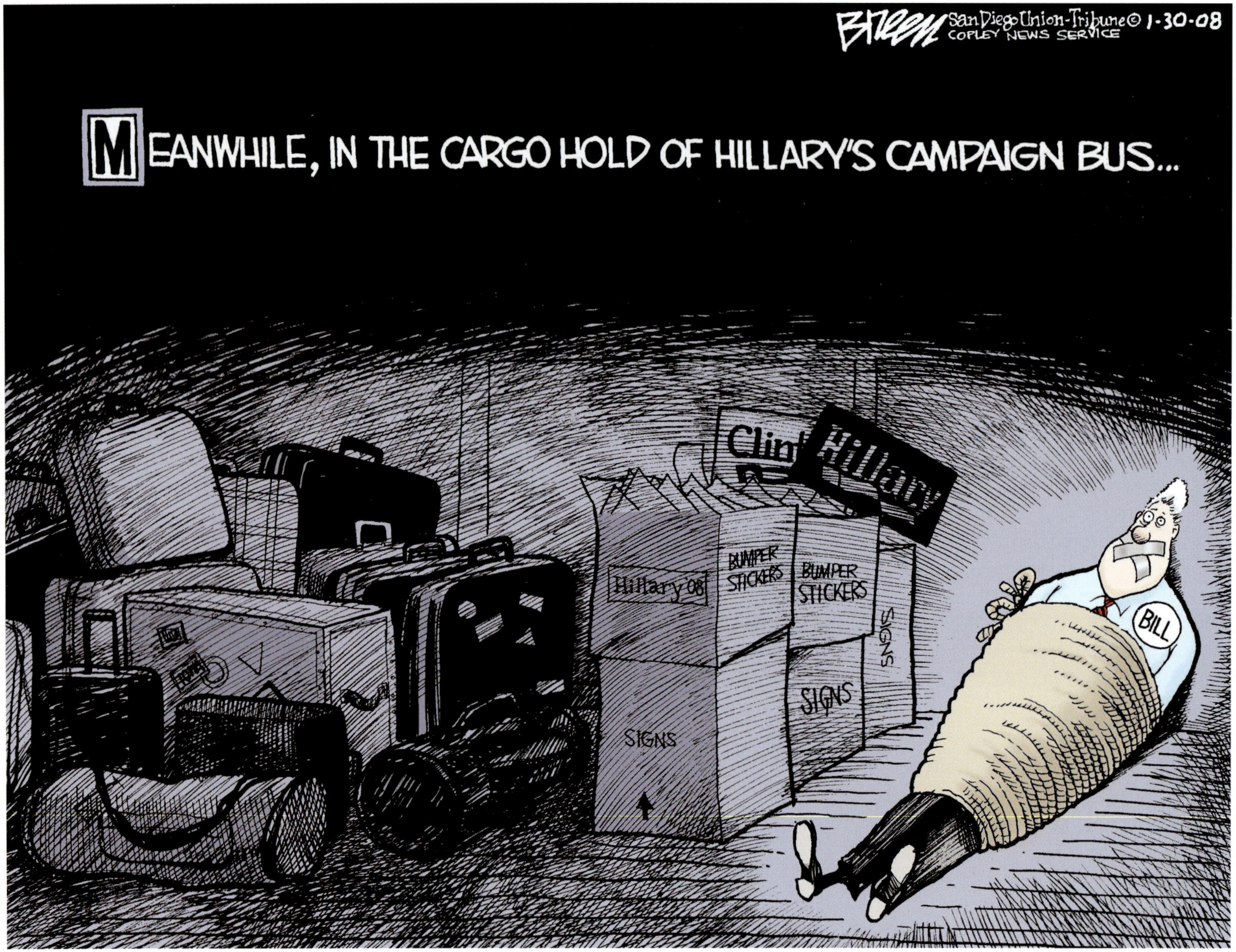
BREEN San Diego Union-Tribune © 1-30-08
COPLEY NEWS SERVICE
MEANWHILE, IN THE CARGO HOLD OF HILLARY'S CAMPAIGN BUS...
Hillary '08
BUMPER STICKERS
BUMPER STICKERS
SIGNS
SIGNS
SIGNS
Hillary
BILL

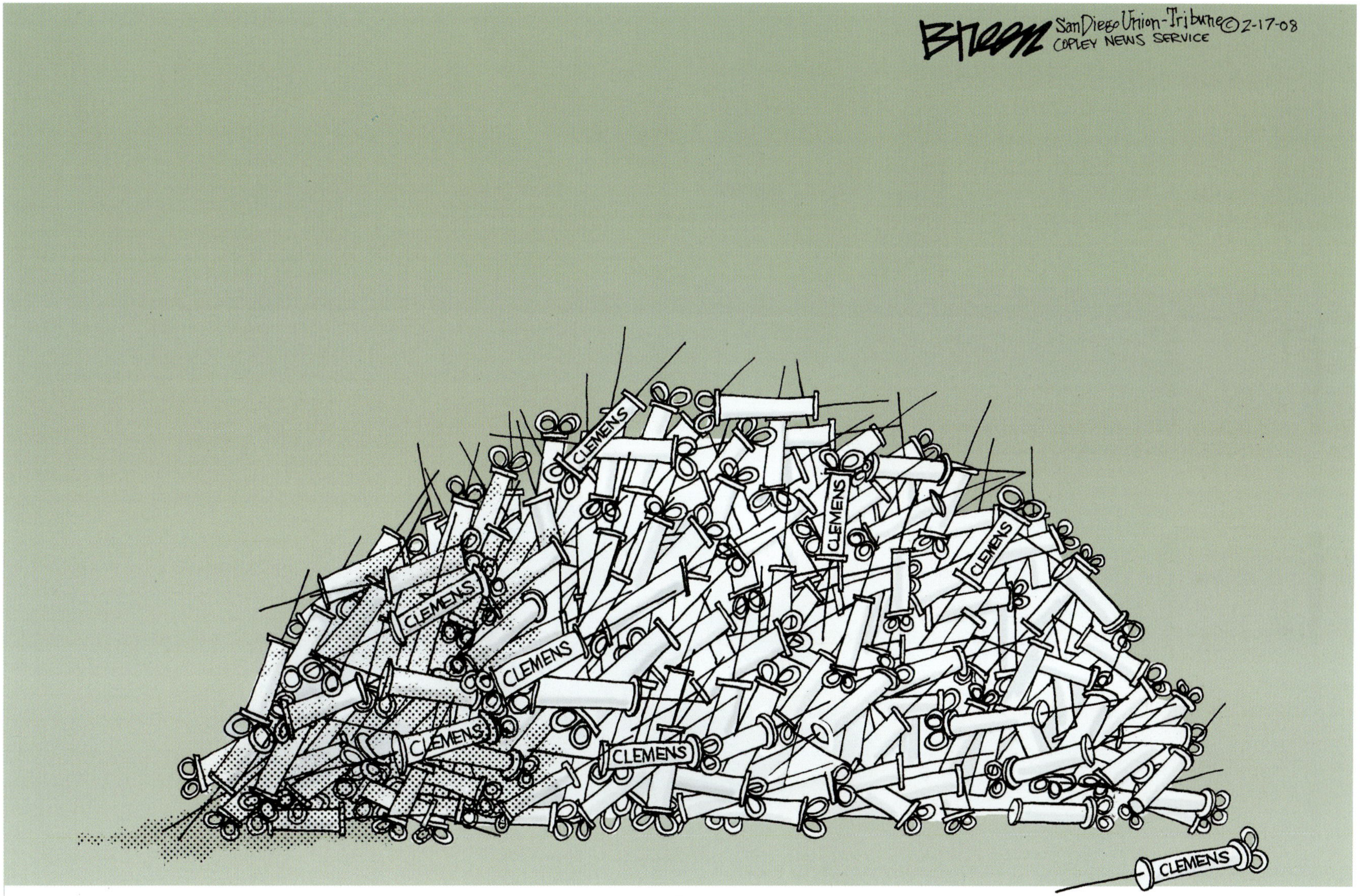
Breen
San Diego Union-Tribune ©2-17-08
COPLEY NEWS SERVICE
CLEMENS
CLEMENS
CLEMENS
CLEMENS
CLEMENS
CLEMENS
CLEMENS
CLEMENS
CLEMENS
CLEMENS

PITCHER'S MOUND

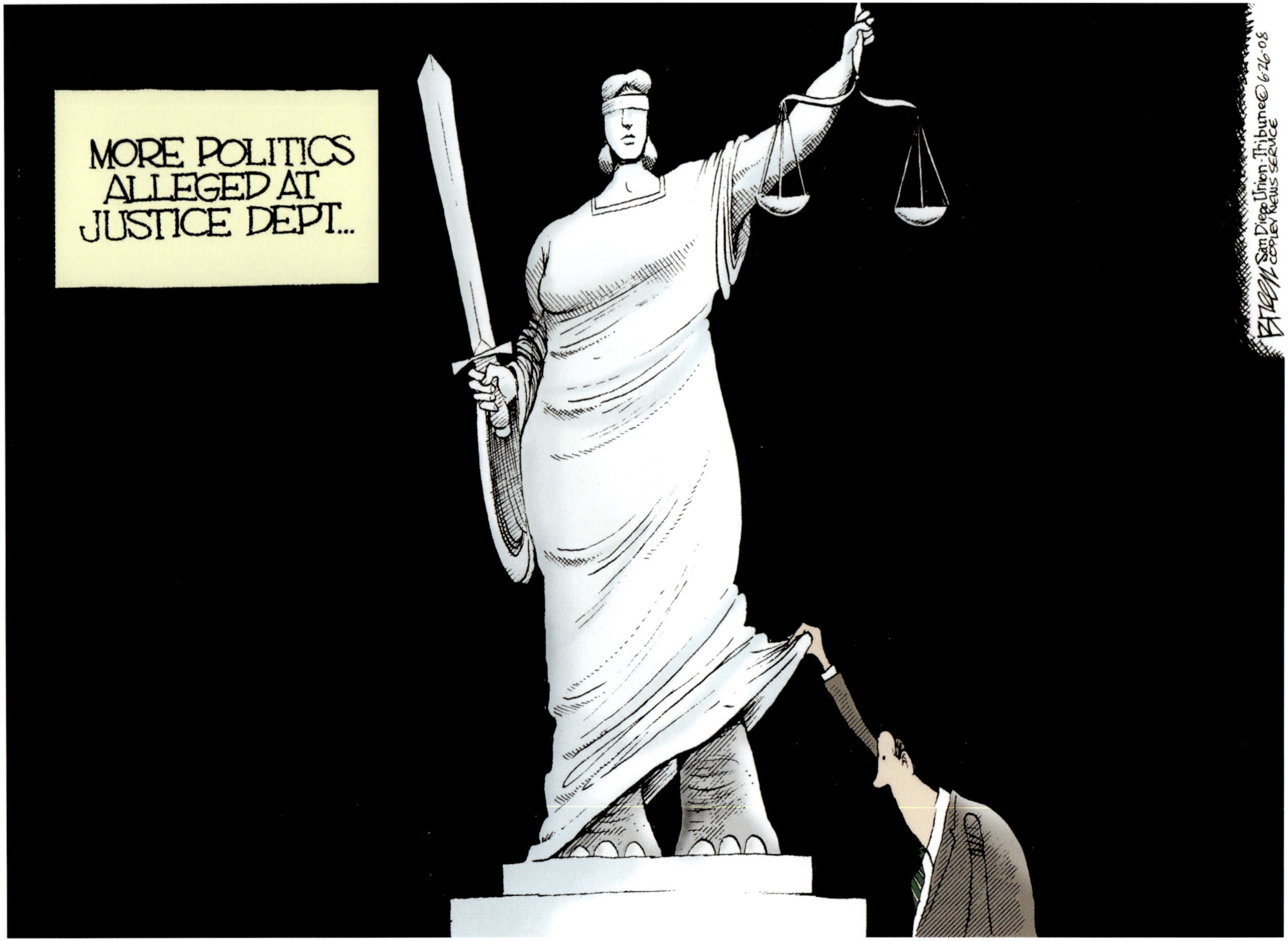
MORE POLITICS ALLEGED AT JUSTICE DEPT...
San Diego Union-Tribune © 6-26-08
COPLEY NEWS SERVICE

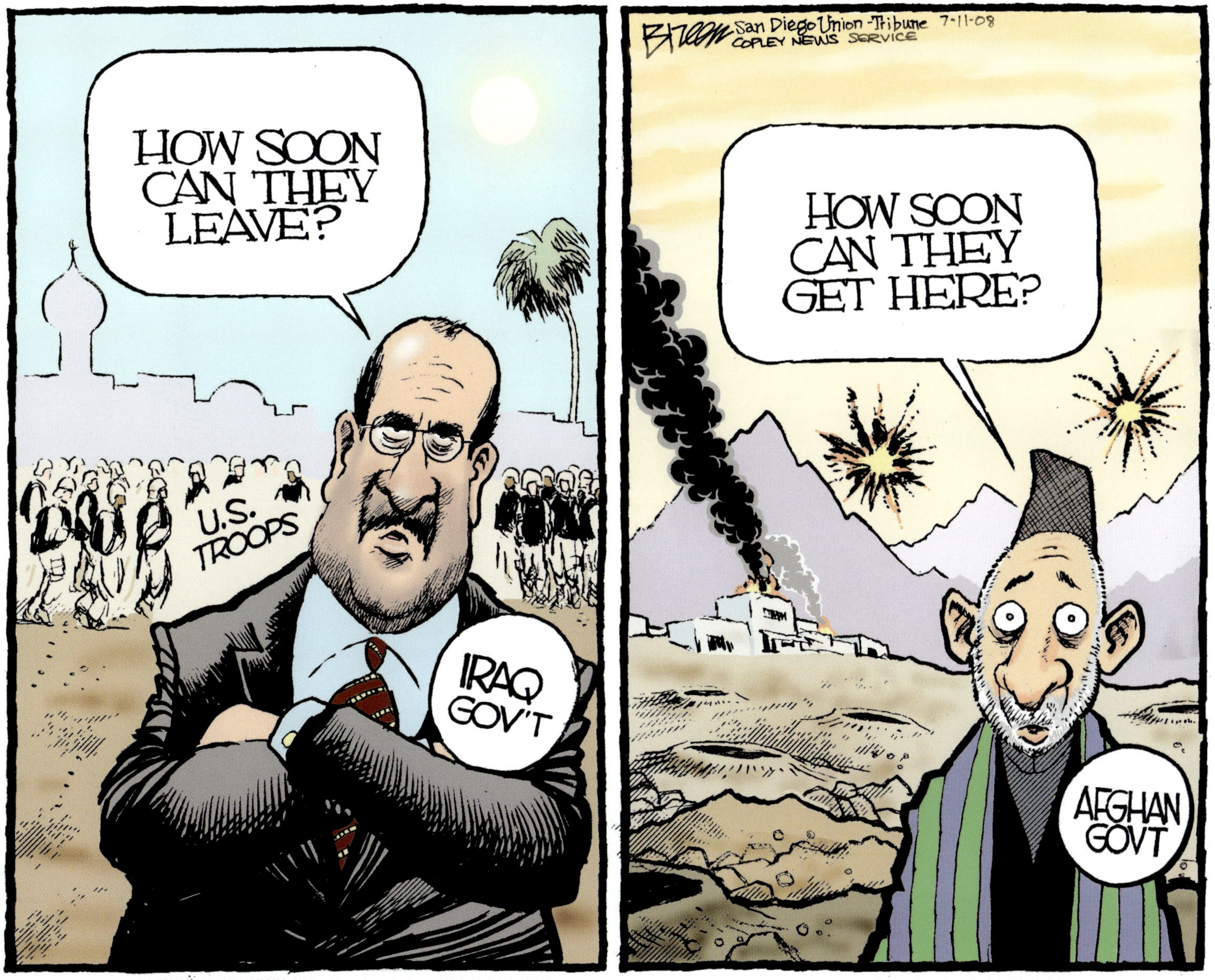
HOW SOON CAN THEY LEAVE?
U.S. TROOPS
IRAQ GOV'T
San Diego Union-Tribune 7-11-08
COPLEY NEWS SERVICE
HOW SOON CAN THEY GET HERE?
AFGHAN GOVT

BREEN San Diego Union-Tribune © 7-17-
CREATORS NEWS SERVICE
HEY, BIG LENDER!..
FANNIE MAE

I DITCHED MY MILITARY FATIGUES, PUT ON GLASSES, GREW A BEARD, BUT THEY **STILL** FOUND ME.
RADOVAN KARADZIC

Breen San Diego Union-Tribune © 7-24-08
CREATORS NEWS SERVICE
...I WONDER WHAT TIPPED THEM OFF.

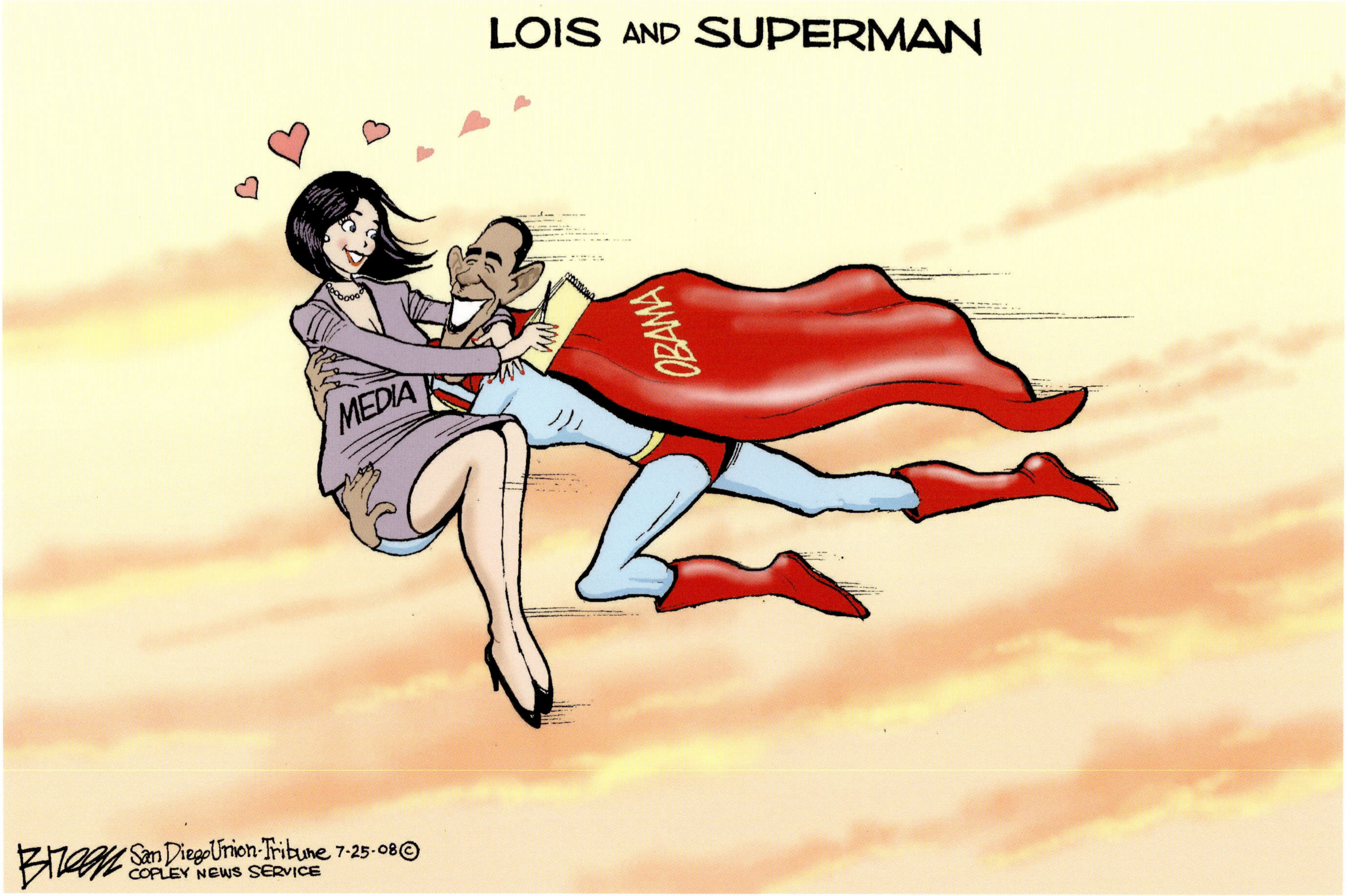
LOIS AND SUPERMAN
MEDIA
OBAMA
San Diego Union-Tribune 7-25-08©
COPLEY NEWS SERVICE

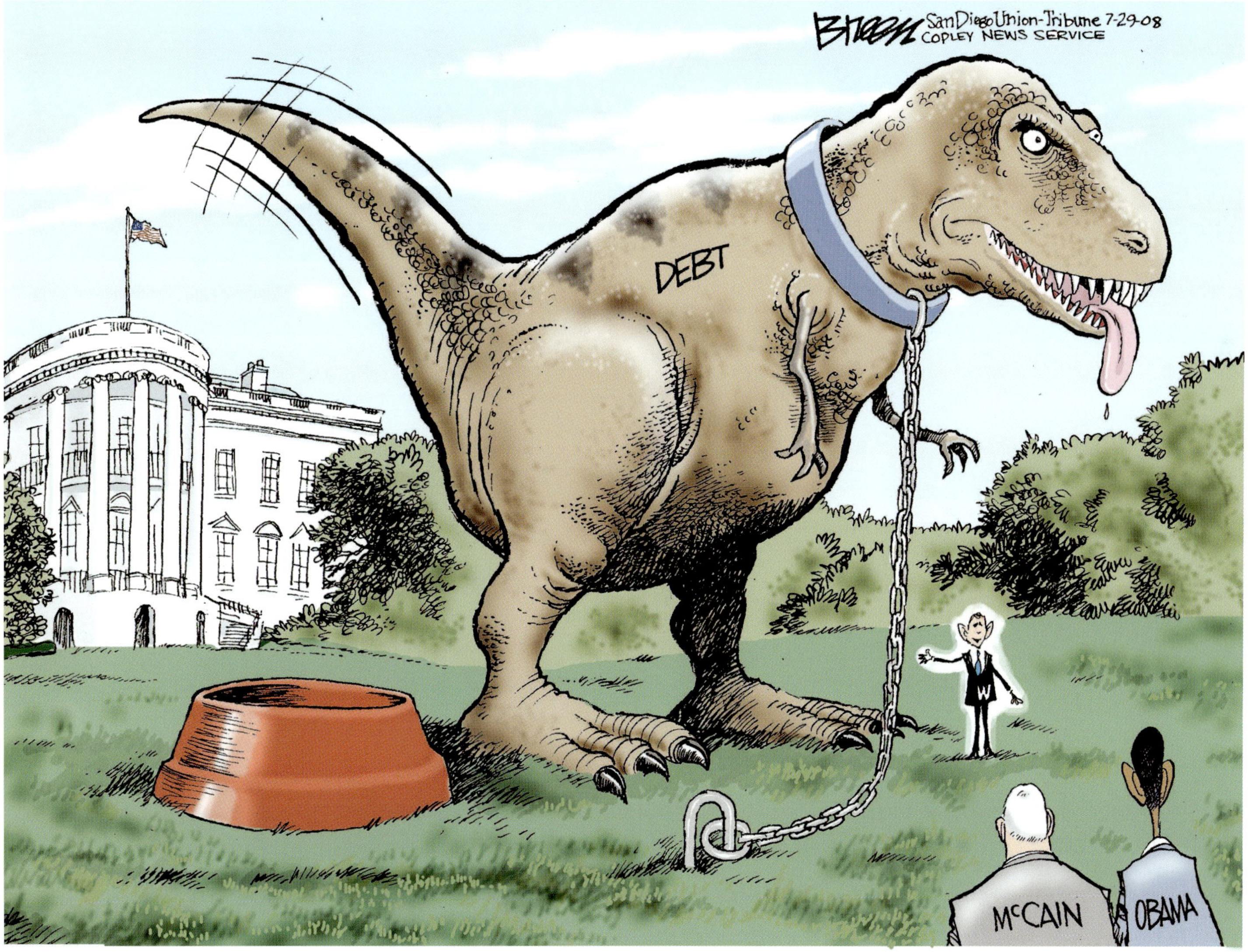
BREEN San Diego Union-Tribune 7-29-08
COPLEY NEWS SERVICE
DEBT
W
McCAIN
OBAMA

" REX COMES WITH THE HOUSE..."

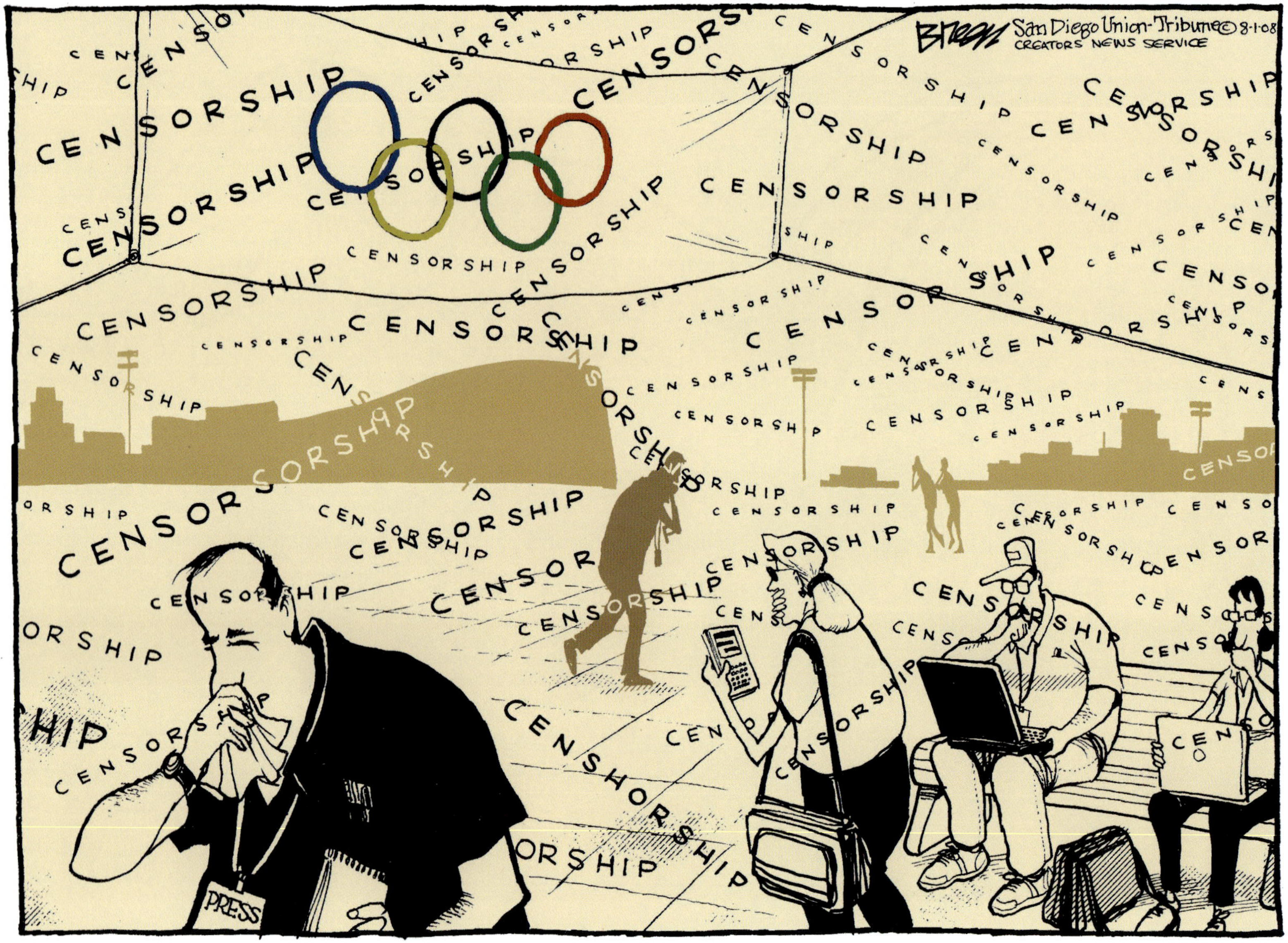
San Diego Union-Tribune © 8-1-08
CREATORS NEWS SERVICE
CENSORSHIP
PRESS

BEIJING POLLUTION

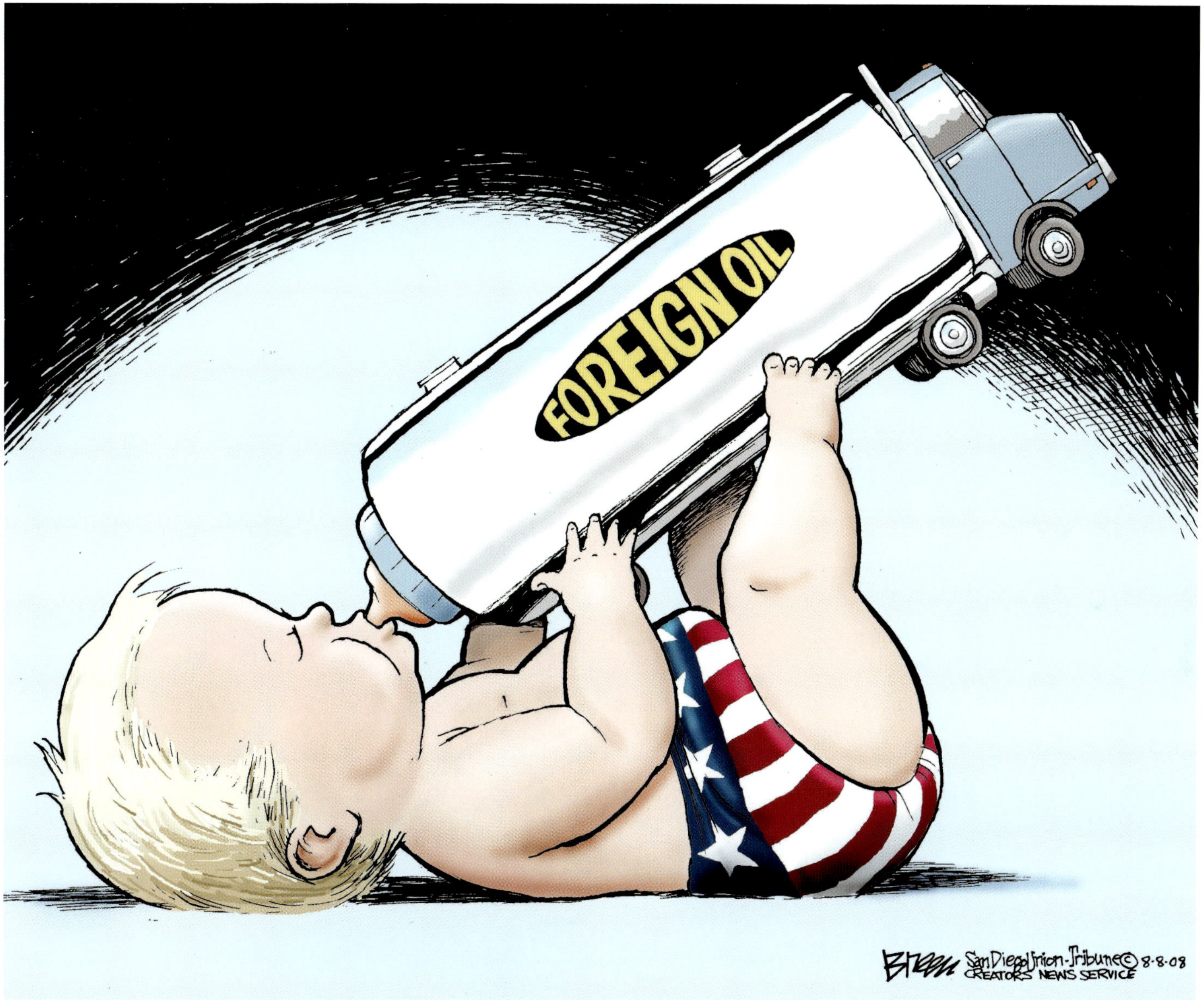
FOREIGN OIL
Breen San Diego Union-Tribune © 8-8-08
CREATORS NEWS SERVICE

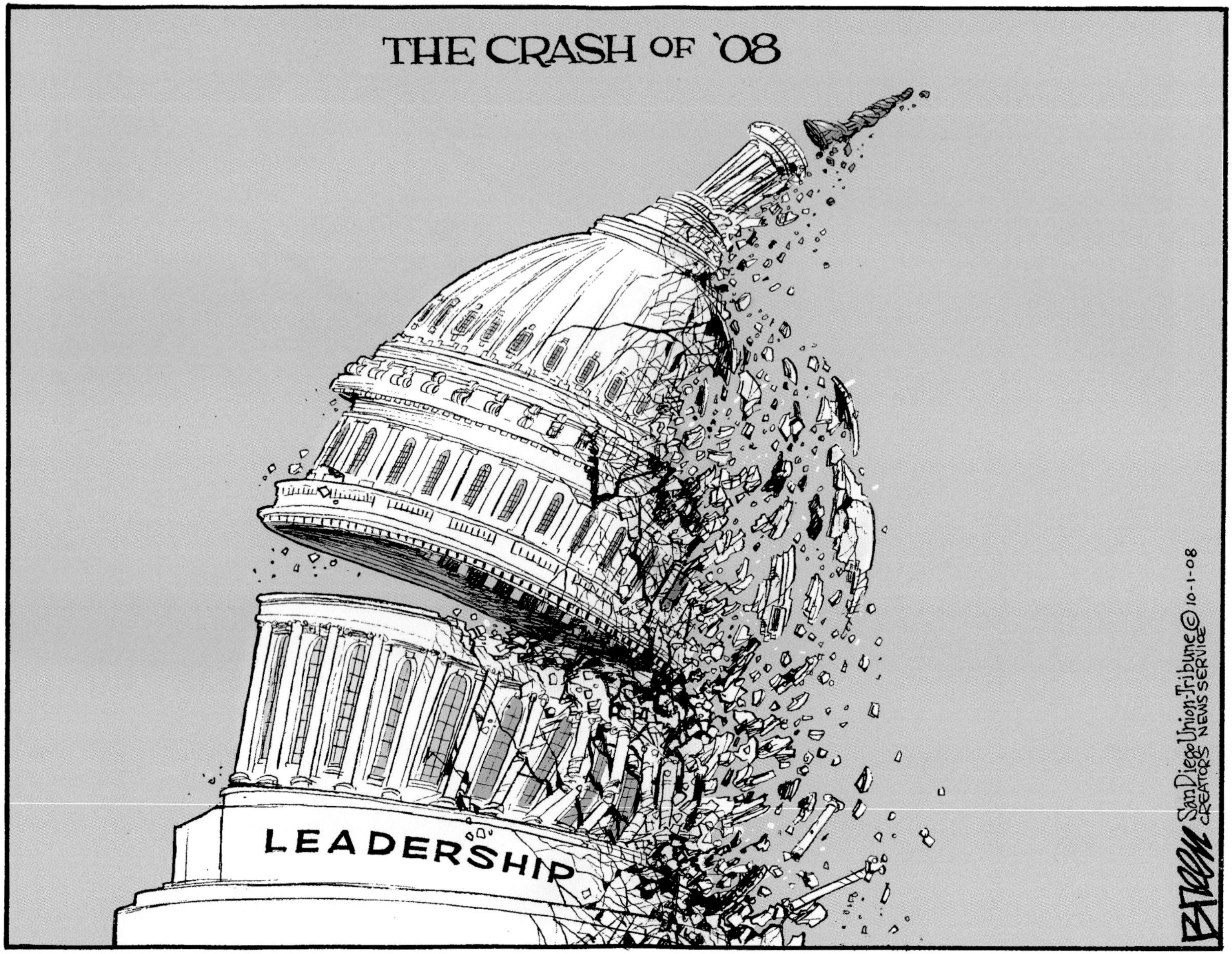

THE CRASH OF '08
LEADERSHIP
San Diego Union-Tribune © 10-1-08
CREATORS NEWS SERVICE

SEVEN DEADLY SINS
OF THE
MELTDOWN
ENVY
GLUTTONY
HOME EQUITY LINE OF CREDIT
HOT TUB
PLASMA TV
GREED & LUST
WALL STREET
SLOTH
Z
REGULATORS
PRIDE
HIS FAULT
HIS FAULT
WRATH
TAX-PAYERS
BAILOUT
NATIONAL DEBT
401(k)

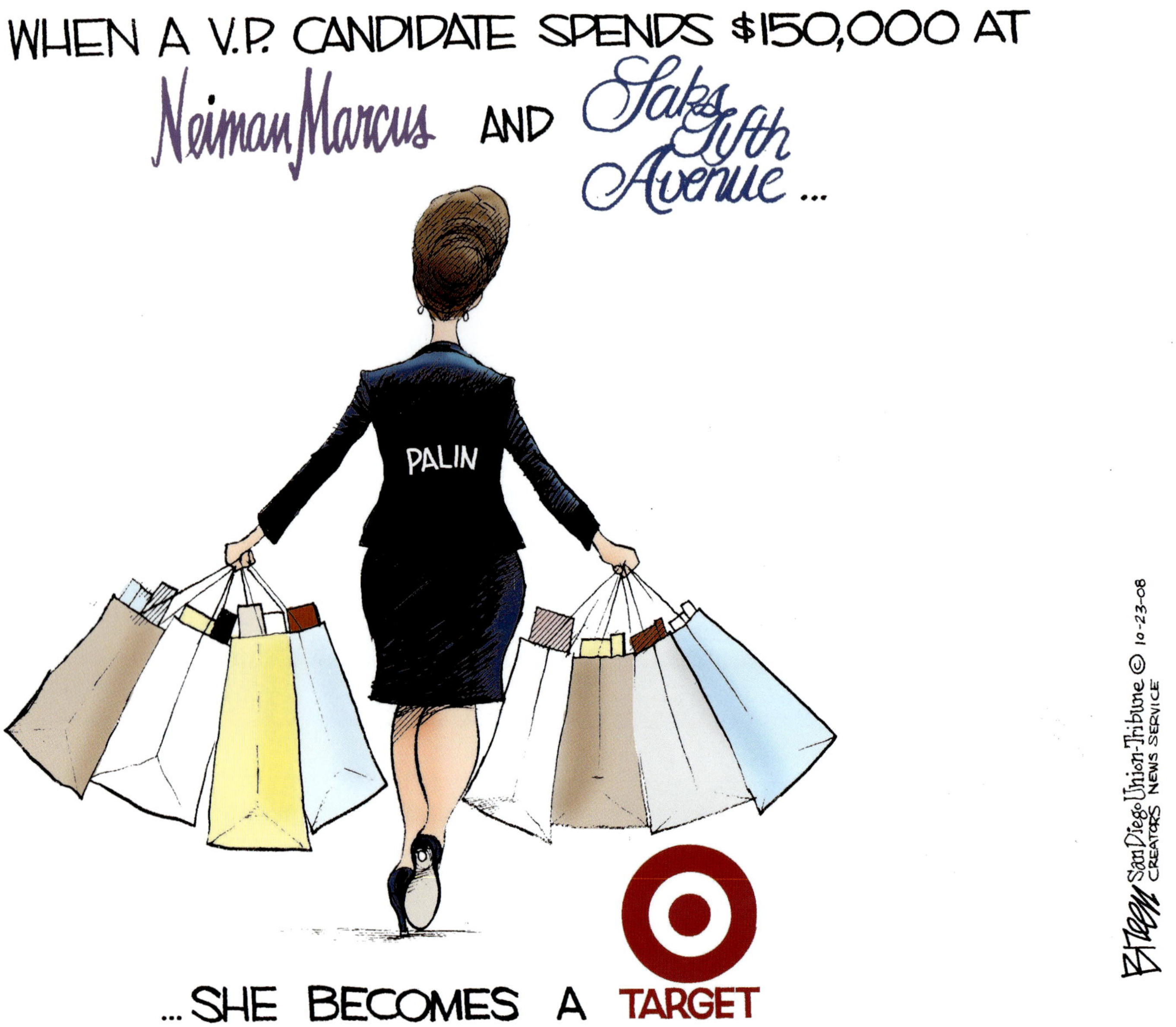
WHEN A V.P. CANDIDATE SPENDS $150,000 AT
Neiman Marcus AND Saks Fifth Avenue ...
PALIN
...SHE BECOMES A TARGET
San Diego Union-Tribune © 10-23-08
CREATORS NEWS SERVICE

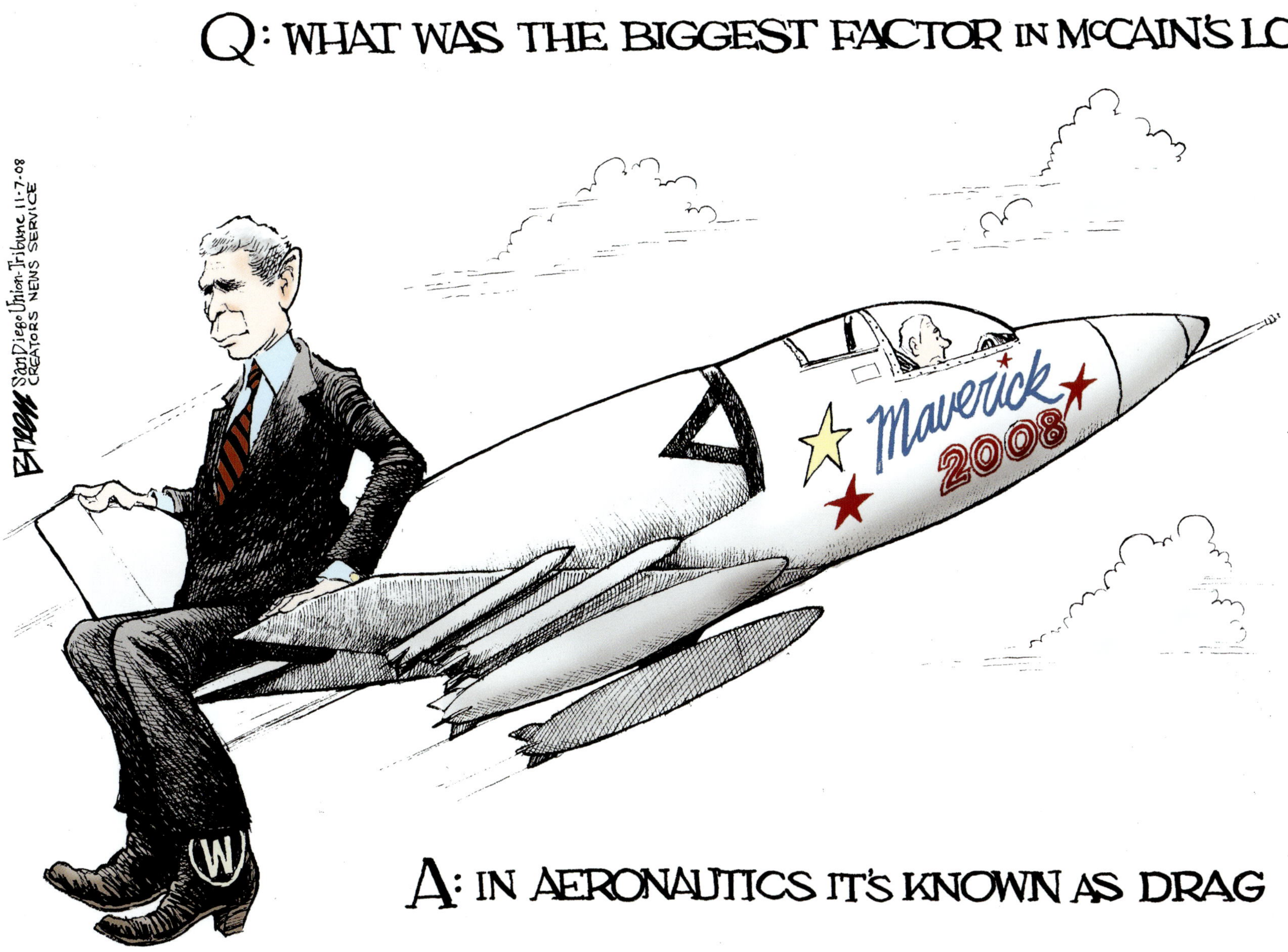
Q: WHAT WAS THE BIGGEST FACTOR IN McCAIN'S LOSS?
BREEN San Diego Union-Tribune 11-7-08
CREATORS NEWS SERVICE
Maverick
2008
W
A: IN AERONAUTICS IT'S KNOWN AS DRAG

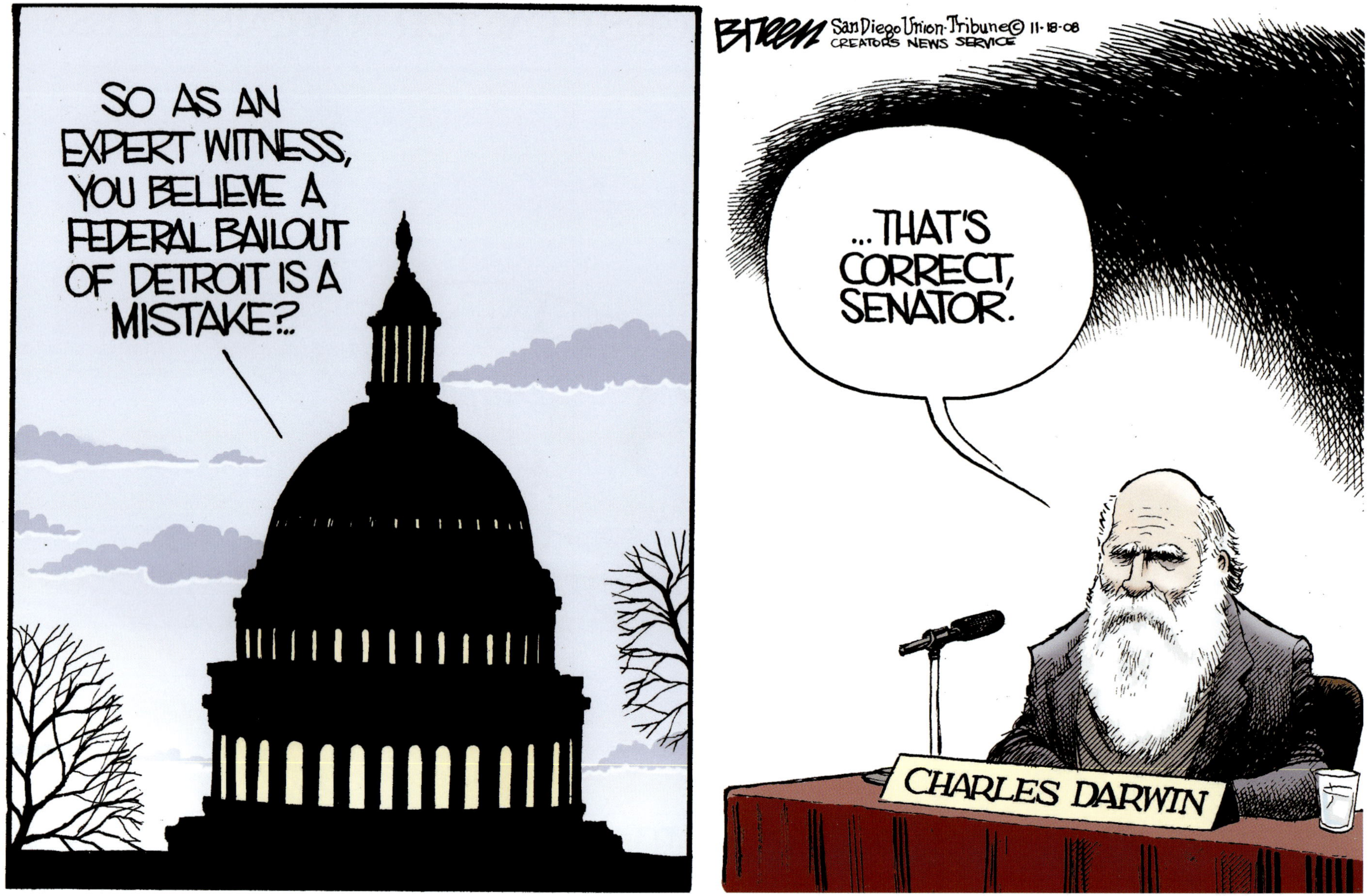
SO AS AN EXPERT WITNESS, YOU BELIEVE A FEDERAL BAILOUT OF DETROIT IS A MISTAKE?..
San Diego Union-Tribune © 11-18-08
CREATORS NEWS SERVICE
...THAT'S CORRECT, SENATOR.
CHARLES DARWIN

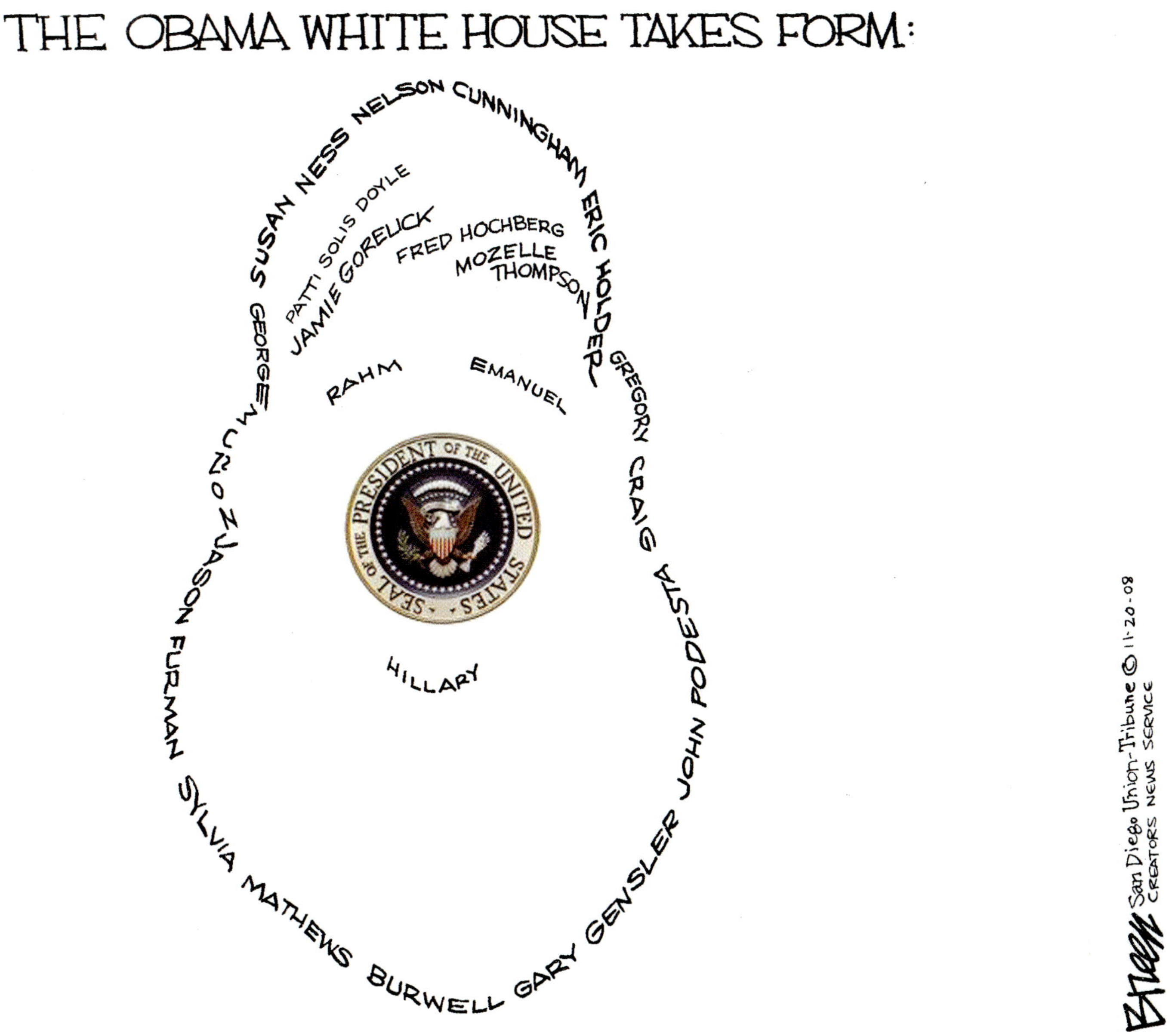
THE OBAMA WHITE HOUSE TAKES FORM:
SUSAN NESS NELSON CUNNINGHAM ERIC HOLDER
PATTI SOLIS DOYLE
JAMIE GORELICK
FRED HOCHBERG
MOZELLE THOMPSON
GEORGE MUÑOZ JASON FURMAN SYLVIA MATHEWS BURWELL GARY GENSLER JOHN PODESTA GREGORY CRAIG
RAHM EMANUEL
SEAL OF THE PRESIDENT OF THE UNITED STATES
HILLARY
BREEN
San Diego Union-Tribune © 11-20-08
CREATORS NEWS SERVICE

BREEN San Diego Union-Tribune © 12-14-08
CREATORS NEWS SERVICE
NEW JERSEY POLITICS
LOUISIANA POLITICS
ILLINOIS POLITICS

GUARD DOG
ON DUTY
S.E.C.
Breen San Diego Union-Tribune ©12-21
CREATORS NEWS SERVICE

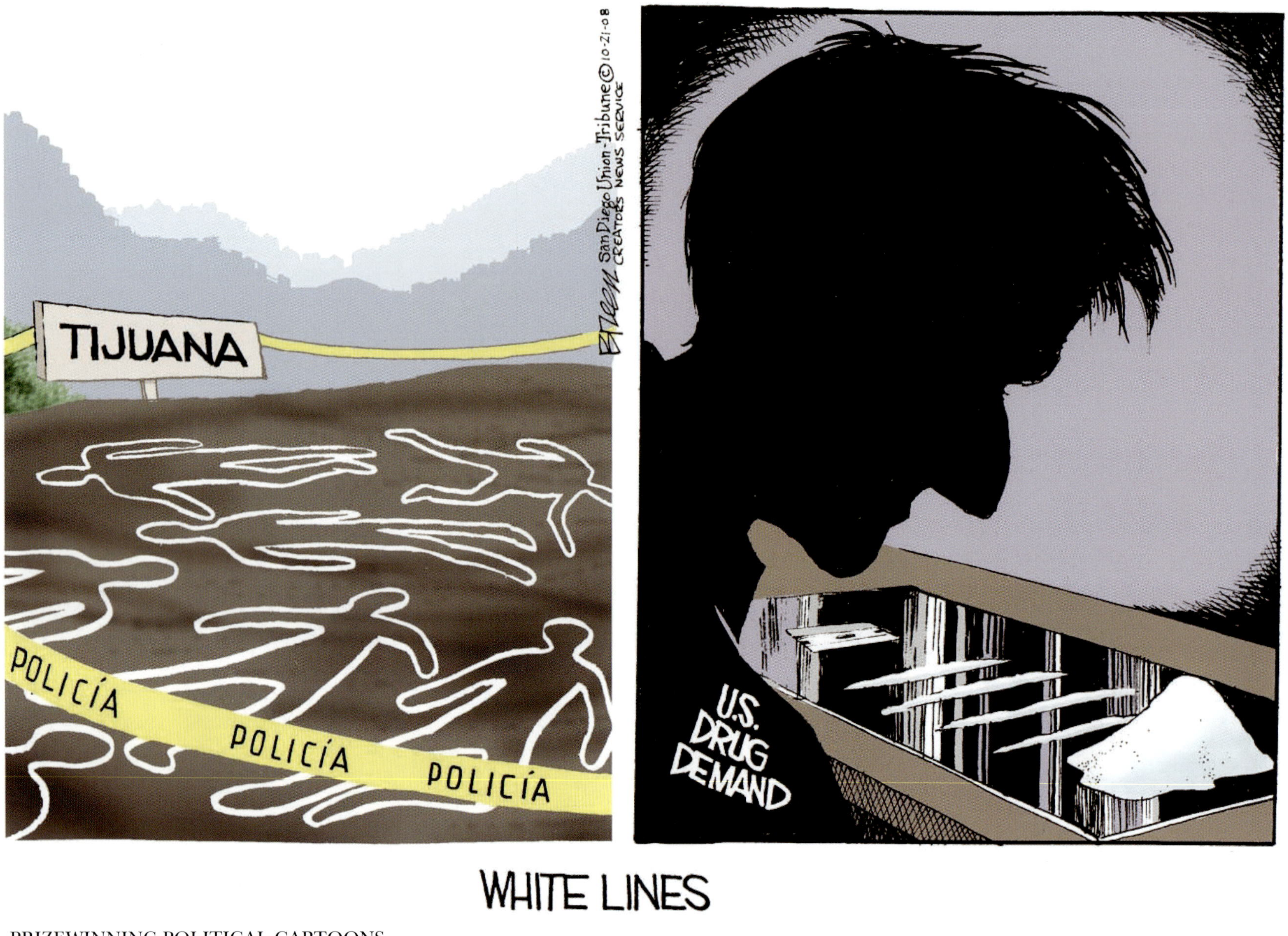
TIJUANA
POLICÍA
POLICÍA
POLICÍA
Breen San Diego Union-Tribune © 10-21-08
CREATORS NEWS SERVICE
U.S. DRUG DEMAND
WHITE LINES

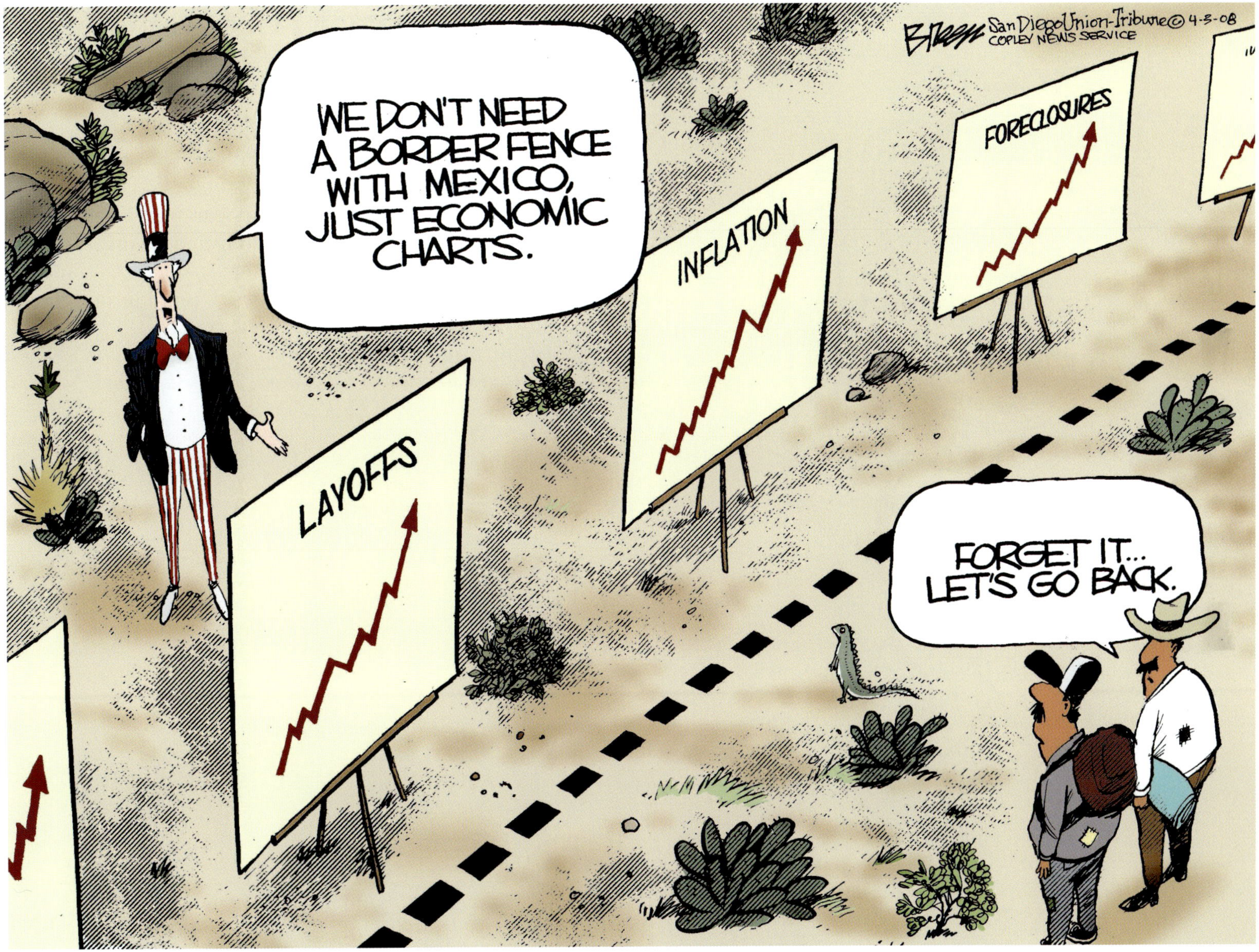
San Diego Union-Tribune © 4-3-08
COPLEY NEWS SERVICE
WE DON'T NEED A BORDER FENCE WITH MEXICO, JUST ECONOMIC CHARTS.
LAYOFFS
INFLATION
FORECLOSURES
FORGET IT... LET'S GO BACK.

2009 Pulitzer Prize Nominee
Matt Wuerker—Politico.com

Nomination for the Pulitzer is the next best thing to winning. Matt Wuerker, staff cartoonist for the newspaper/Web site Politico.com can take great pride in this honor. Wuerker is a political cartoonist based in Washington, D.C.

Wuerker has been a successful freelance cartoonist for more than twenty-five years, and his cartoons have been published in the *Los Angeles Times*, the *Washington Post*, the *Christian Science Monitor*, the *Nation*, and *Smithsonian* magazine. His caricature and illustration work is syndicated internationally by both Tribune Media Service and NewsArt.com.

Wuerker is the author of two cartoon collections, *Standing Tall in Deep Doo Doo: A Cartoon Chronicle of Campaign '92 Bush/Quayle Years* and *Meanwhile in Other News: A Graphic Look at Politics in the Empire of Money, Sex and Scandal.*

Matt Wuerker Interview

Dean: With the continuing decline of newspaper readership, what do you believe the future holds for the fate of the editorial cartoonist?

Matt: I think the future will be tricky for cartoonists, but for the adaptable ones, I think it's a bright one. Someone recently summed up our dire situation as akin to the vaudevillians facing the advent of radio. Vaudeville theaters were to vaudevillians as newspapers are to cartoonists, or so some would have it. The pessimists are sure all our stages are disappearing and it's the end of political cartooning.

That's only true if you're rigid about where and how cartoons work. The end of vaudeville was not the end of comedy entertainment. The stages just changed. In reality, radio and TV actually brought in an explosion of entertainment platforms and in the long run made comedy and entertainment a much bigger industry. I think the jump for cartoons from newsprint to the Internet is kind of similar, and the platforms are just multiplying and getting more flexible. Adapting won't be easy, cartoonists will need to learn to swim in a new media and this will require updating our skills. The old model of an office and a salary from a newspaper publisher was wonderful, but that's pretty much gone except for a lucky few of us.

Dean: What do you feel distinguishes your work from that of your peers?

Matt: Having said all the above about new technologies I think I'm distinguished by generally being a serious throwback. I do very old-fashioned, highly rendered, and even painted work on paper that would be right at home in the nineteenth century. From time to time, I also throw in some Flash animation and interactive games so as not to be a complete anachronism.

THE IDEA OF THE FIRST WOMAN PRESIDENT IS VERY EXCITING... BUT THERE'S JUST SOMETHING ABOUT HER...
Billary
Billary
Billary
Billary
Billary
Billary
M. WUERKER POLITICO

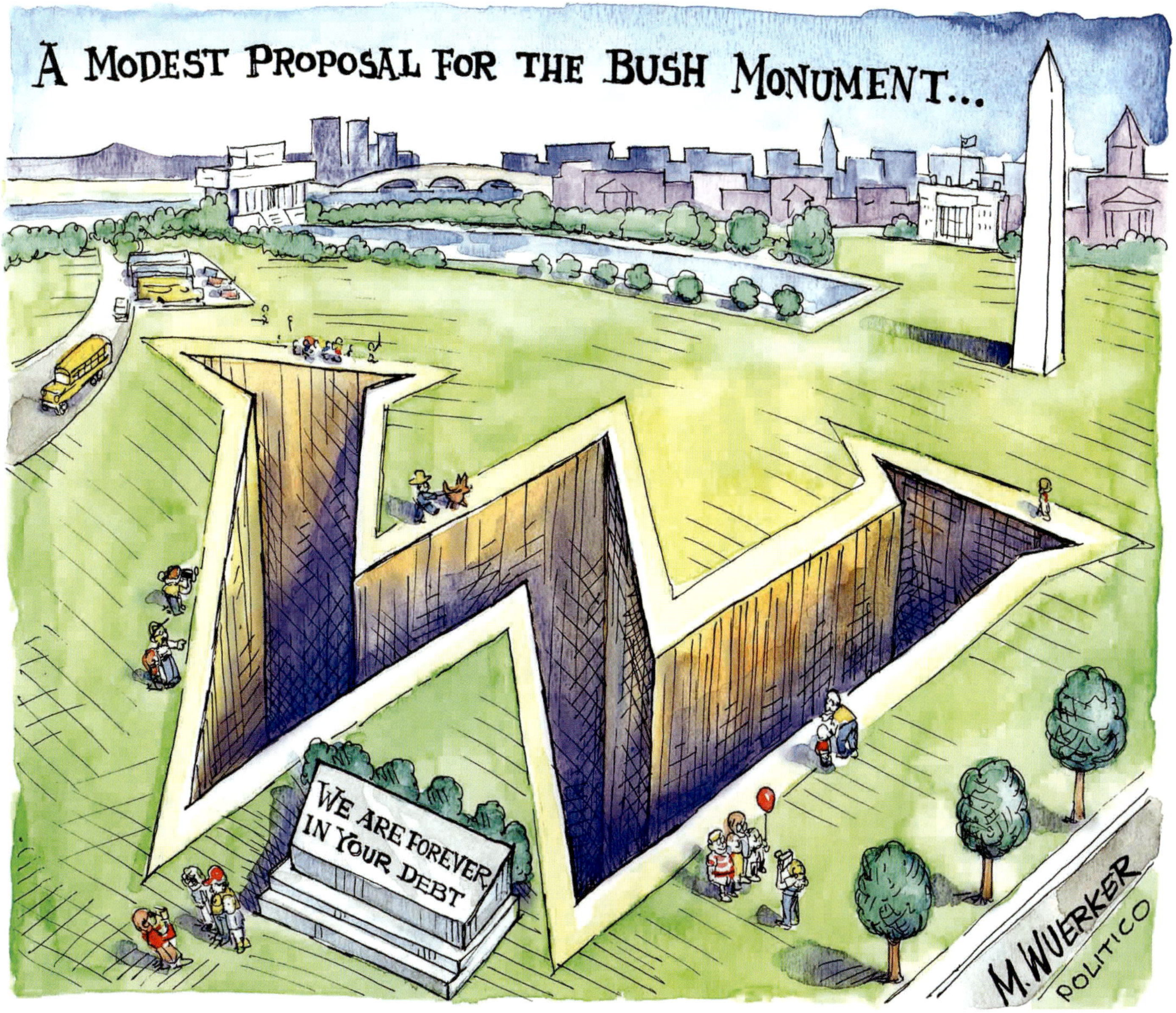
A MODEST PROPOSAL FOR THE BUSH MONUMENT...
WE ARE FOREVER IN YOUR DEBT
M. WUERKER
POLITICO

RACE... GENDER... THOSE DEMOCRATS ARE SO DARN DIVISIVE!
M.WUERKER POLITICO

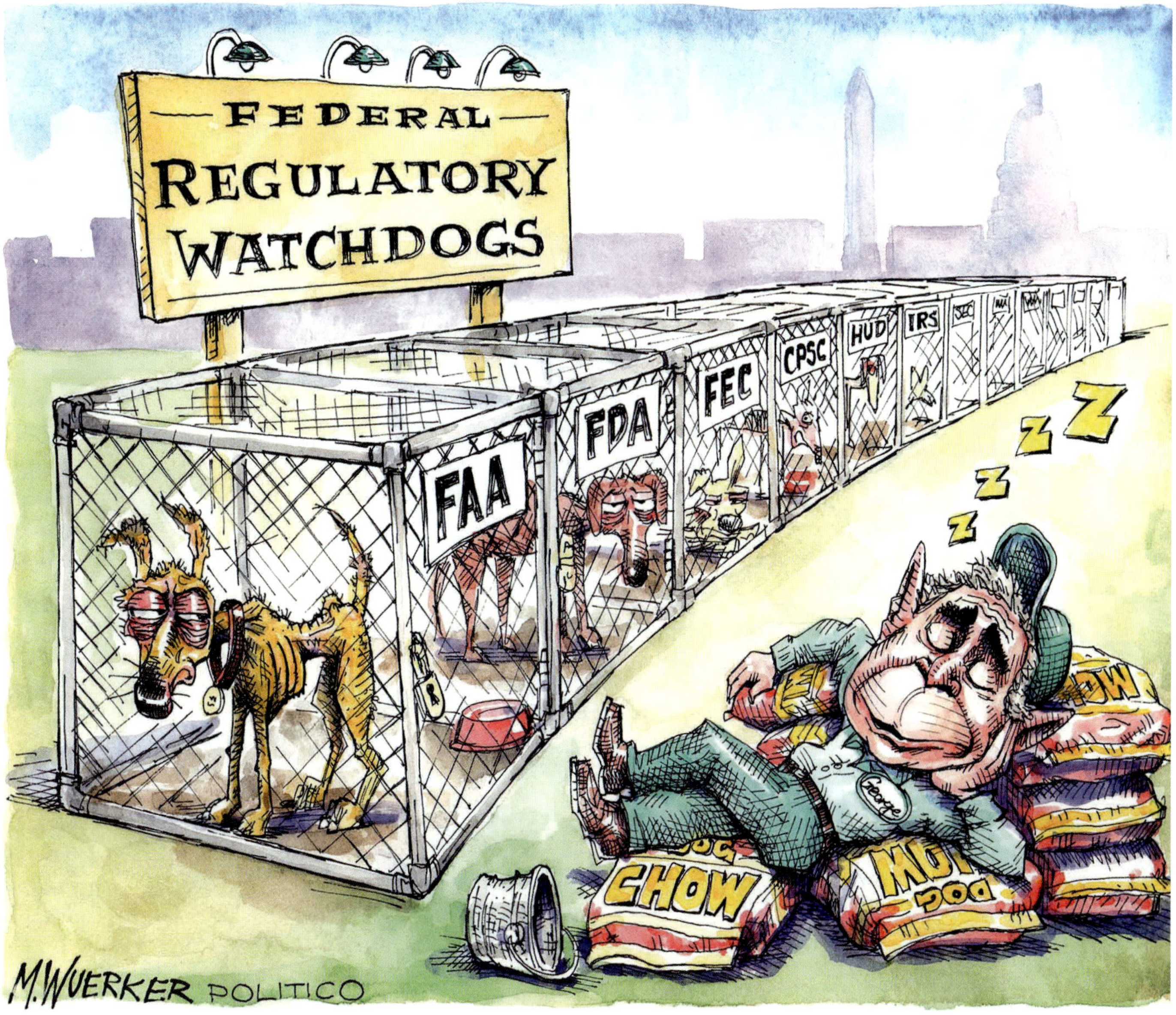
FEDERAL
REGULATORY
WATCHDOGS
FAA
FDA
FEC
CPSC
HUD
IRS
SEC
Z
Z
Z
Z
Z
CHOW
DOG
George
M.WUERKER POLITICO

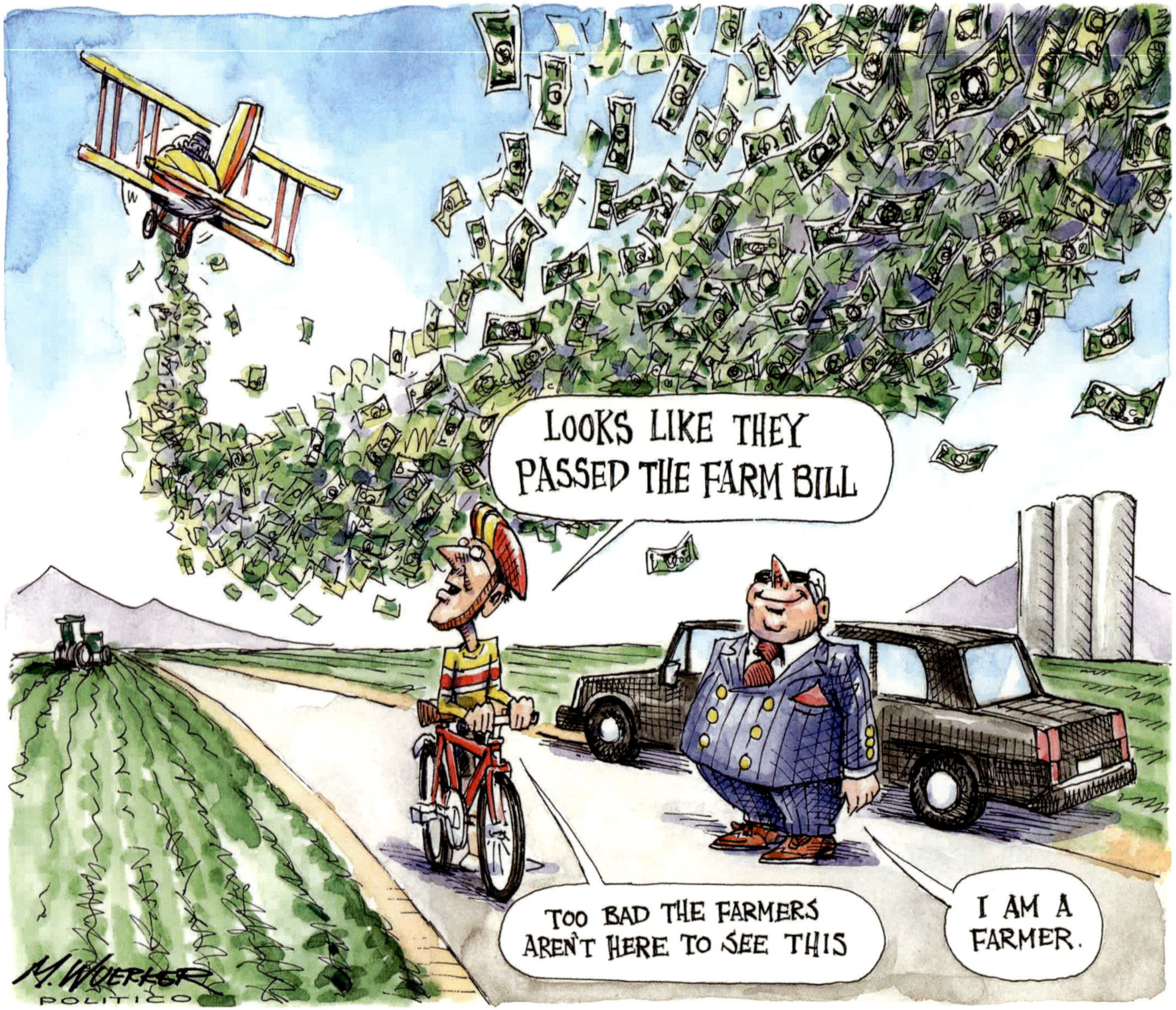
LOOKS LIKE THEY PASSED THE FARM BILL
TOO BAD THE FARMERS AREN'T HERE TO SEE THIS
I AM A FARMER.
M. WUERKER
POLITICO

YA KNOW HE'S A MUSLIM
... AND REFUSES TO SAY THE PLEDGE!
... AND TOOK HIS OATH ON A QURAN!
... AND WHAT'S WORSE, HE'S AN ELITIST WHO THINKS WE'RE GULLIBLE IGNORAMUSES!!
M. WUERKER
POLITICO

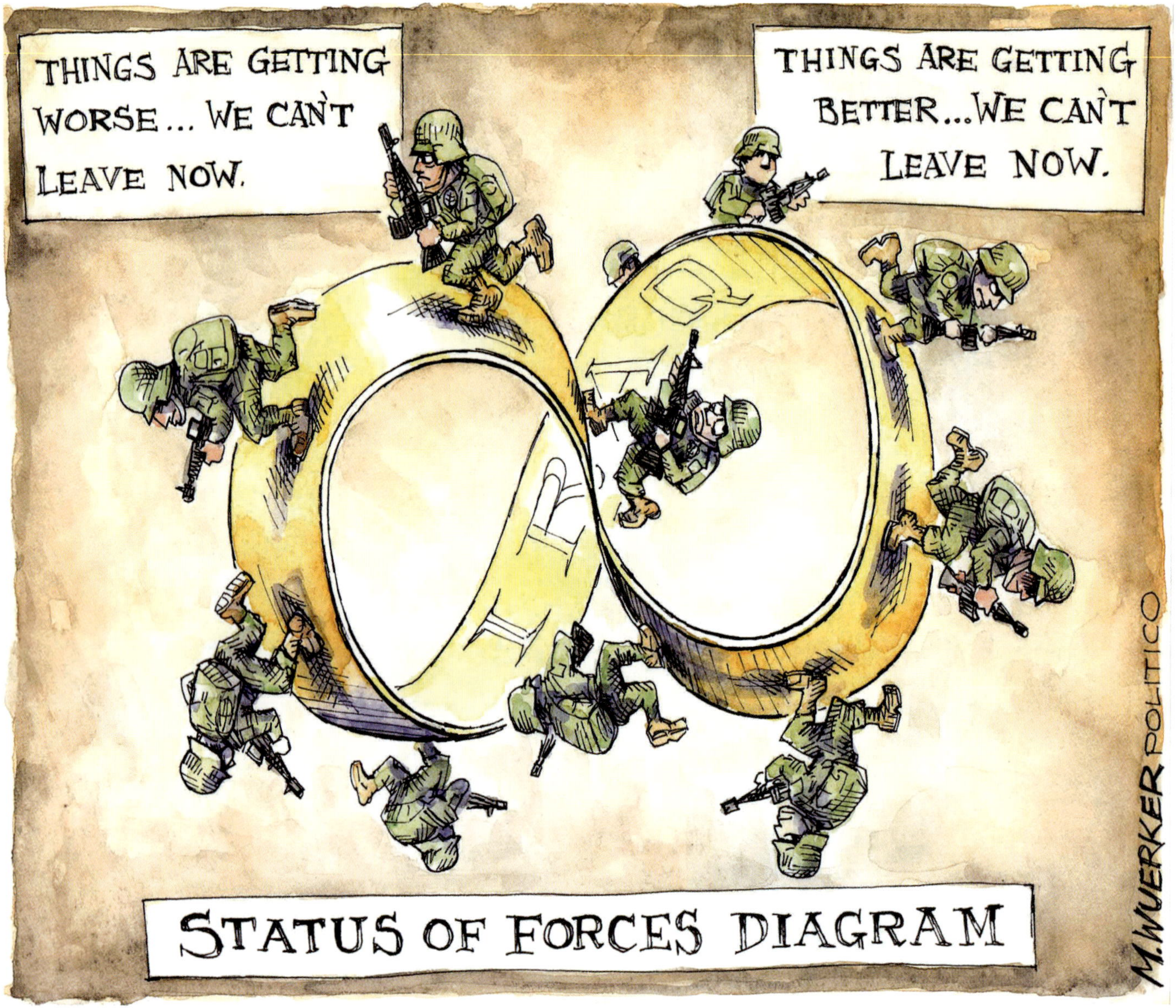
THINGS ARE GETTING WORSE... WE CAN'T LEAVE NOW.
THINGS ARE GETTING BETTER...WE CAN'T LEAVE NOW.
IRAQ
STATUS OF FORCES DIAGRAM
M.WUERKER POLITICO

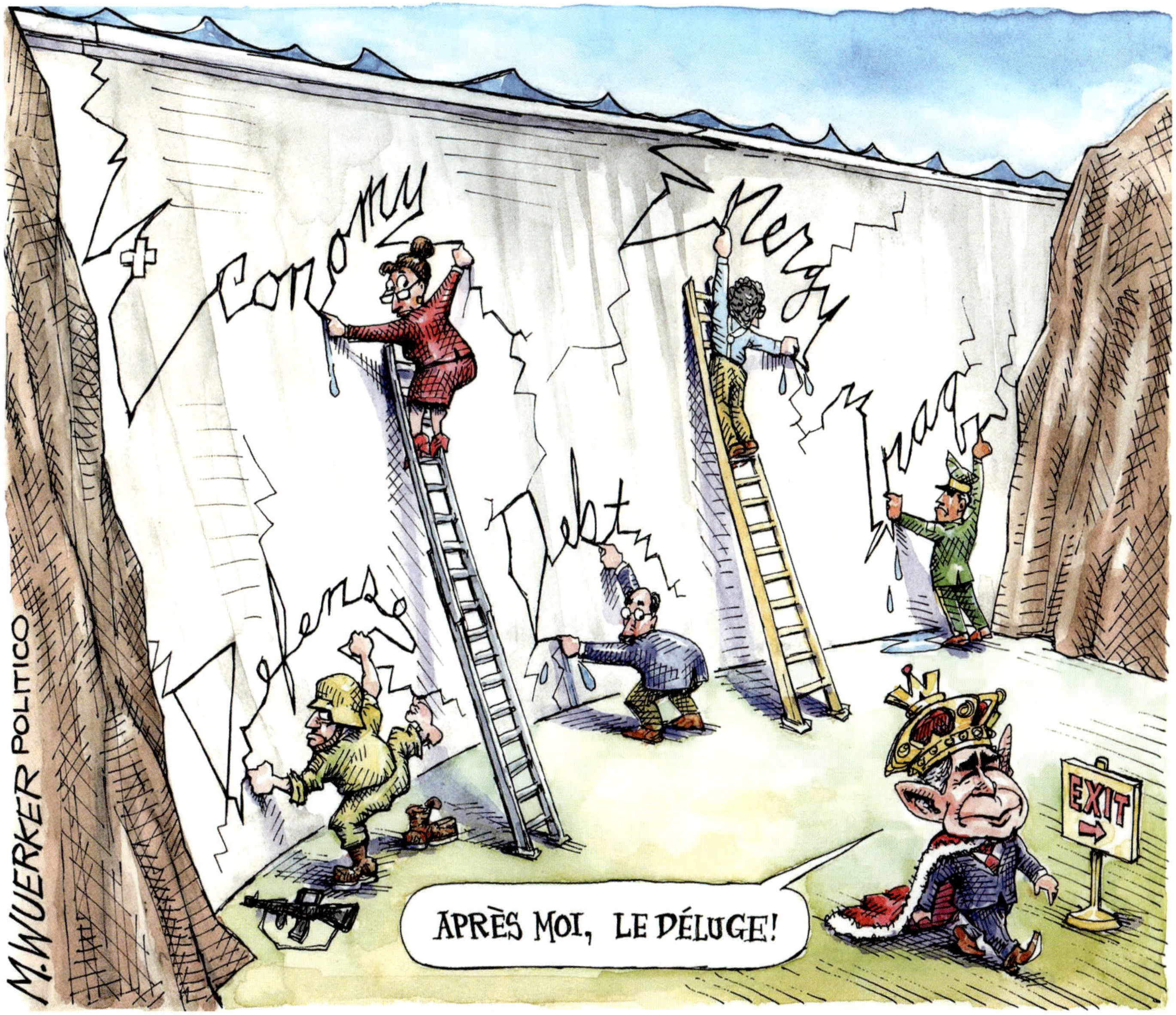
Economy
Energy
Debt
Iraq
Defense
EXIT
APRÈS MOI, LE DÉLUGE!
M.WUERKER POLITICO

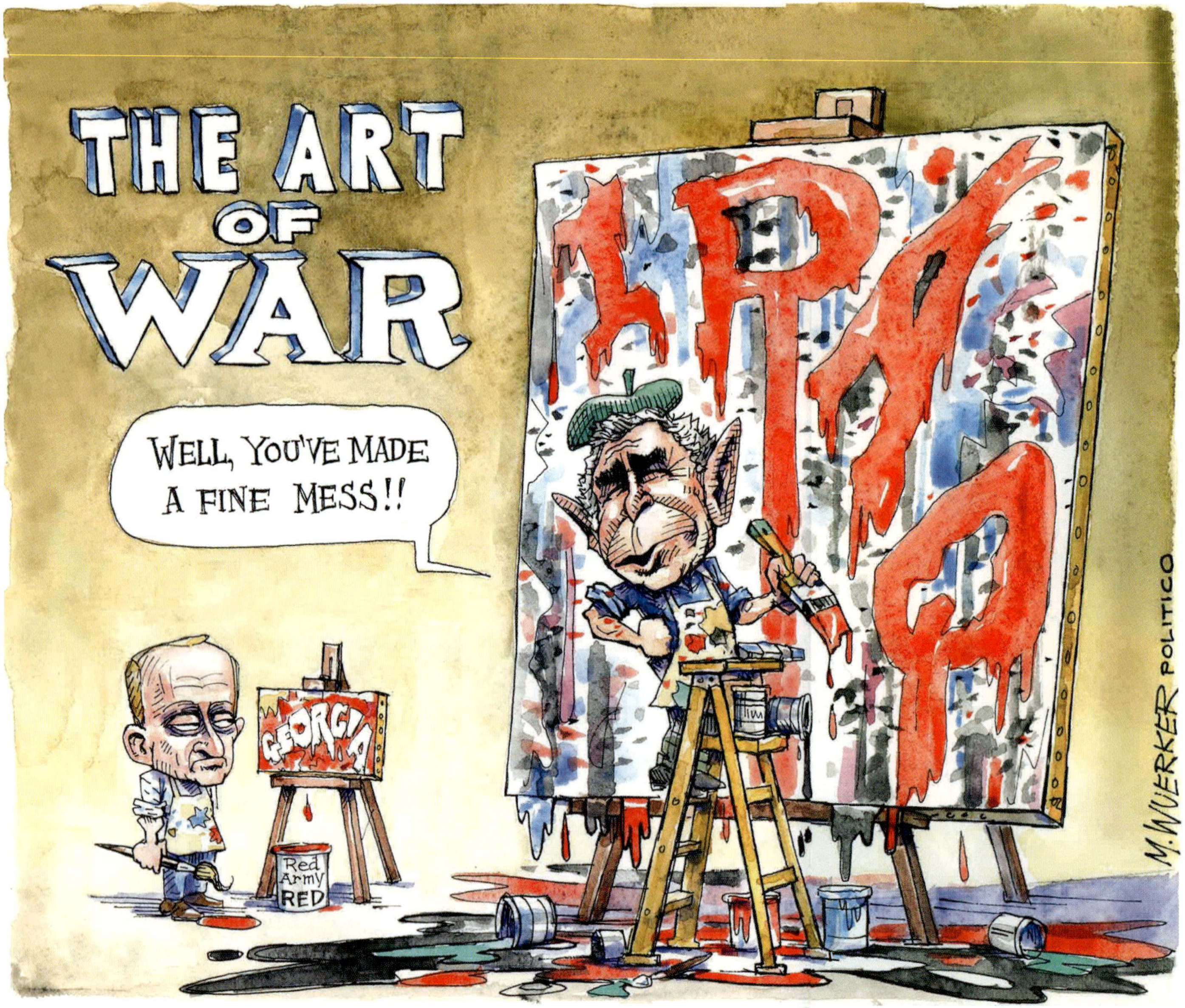
THE ART OF WAR
WELL, YOU'VE MADE A FINE MESS!!
GEORGIA
Red Army RED
M. WUERKER POLITICO

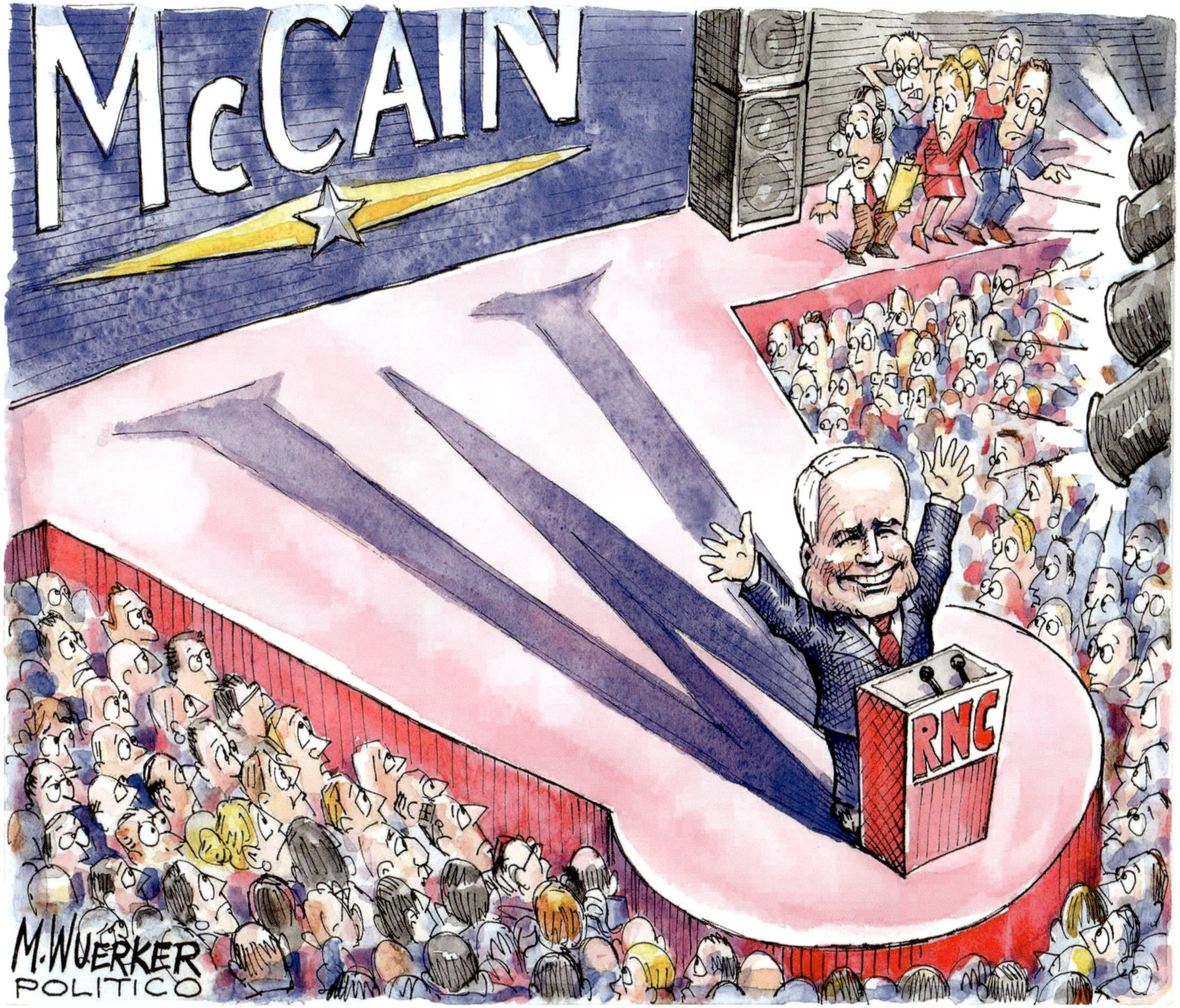
McCAIN
RNC
M. WUERKER
POLITICO

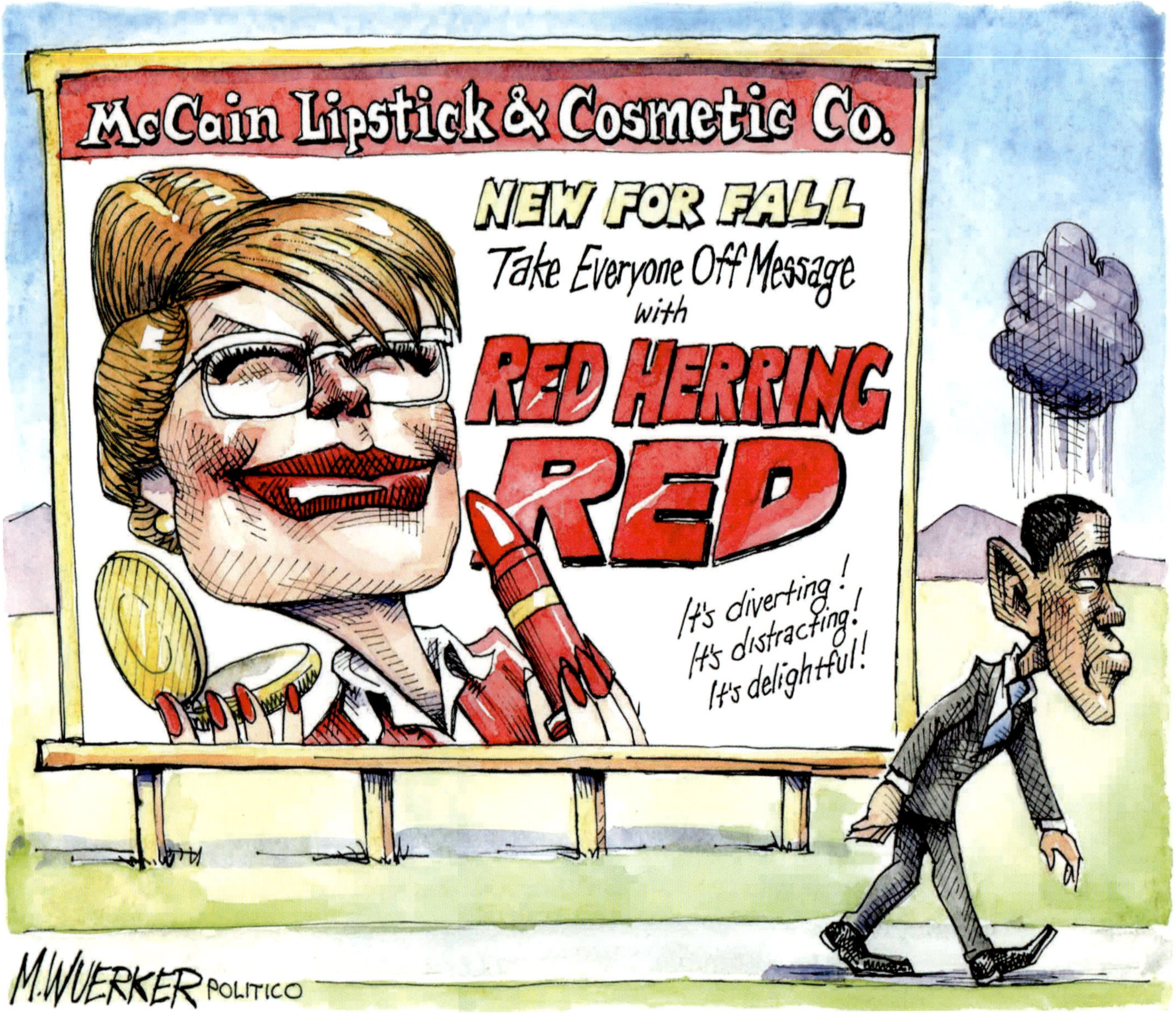
McCain Lipstick & Cosmetic Co.
NEW FOR FALL
Take Everyone Off Message
with
RED HERRING
RED
It's diverting!
It's distracting!
It's delightful!
M.WUERKER POLITICO

THE
FAR NORTHERNER
MEXICO
CHINA
PACIFIC
OCEAN
GOMORRAH
SODOM
OHIO
BOISE
RUSSIA
CANADA
HOCKEY!
WAL*MART
MAIN ST
MOOSE
BURGER
CITY
HALL
TAVERN
STOP
ZZ
WASILLA HWY
M. WUERKER
POLITICO

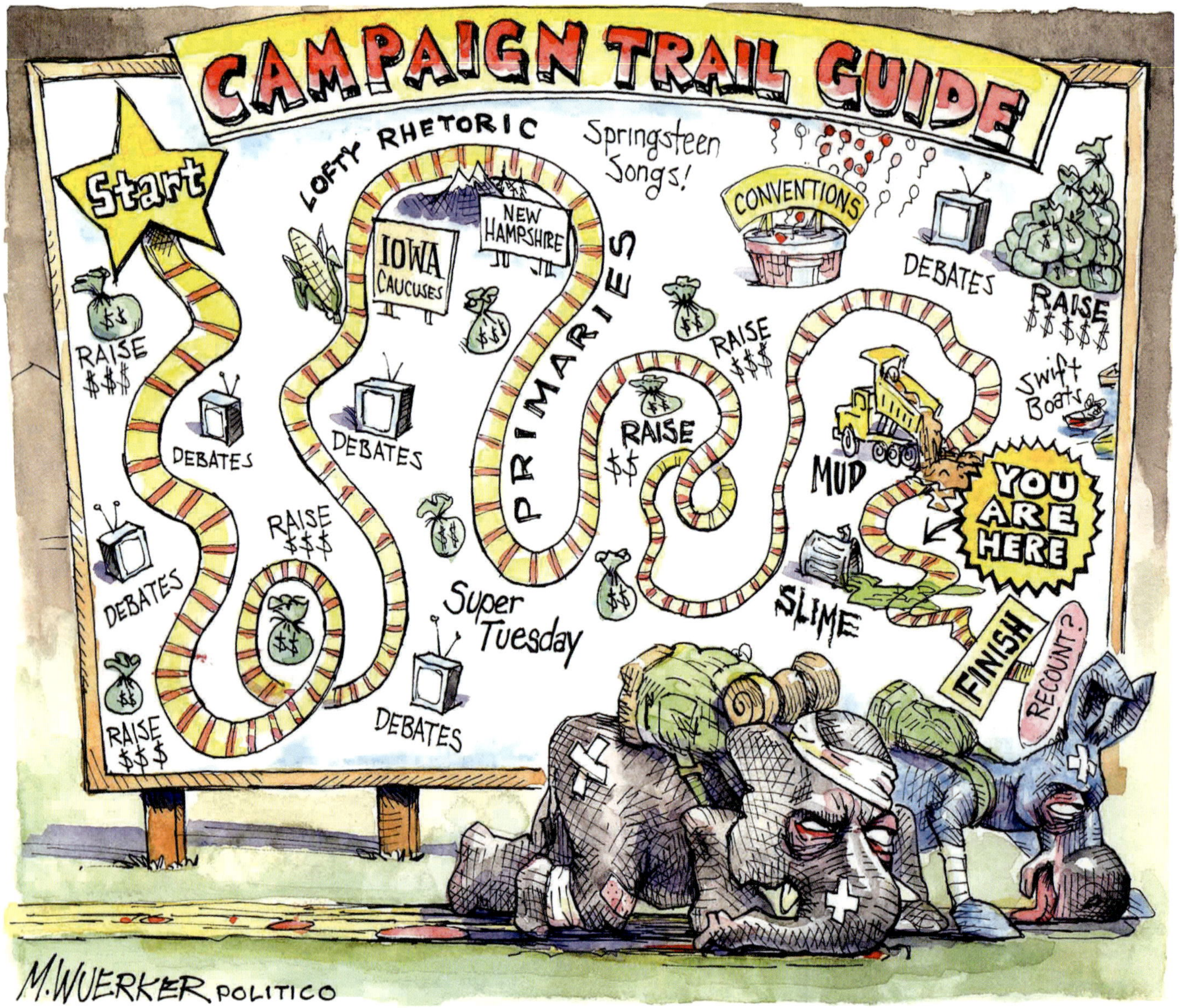
CAMPAIGN TRAIL GUIDE
Start
LOFTY RHETORIC
Springsteen Songs!
CONVENTIONS
IOWA CAUCUSES
NEW HAMPSHIRE
PRIMARIES
RAISE $$$
DEBATES
RAISE $$$
DEBATES
DEBATES
RAISE $$$
DEBATES
Super Tuesday
DEBATES
RAISE $$$
RAISE $$
RAISE $$$
MUD
SLIME
DEBATES
RAISE $$$$$
Swift Boats
YOU ARE HERE
FINISH
RECOUNT?
M.WUERKER POLITICO

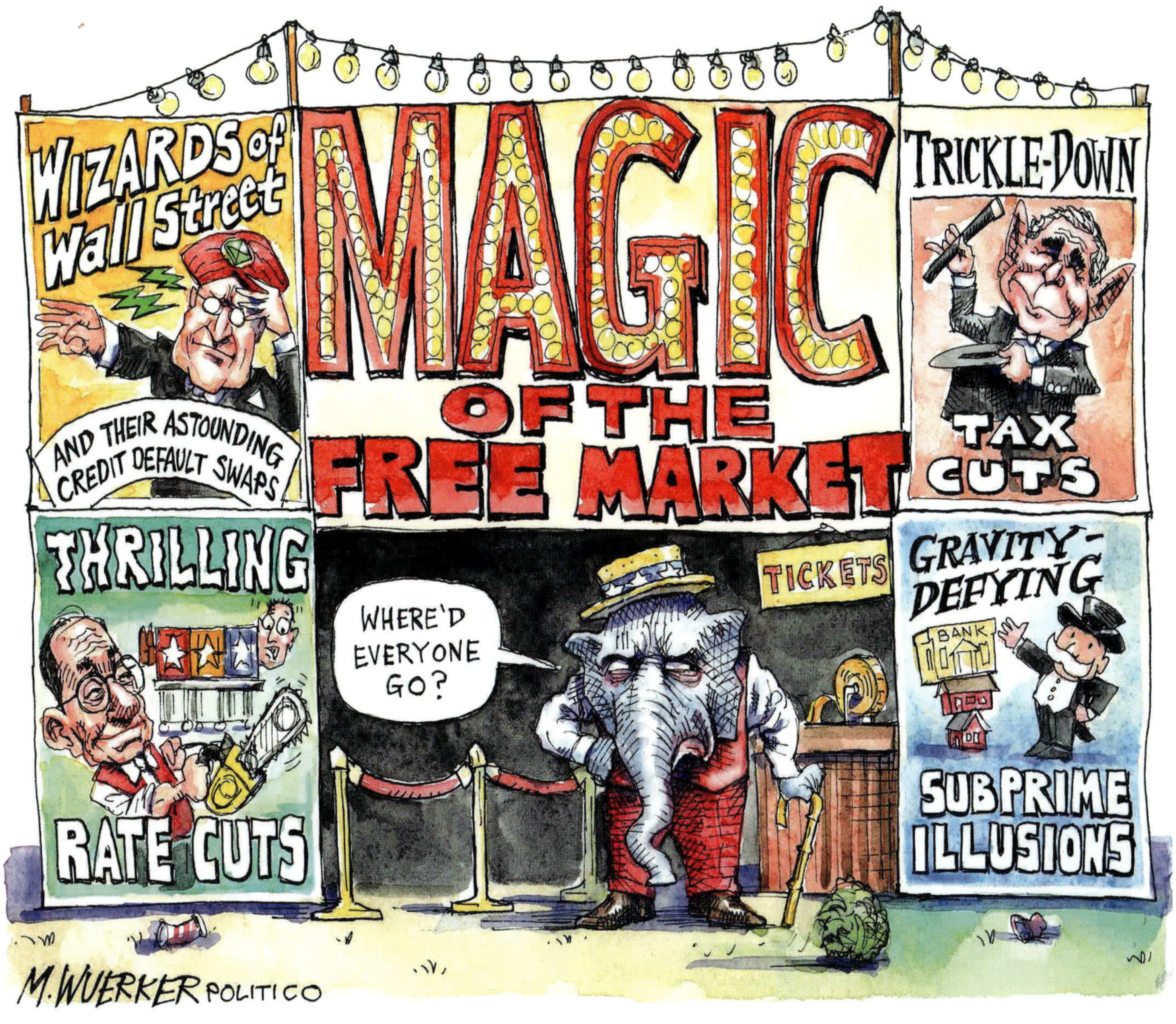
WIZARDS of Wall Street
AND THEIR ASTOUNDING CREDIT DEFAULT SWAPS
MAGIC
OF THE
FREE MARKET
TRICKLE-DOWN
TAX CUTS
THRILLING
RATE CUTS
TICKETS
WHERE'D EVERYONE GO?
GRAVITY-DEFYING
BANK
SUBPRIME ILLUSIONS
M.WUERKER POLITICO

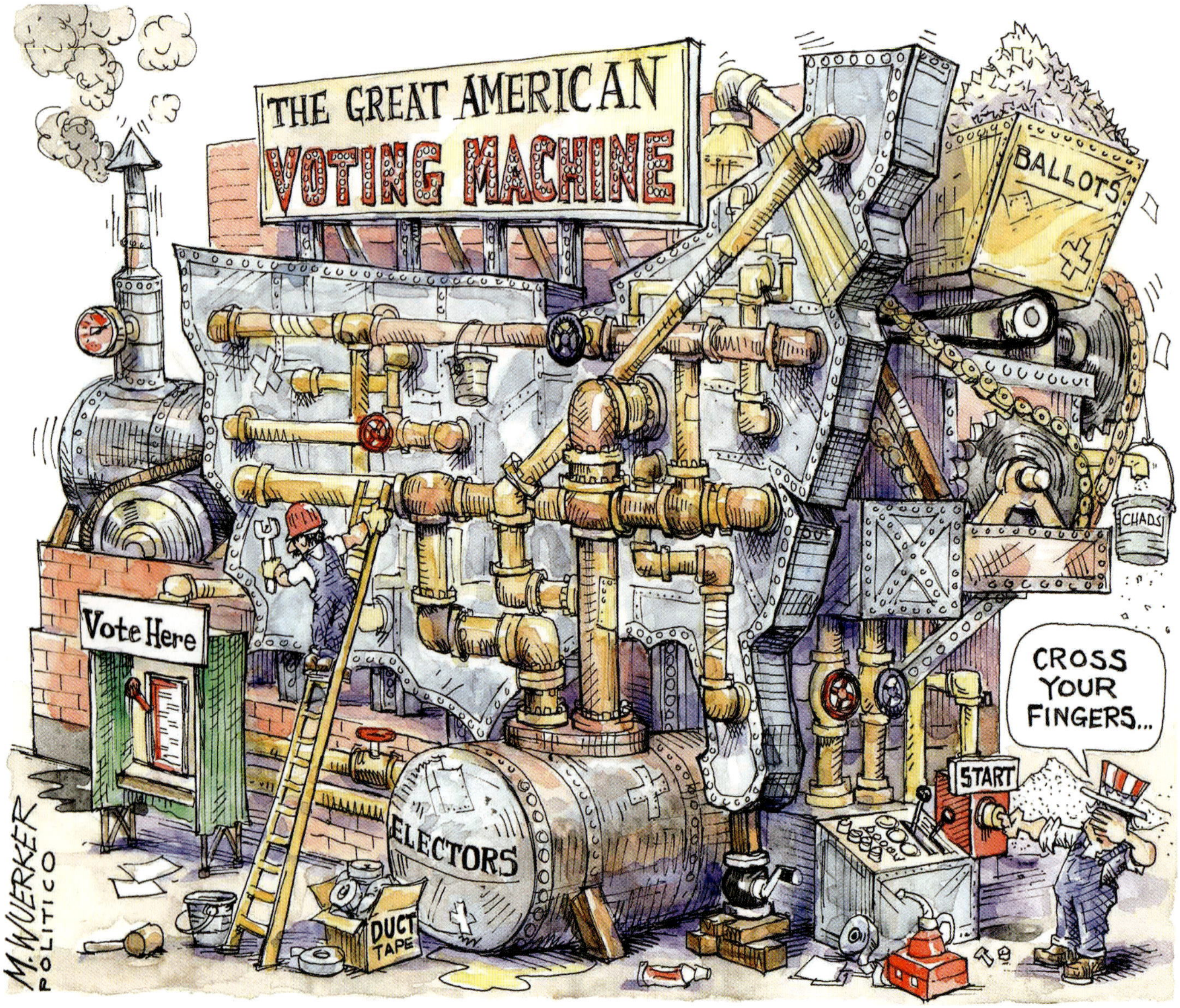
THE GREAT AMERICAN
VOTING MACHINE
BALLOTS
CHADS
Vote Here
CROSS YOUR FINGERS...
START
ELECTORS
DUCT TAPE
M. WUERKER
POLITICO

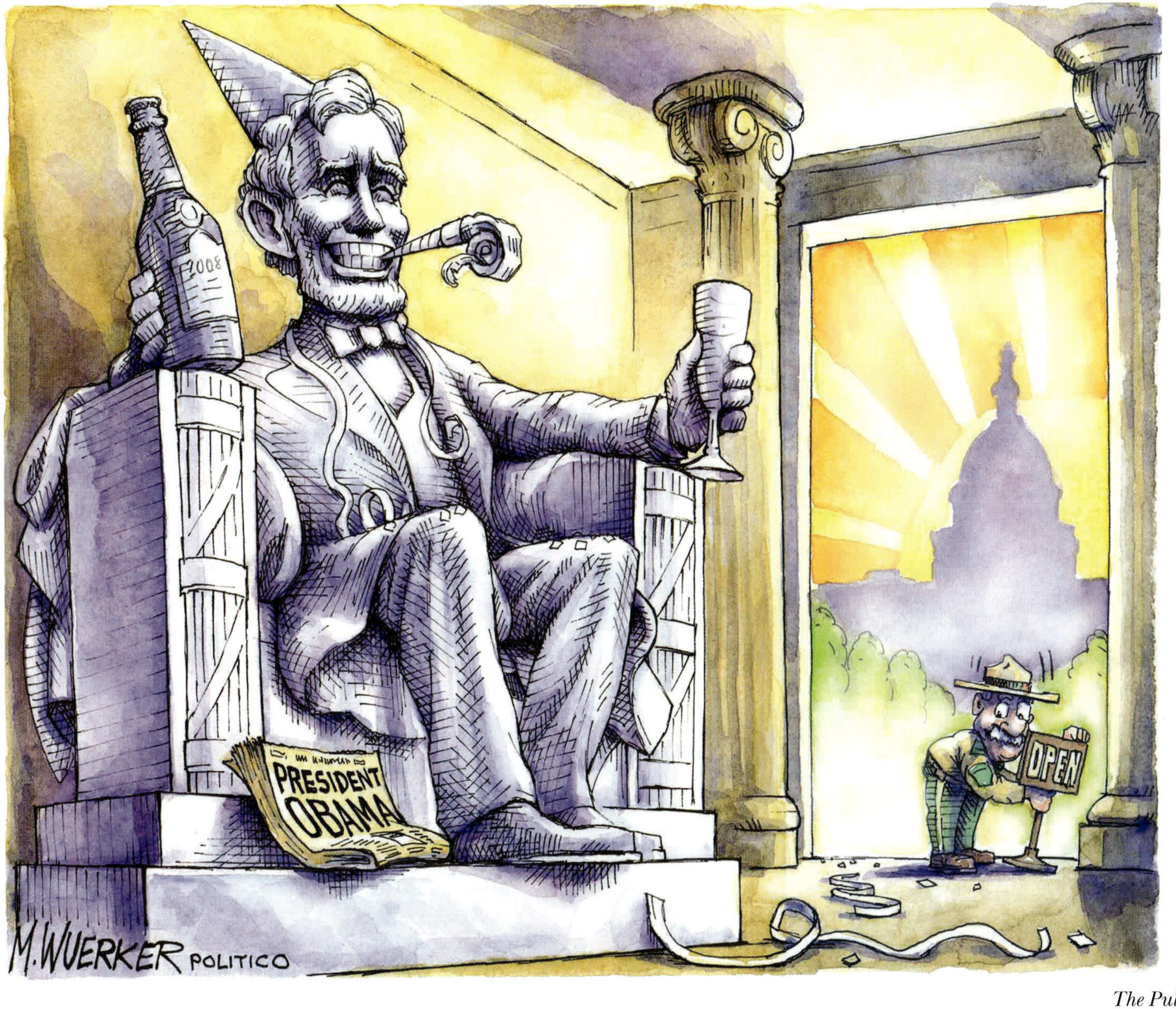
2008
PRESIDENT OBAMA
OPEN
M.WUERKER POLITICO

ALL THE WATER BOARDS?! CAN'T I KEEP JUST ONE?
MOVING SALE
(DUE TO FORECLOSURE
MISSION
LIBBY
SHOCK
FEAR
AWE
ASHCROFT Soars like an Eagle!
PLAN A Permanent GOP Majority
Rummy Rules
FREE
Wedge Issue
We the People
Flag Pins
Shred-O-Matic
BROKEN
COLLECTED WISDOM OF KARL ROVE
50¢ 25¢ 15¢
WIRETAP KIT
M. WUERKER
POLITICO

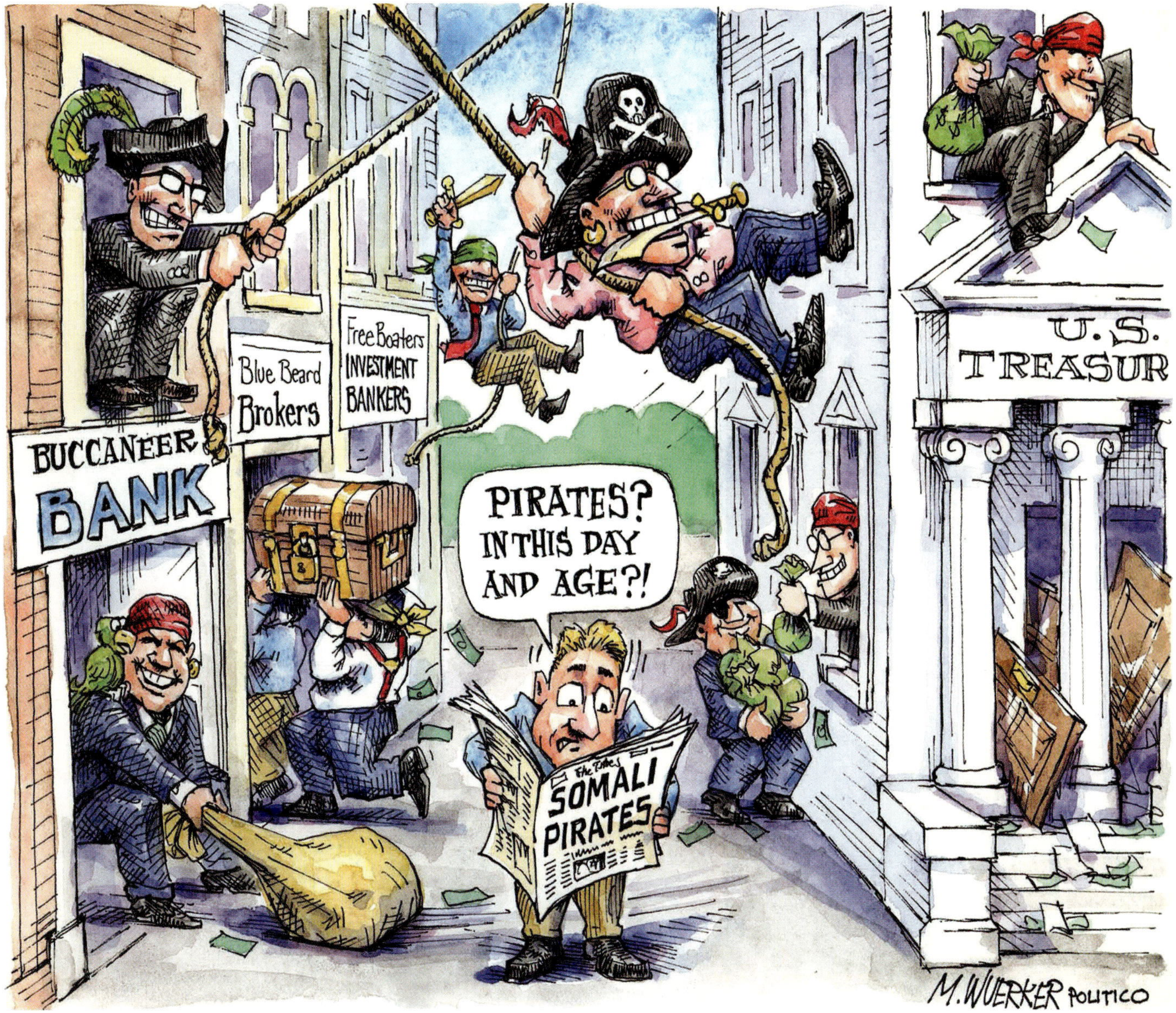
BUCCANEER
BANK
Blue Beard
Brokers
Free Boaters
INVESTMENT
BANKERS
U.S.
TREASUR
PIRATES?
IN THIS DAY
AND AGE?!
SOMALI
PIRATES
M.WUERKER POLITICO

2009 Pulitzer Prize Nominee
Mike Thompson—*Detroit Free Press*

Mike Thompson has been a Pulitzer nominee for two years running. He is syndicated to more than four hundred publications by Creators Syndicate and has been the editorial cartoonist for the *Detroit Free Press* since 1998. Aside from the *Detroit Free Press,* Thompson regularly draws for *USA Today.* His work has been featured on C-SPAN, CNN, the *CBS Evening News,* PBS, the Fox News Network, and the *Today Show*.

Thompson began his career at the *Milwaukee Journal* as a contributing cartoonist, then became the staff cartoonist for the *St. Louis Sun* and Copley, Illinois, newspapers before taking his present job.

Thompson's awards include the National Press Foundation's Berryman Award (1999), the Overseas Press Club's Thomas Nast Award (2001), and the Society of Professional Journalists' Sigma Delta Chi Award (1999 and 2002).

Mike Thompson Interview

Dean: Turn-of-the-century journalist Finley Peter Dunne is quoted as saying, "The job of the newspaper is to comfort the afflicted and afflict the comfortable." What do you see as the role of the editorial cartoonist?

Mike: An editorial cartoonist is a visual columnist. Hopefully, the "comforting the afflicted and afflicting the comfortable" sentiment is reflected in the work of editorial cartoonists as well.

Dean: With the continuing decline of newspaper readership, what do you believe the future holds for the fate of the editorial cartoonist?

Mike: Editorial cartoonists, like everyone else in the newsroom, will wear many hats. Animation, blogging and video will increasingly become tools cartoonists use to express their opinions.

Dean: Although the bulk of this book is dedicated to editorial contests in the U.S., the final section of this book deals with international Lurie Award. How do you think U.S. cartoons differ from those of other countries?

Mike: American political cartoons tend to be verbally oriented. International cartoons tend to be visually oriented.

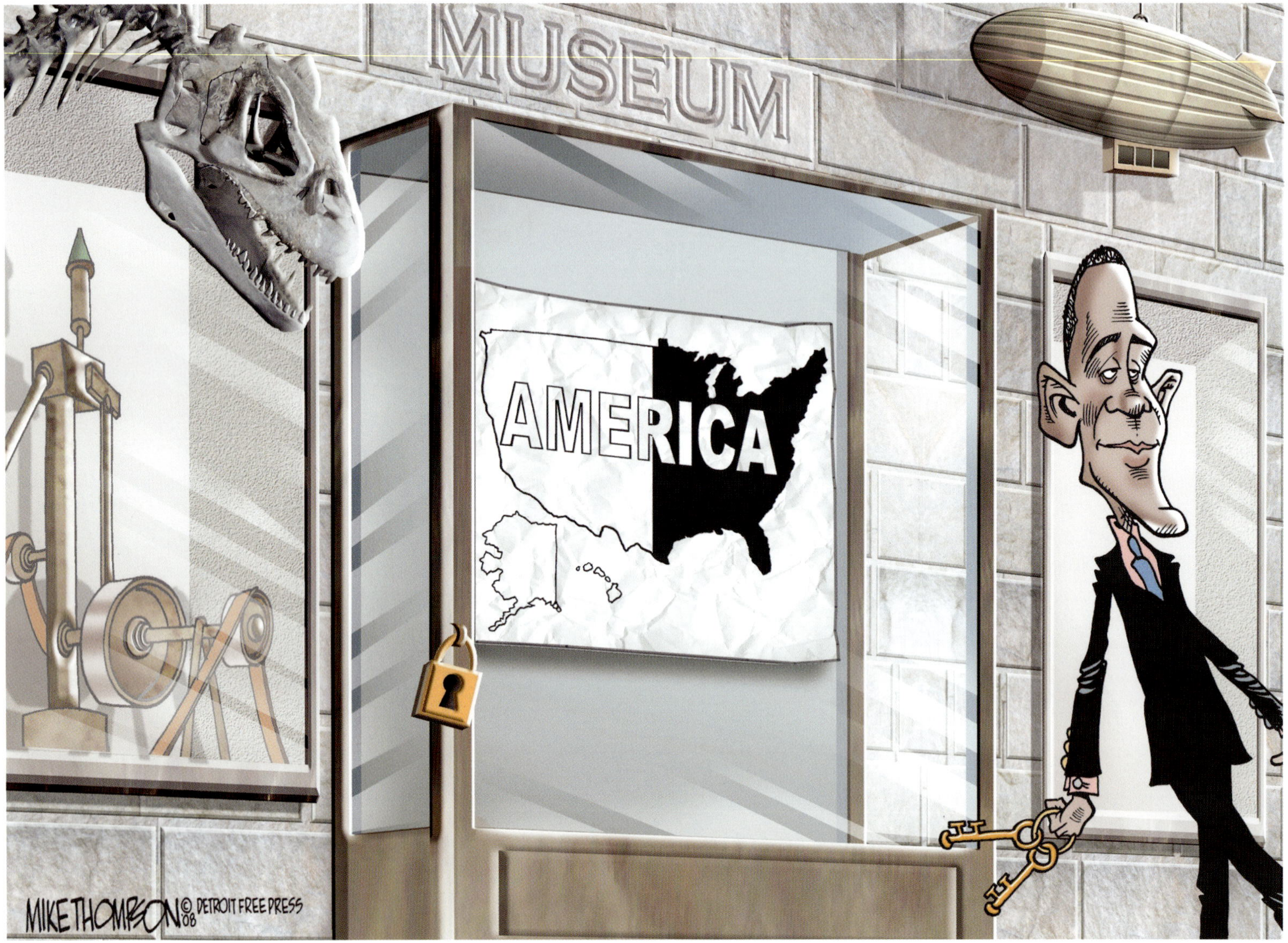
MUSEUM
AMERICA
MIKE THOMPSON © '08 DETROIT FREE PRESS

IT'S HISTORY

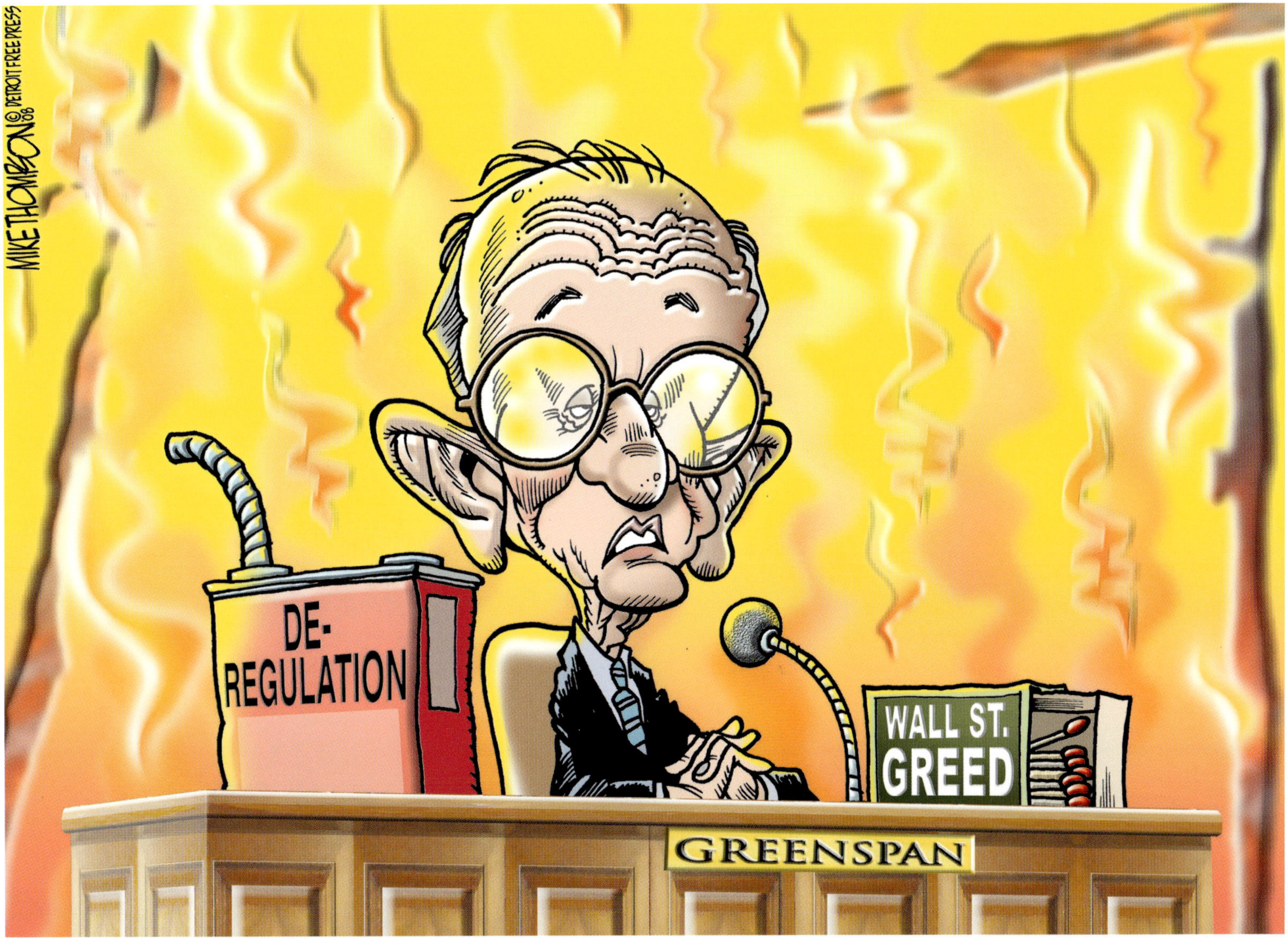
MIKE THOMPSON © '08 DETROIT FREE PRESS
DE-
REGULATION
WALL ST.
GREED
GREENSPAN

"WHO COULD HAVE FORESEEN THAT MIXING GASOLINE AND MATCHES WOULD RESULT IN FIRE?"

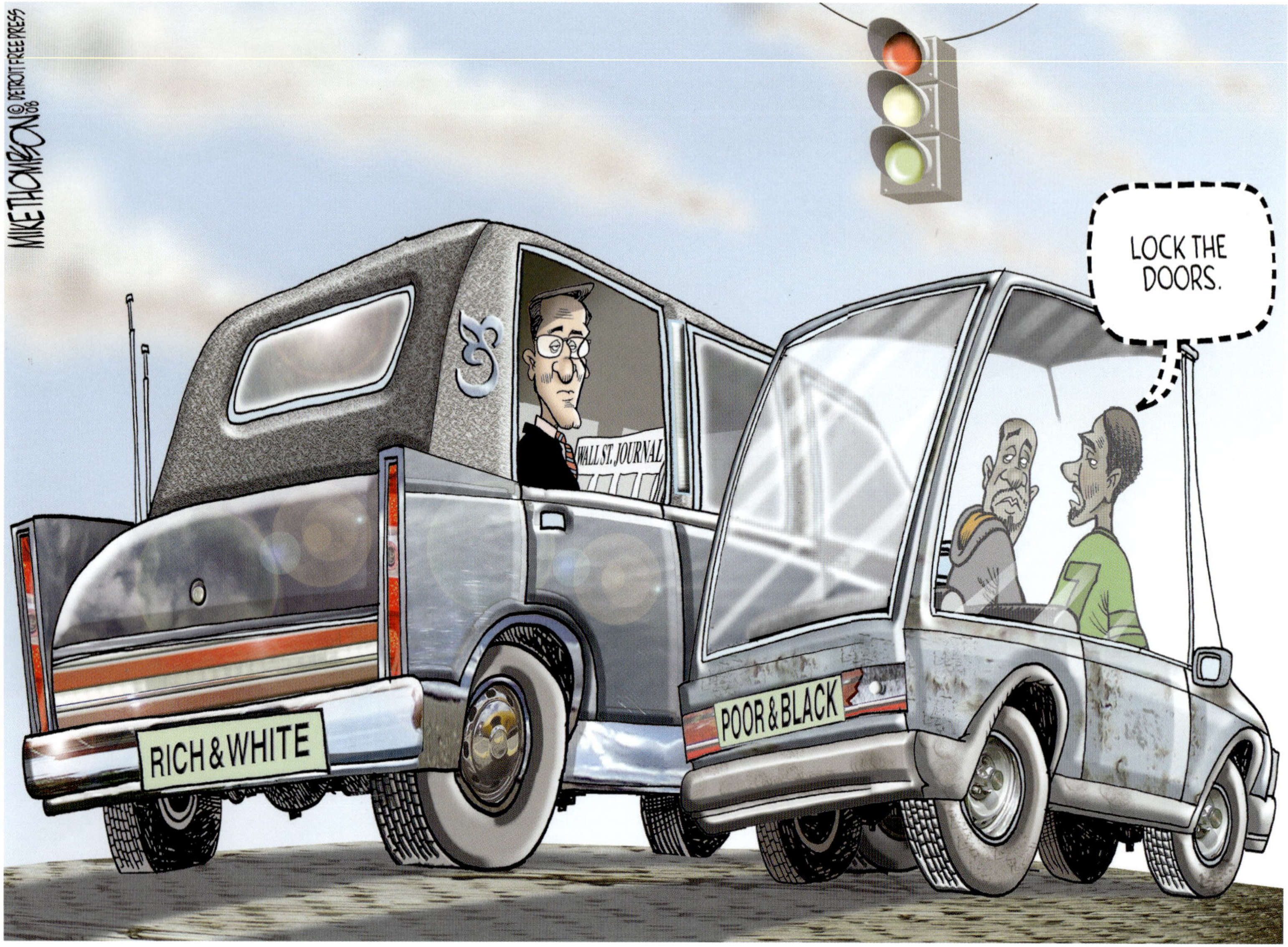
MIKE THOMPSON © DETROIT FREE PRESS '08
WALL ST. JOURNAL
RICH & WHITE
POOR & BLACK
LOCK THE DOORS.

DID I FORGET TO ALSO MENTION THAT WHAT'S BAD FOR GENERAL MOTORS IS WHAT'S BAD FOR THE COUNTRY?
MIKE THOMPSON © '08 DETROIT FREE PRESS
GM
LIVE NOW, PAY LATER
LIVE NOW, PAY LATER

THAT COURT WAS WRONG TO OVERTURN A GAY MARRIAGE BAN. THE ORIGINAL CONCEPT OF MARRIAGE SHOULDN'T BE CHANGED!
RIGHT. I NOW PRONOUNCE YOU HUSBAND AND PROPERTY.
MIKE THOMPSON © '08 DETROIT FREE PRESS

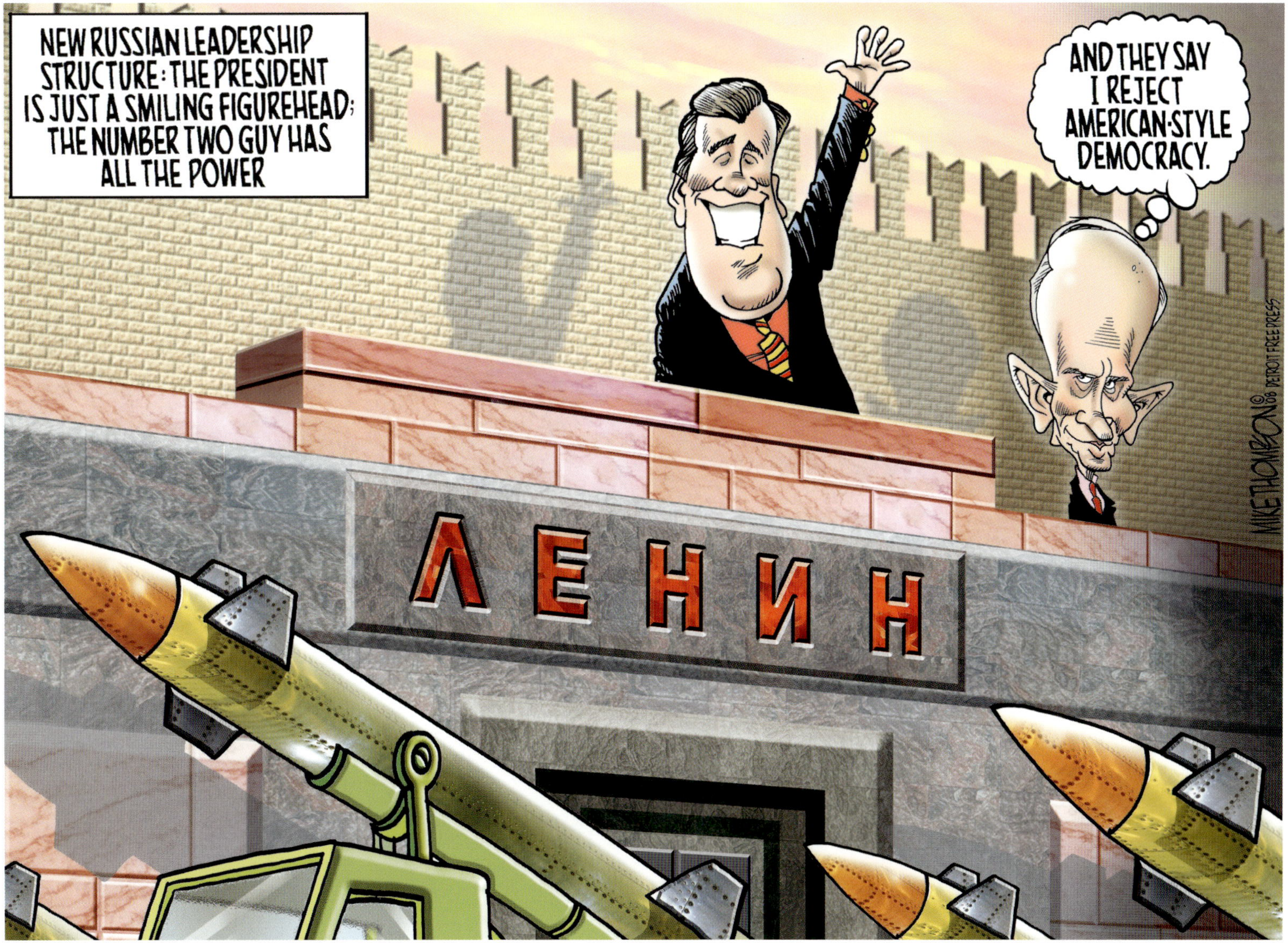
NEW RUSSIAN LEADERSHIP STRUCTURE: THE PRESIDENT IS JUST A SMILING FIGUREHEAD; THE NUMBER TWO GUY HAS ALL THE POWER
AND THEY SAY I REJECT AMERICAN-STYLE DEMOCRACY.
ЛЕНИН
MIKE THOMPSON © '08 DETROIT FREE PRESS

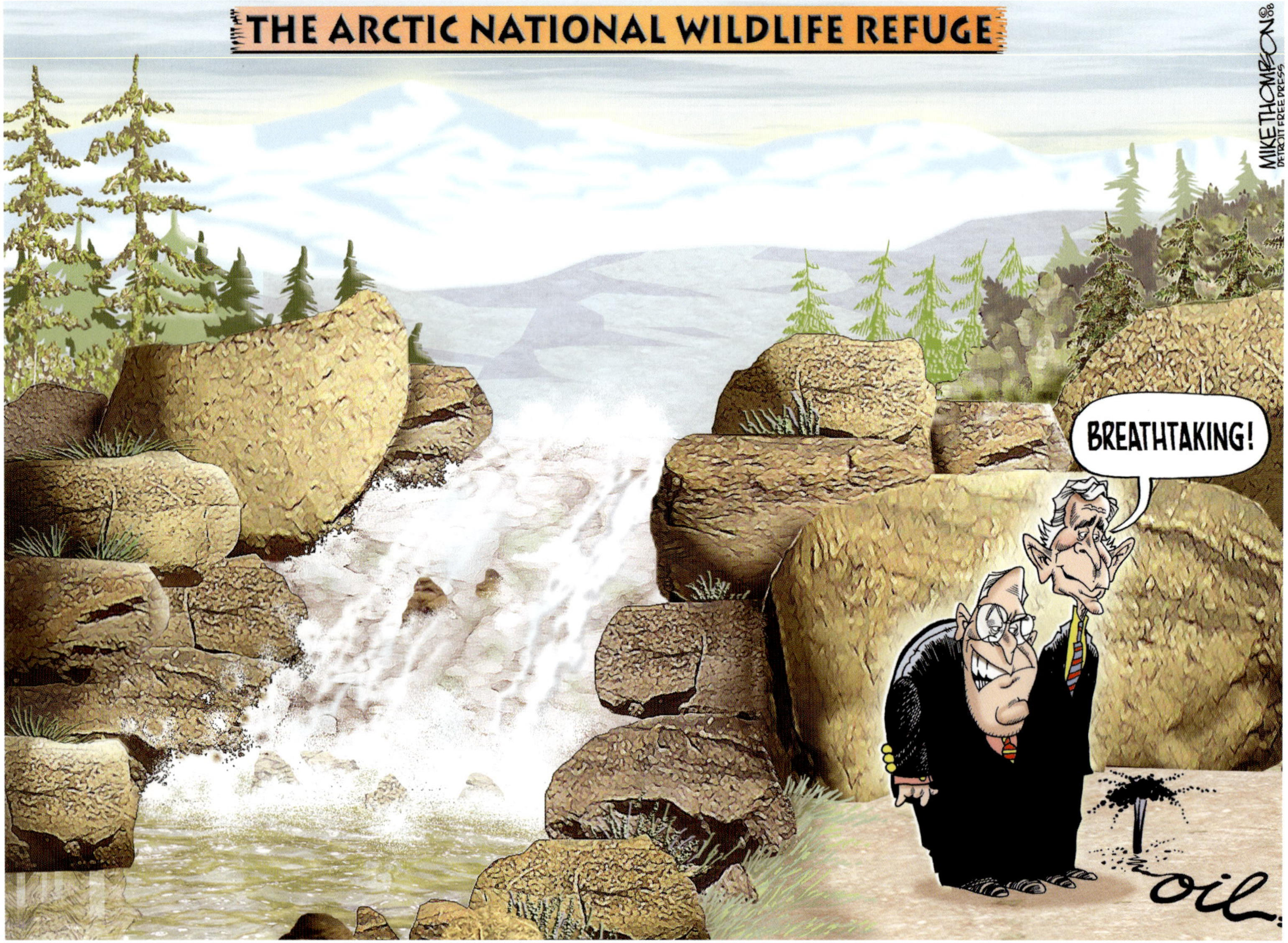
THE ARCTIC NATIONAL WILDLIFE REFUGE
MIKE THOMPSON ©08
DETROIT FREE PRESS
BREATHTAKING!
oil

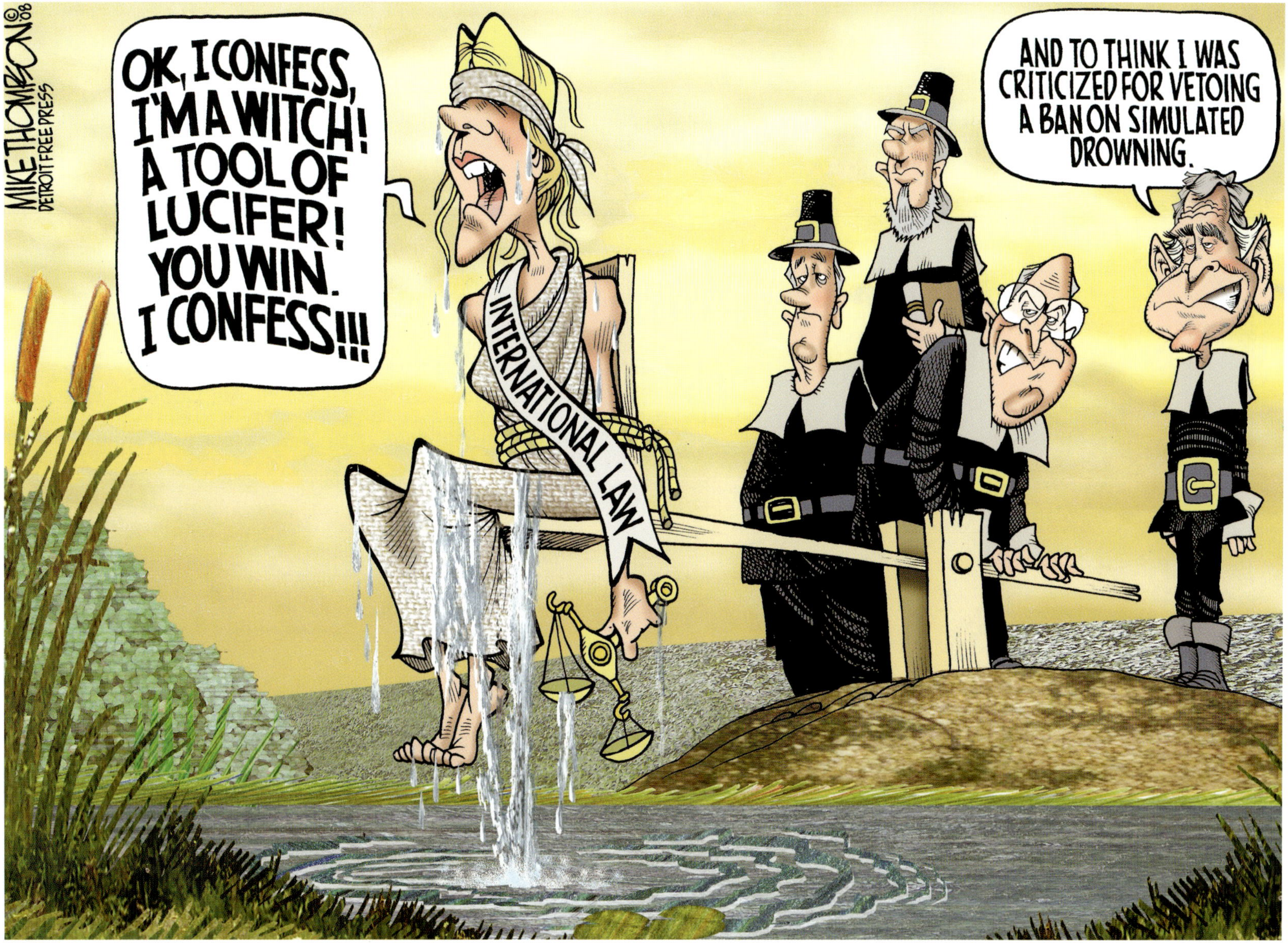
MIKE THOMPSON © '08 DETROIT FREE PRESS
OK, I CONFESS, I'M A WITCH! A TOOL OF LUCIFER! YOU WIN. I CONFESS!!!
INTERNATIONAL LAW
AND TO THINK I WAS CRITICIZED FOR VETOING A BAN ON SIMULATED DROWNING.

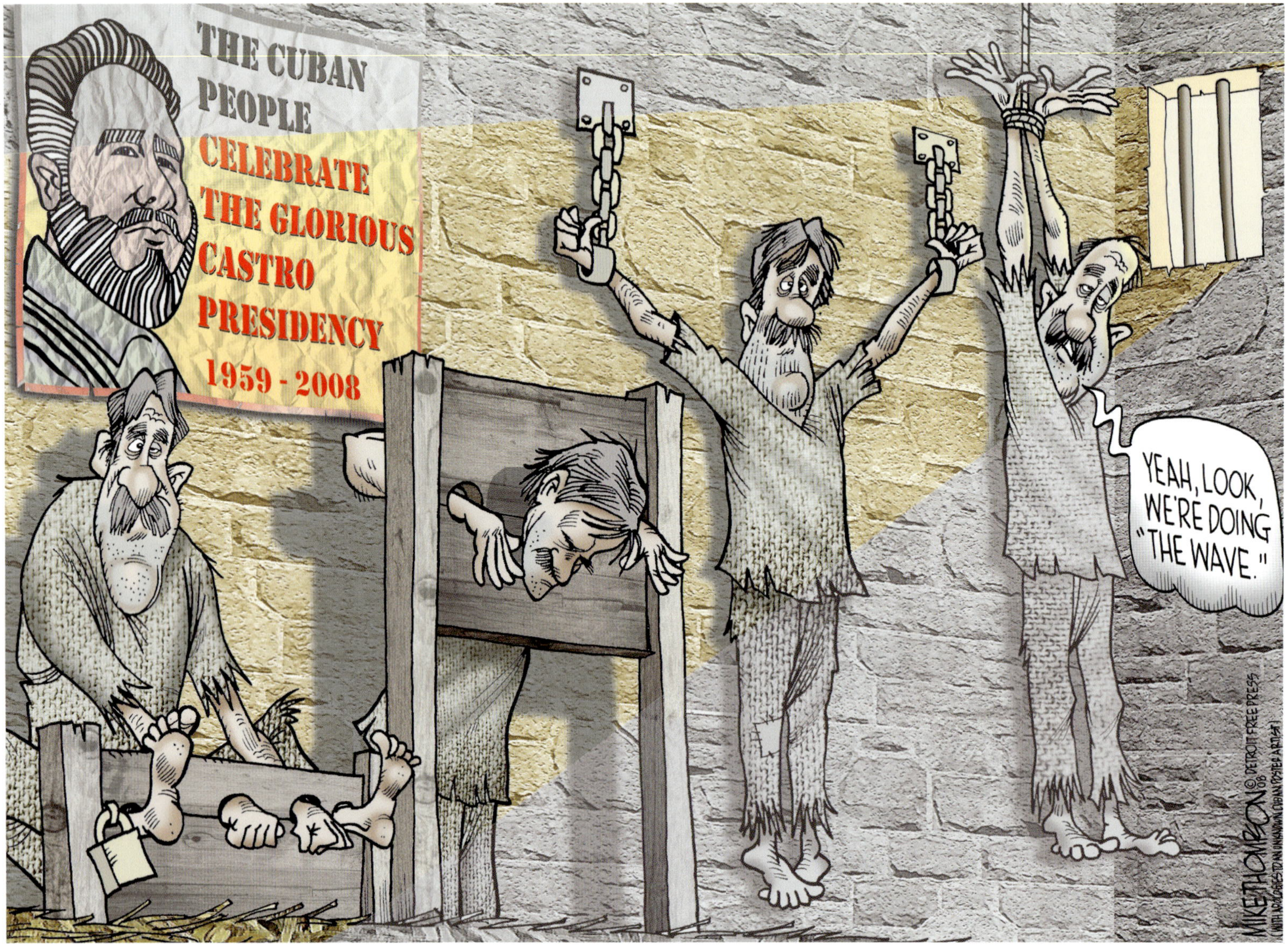
THE CUBAN PEOPLE
CELEBRATE THE GLORIOUS CASTRO PRESIDENCY
1959 - 2008
YEAH, LOOK, WE'RE DOING "THE WAVE."
MIKE THOMPSON © DETROIT FREE PRESS '08
(WITH APOLOGIES TO AN UNKNOWN CUBAN POSTER ARTIST)

MIKETHOMPSON © DETROIT 08 FREE PRESS
POLITICAL SIBERIA
DNC
I WAS EXILED FOR DARING TO CHALLENGE THE PARTY.
MICHIGAN PRIMARY

WALL ST.
TERRORISM
ECONOMY
IRAN
I'D OFFER YOU A LAST CIGARETTE, BUT I HEARD YOU QUIT.
WAR
WALL ST.
CHINA

JOURNALISM
NEWSPAPER
RADIO
MAGAZINE
NEWS
PHOTOGRAPHY
TELEVISION

The National Headliner Awards

In 1934, the Press Club of Atlantic City founded the National Headliner Awards, making it one of the oldest and largest national contests recognizing journalism merit. These cherished medallions were first presented in 1935, and since that time, more than sixteen hundred have been received by outstanding writers, photographers, daily newspapers, radio and television stations, and news syndicates.

It wasn't until 1938 that the first National Headliner Award was presented to an editorial cartoonist, C. D. Batcher of the *New York Daily News.* Today, editorial cartooning is one of sixteen subcategories in the Daily Newspapers and News Syndicates division of the Print and Graphics category.

The majority of the work related to the National Headliner Awards is done by unpaid volunteers, distinguishing it from those award programs supported by universities or foundations. These volunteers sift through hundreds of entries in three main categories and sixty-two subcategories. The main categories are Print and Graphics, Online Journalism, and Radio and Television (Broadcast). The entries are painstakingly catalogued and prepared for judging. Each is prescreened before being seen by the final judging panel in order to distill the strongest entries.

2009 National Headliner Award Winner
Steve Breen—*San Diego Union-Tribune*

The National Headliner Award is the second of three major editorial cartooning awards Steve Breen has won this year.

As the Pulitzer winner this year, Breen was asked and graciously accepted the task of writing the foreword for this book. As noted before, Breen was born in Los Angeles in 1970 and attended the University of California, Riverside. Editorial cartoonist for the *San Diego Union-Tribune* since ,2001 his work is nationally syndicated by Creators News Service and regularly appears in *USA Today*, the *New York Times*, and *Newsweek*.

In his spare time, he writes and illustrates picture books. Breen lives in San Diego with his wife and four children. He enjoys reading, running, playing the guitar and piano, and watching old movies on cable.

Steve Breen Interview

Dean: With the continuing decline of newspaper readership, what do you believe the future holds for the fate of the editorial cartoonist?

Steve: Cartoons will always exist. As long as there is news, there will be people who create static images commenting on that news. The question is, how many will be pros and how many will be part-time cartoonists/amateurs. The trend looks like there will be fewer full-time professionals because the old newspaper model is unsustainable. Because there are likely to be fewer full-time pros, the overall quality of the work out there on the Internet will probably decrease. That said, I'm sure the Internet will provide a platform for some talented cartoonists here and there.

Dean: It has been said that how a person entertains him/herself speaks volumes of their character. Please name your favorite three books, three movies, three actors/actresses, and three musical performers.

Steve: Books—The Bible, *The Giving Tree, Robinson Crusoe*
Movies—*Raiders of the Lost Ark, The Godfather* (I, II), anything by Pixar
Actors—Nicholson, Crowe, DiCaprio
Acresses—Streep, Winslet, Blanchett
Musical—The Beatles, Stevie Wonder, Mozart

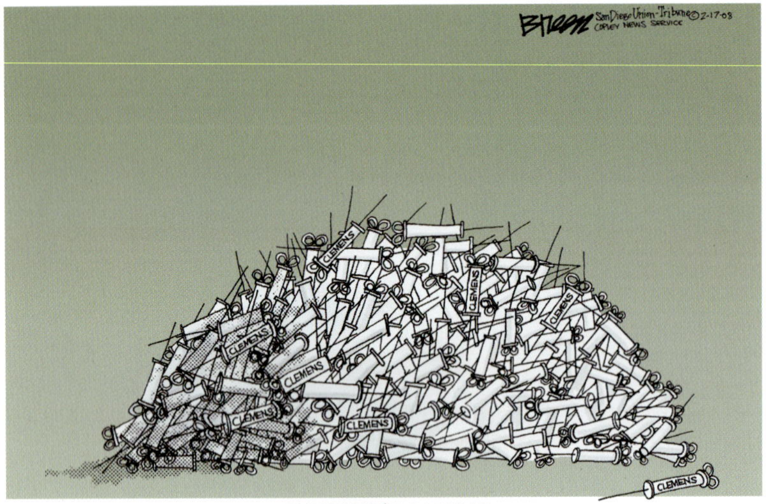

Breen San Diego Union-Tribune © 2-17-08
COPLEY NEWS SERVICE
CLEMENS

PITCHER'S MOUND

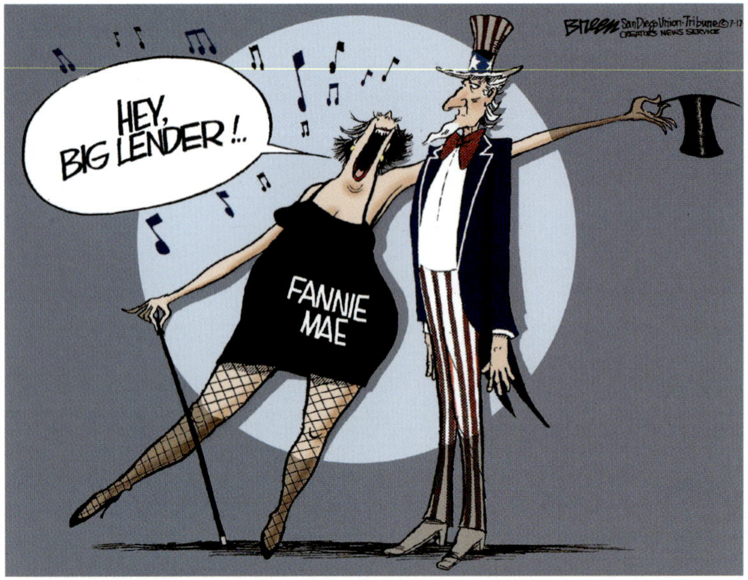

Breen San Diego Union-Tribune © 7-17
CREATORS NEWS SERVICE
HEY, BIG LENDER!..
FANNIE MAE

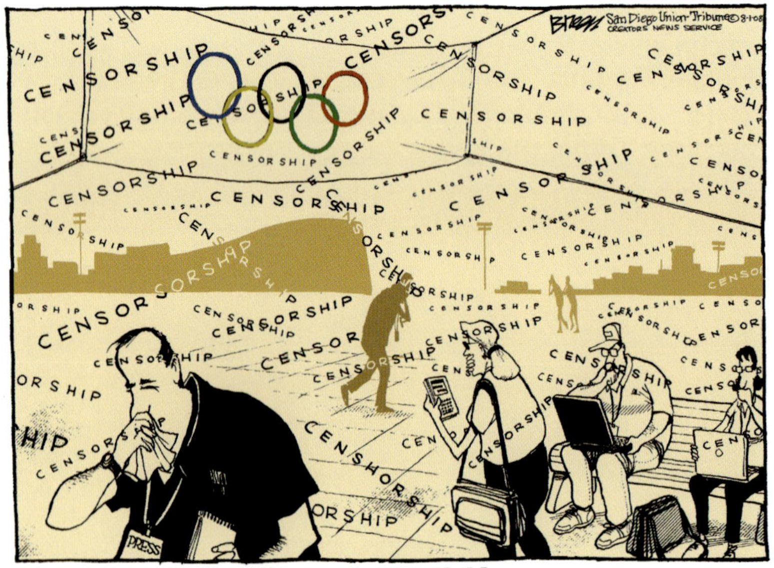

Breen San Diego Union-Tribune © 8-08
CREATORS NEWS SERVICE
CENSORSHIP
PRESS

BEIJING POLLUTION

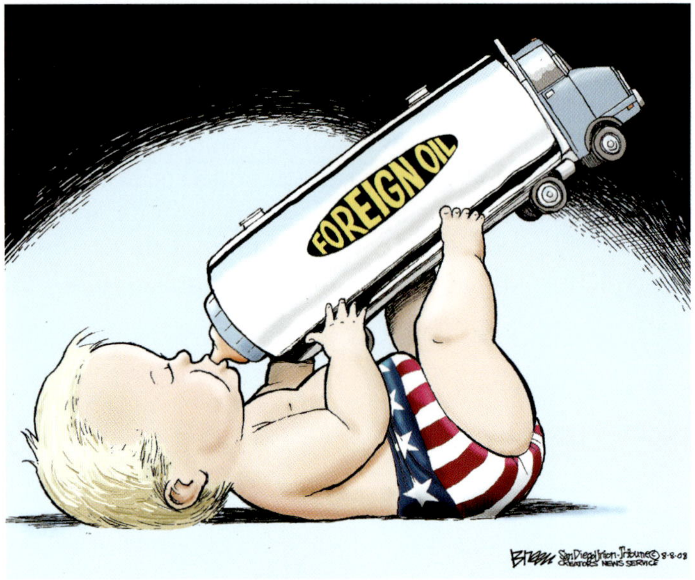

FOREIGN OIL
Breen San Diego Union-Tribune © 8-8-08
CREATORS NEWS SERVICE

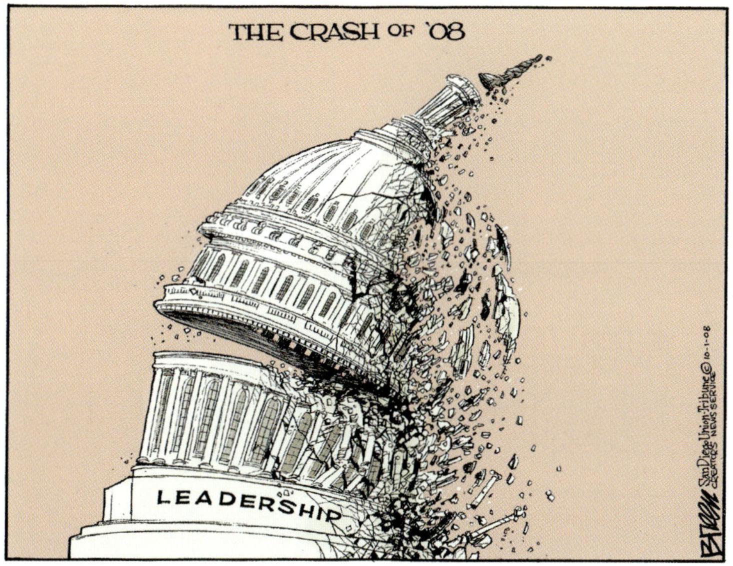
THE CRASH OF '08
LEADERSHIP
San Diego Union-Tribune © 10-1-08
CREATORS NEWS SERVICE

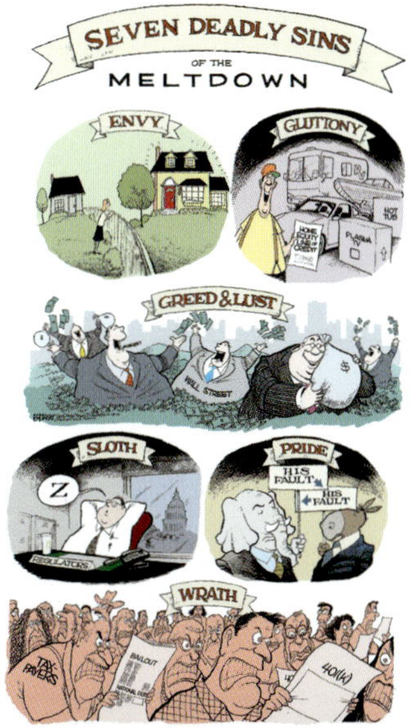
SEVEN DEADLY SINS
OF THE
MELTDOWN
ENVY
GLUTTONY
HOT TUB
PLASMA TV
GREED & LUST
WALL STREET
SLOTH
Z
REGULATORS
PRIDE
HIS FAULT
HIS FAULT
WRATH
TAX-PAYERS
BAILOUT
401(k)

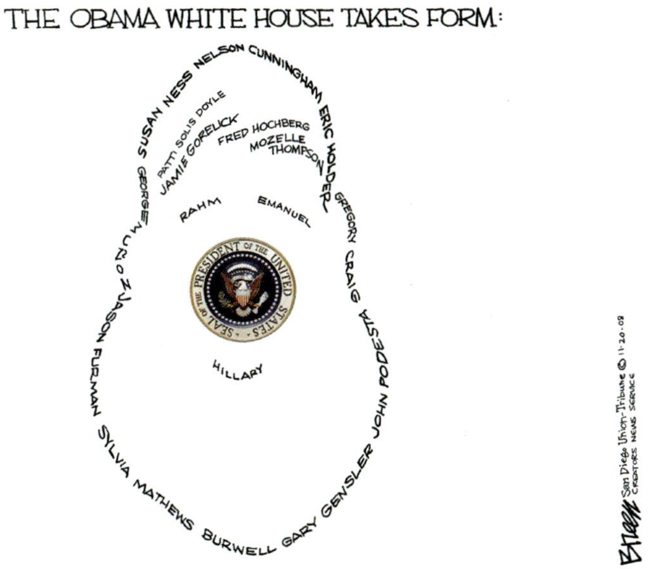
THE OBAMA WHITE HOUSE TAKES FORM:
SUSAN NESS NELSON CUNNINGHAM ERIC HOLDER
PATTI SOLIS DOYLE
JAMIE GORELICK
FRED HOCHBERG
MOZELLE THOMPSON
GEORGE MUÑOZ
RAHM
EMANUEL
GREGORY CRAIG
HILLARY
JASON FURMAN
JOHN PODESTA
SYLVIA MATHEWS BURWELL GARY GENSLER
San Diego Union-Tribune © 11-20-08
CREATORS NEWS SERVICE

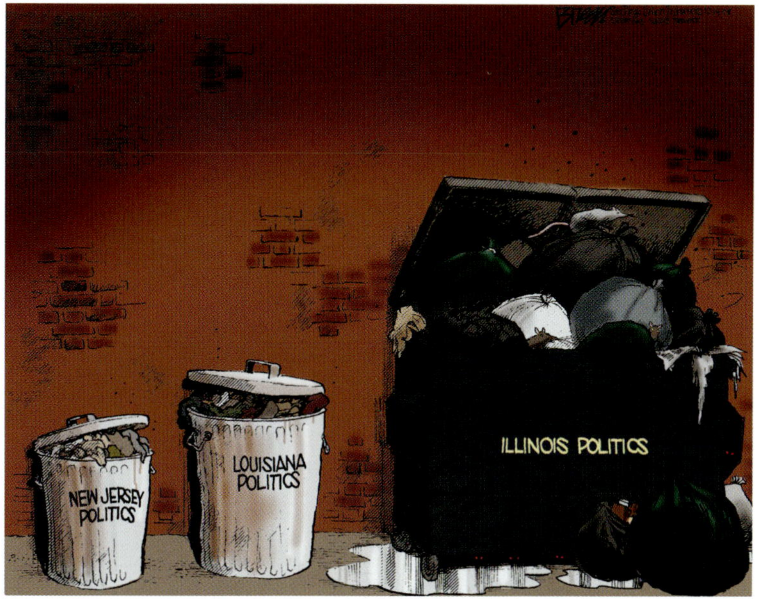
NEW JERSEY POLITICS
LOUISIANA POLITICS
ILLINOIS POLITICS

San Diego Union-Tribune © 10-21-08
Creators News Service
TIJUANA
POLICÍA
POLICÍA
POLICÍA
U.S. DRUG DEMAND

WHITE LINES

San Diego Union-Tribune © 4-5-08
COPLEY NEWS SERVICE
WE DON'T NEED A BORDER FENCE WITH MEXICO, JUST ECONOMIC CHARTS.
LAYOFFS
INFLATION
FORECLOSURES
FORGET IT... LET'S GO BACK.

2009 National Headliner Award—Second Place

Don Asmussen—*San Francisco Chronicle*

Second place for the National Headliner Award this year goes to Don Asmussen, the creator of *Bad Reporter*, a twice-weekly strip syndicated by Universal Press Syndicate.

Asmussen has worked at the *San Francisco Chronicle*, the *Detroit News*, the *San Diego Union-Tribune*, and *Portland Press Herald*.

His work has been profiled in *Communication Arts* and *Step-by-Step Magazine* and on Poynter.org. Asmussen had a regular strip in *Time* magazine from 1997 to 2002 and is the creator of the weekly Web animation *Like, News* and the strip *The Hero Santon* for *Mad* magazine and Salon.com.

Don Asmussen Interview

Dean: Turn-of-the-century journalist Finley Peter Dunne is quoted as saying, "The job of the newspaper is to comfort the afflicted and afflict the comfortable." What do you see as the role of the editorial cartoonist?

Don: To stay in as many papers as possible during this recession or death of newspapers.

Dean: With the continuing decline of newspaper readership, what do you believe the future holds for the fate of the editorial cartoonist?

Don: Working for free. The Internet is doing what greedy publishers have wanted to do for decades—get free content. Arianna Huffington has done more damage for the worth of content than anyone, yet she's a liberal hero. Unbelievable.

Dean: What do you feel distinguishes your work from that of your peers?

Don: I cannot draw as well. But at least I don't crosshatch. Too many political cartoons look alike, are in the same shape, etc. Lack of diversity killed political cartooning. Toles is still a god, though. And Mark Alan Stamaty should have gotten at least one Pulitzer instead of others winning three or four. Shake it the f*** up.

Don Asmussen
BAD REPORTER
The LIES behind the TRUTH, and the TRUTH behind those LIES that are behind that TRUTH.
The Chronicle
HOPEFUL 3-YEAR-OLD DREAMS OF SEEING FIRST WHITE PRESIDENT ELECTED IN HIS LIFETIME
YOUNGSTER REFUSES TO LET ENTIRE LIFE OF REVERSE RACISM DESTROY HOPE FOR HIS PEOPLE
Can Hillary's new strategy reach these disenfranchised people, or will Obama bring more status quo?
Clinton Still Holding Tough
A test of wills is tearing apart a party ...
The New York Times
FRIDAY, MAY 9, 2008
PICS LEAK OF DEMS PRESSURING HILLARY TO BOW OUT OF RACE
HOWARD DEAN PLEADS FOR ATTORNEY GENERAL TO LOOSEN POLITICAL PRESSURING RESTRICTIONS
Reader poll: If country is at stake, should waterboarding a candidate be allowed?
Hillary Strategy Shift
Opens up to alternatives ...
PUTIN NAMED PM OF RUSSIA — CLINTON STILL INSISTING SHE HAS SHOT
RUSSIANS STUNNED AS RADIOACTIVE POLONIUM 210 ONLY SEEMS TO ENERGIZE HER
© 2008 Don Asmussen/Universal Press Syndicate dasmussen@sfchronicle.com
Send LOVE and HATE e-mails to dasmussen@sfchronicle.com

(Also entered in the Scripps Howard National Journalism contest)

2009 National Headliner Award—Third Place

Clay Bennett—*Chattanooga Times Free Press*

Rounding out the field for this year's National Headliner Award is Clay Bennett. Born January 20, 1958, in Clinton, South Carolina, Bennett served as editorial cartoonist for his college paper and managing editor of the alternative student newspaper while attending the University of North Alabama, where he graduated in 1980 with degrees in art and history.

He joined the staff of the *Chattanooga Times Free Press* in 2008 after having worked for ten years at the *Christian Science Monitor* and thirteen years at the *St. Petersburg Times*.

No stranger to major awards, Bennett was the recipient of the Pulitzer Prize for editorial cartooning in 2002 and has earned almost every honor his profession has to offer, including the Sigma Delta Chi Award (2001), the National Journalism Award (2002), the Robert F. Kennedy Journalism Award (2007), the John Fischetti Award (2001, 2005), the Overseas Press Club's Thomas Nast Award (2005, 2007), and the National Headliner Award three times (1999, 2000, 2004).

Bennett is the husband of artist Cindy Procious and the father of Matt, Ben, and Sarah.

(Editor's note: Mr. Bennett was unavailable for an interview)

BUSINESS
BANK
RETAIL
FORECLOSURE
STOCK MARKET
Chattanooga Times Free Press
Bennett

Disasters Around the World

| Sudan | Indonesia | Chile |
| Myanmar | China | United States |

BENNETT — Chattanooga Times Free Press

FOREIGN
OIL
PRICE
4095
U.S. TROOPS
Bennett Chattanooga Times Free Press

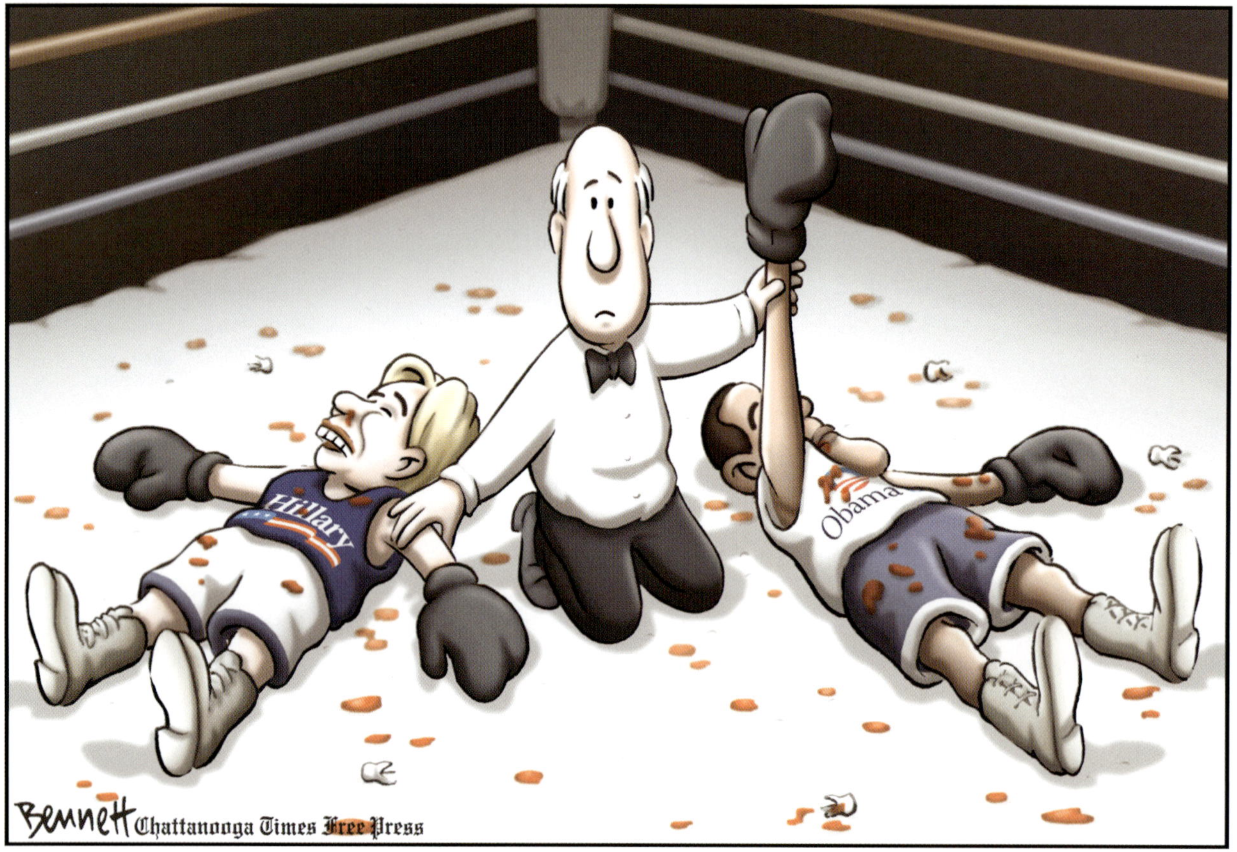
Hillary
Obama
Bennett Chattanooga Times Free Press

ECONOMY
ECONOMY
Bennett Chattanooga Times Free Press

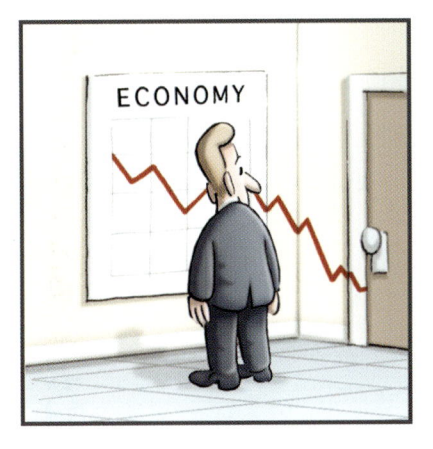

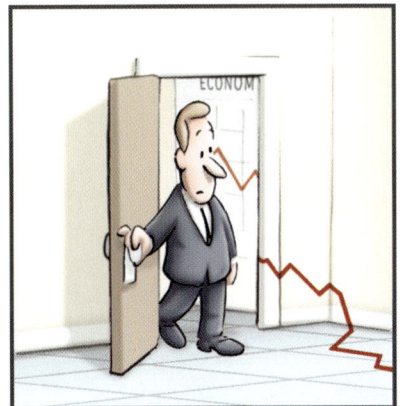

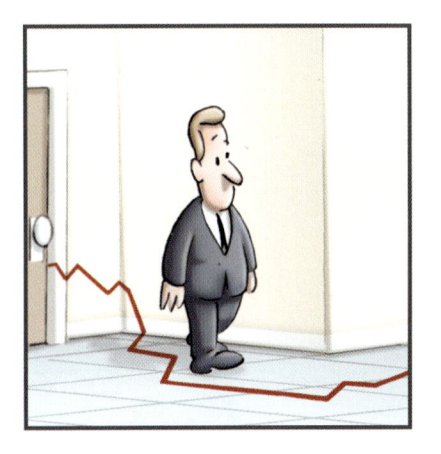

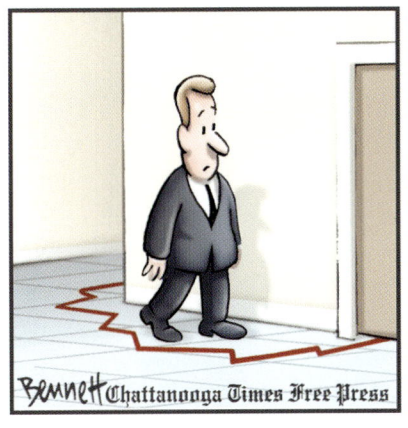

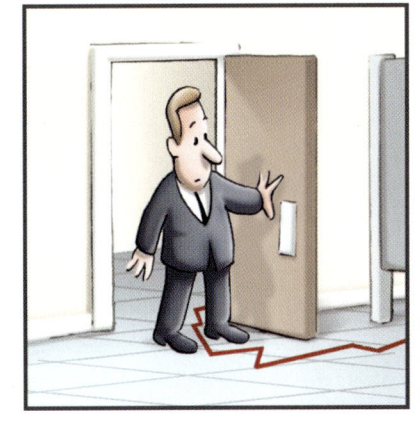

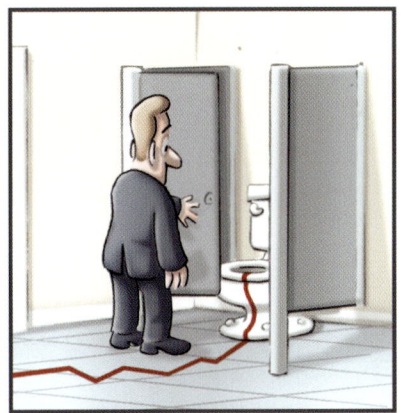

82   PRIZEWINNING POLITICAL CARTOONS

The Rescue Plan

The National Headliner Awards

84   PRIZEWINNING POLITICAL CARTOONS

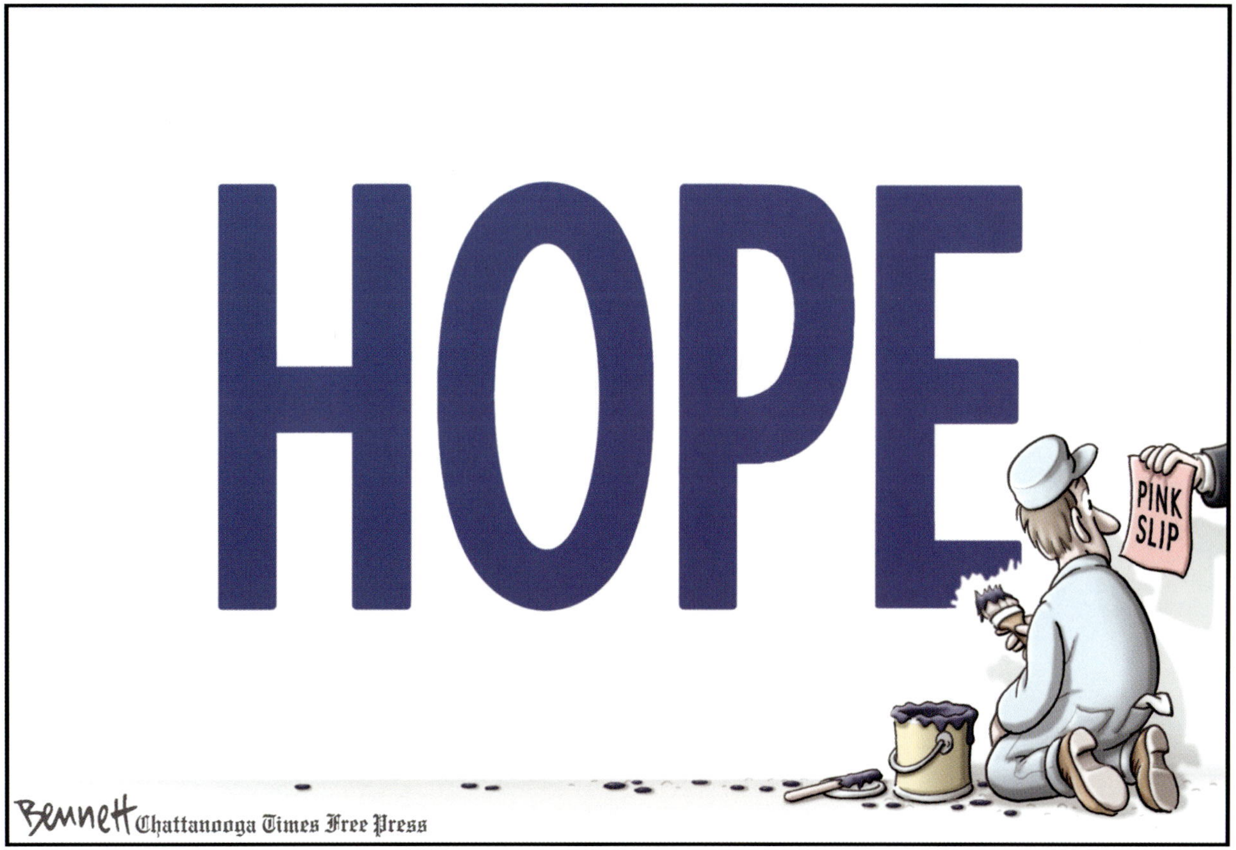
HOPE
PINK SLIP
Bennett Chattanooga Times Free Press

Chattanooga Times Free Press
Bennett
1600

'We've come to help you pack.'

Society of Professional Journalists' Sigma Delta Chi Award

The Society of Professional Journalists, founded in 1909 as Sigma Delta Chi, is dedicated to encouraging the free practice of journalism and stimulating high standards of ethical behavior. It works to inspire and educate current and future journalists through professional development, protecting First Amendment guarantees of freedom of speech and press through its advocacy efforts.

Each year the Society of Professional Journalists sponsors the Sigma Delta Chi Awards, dating back to 1932 when the Society first honored six individuals for their contributions to the field of journalism. The awards in their current form began in 1939 when the first Distinguished Service Awards were awarded and took on the name Sigma Delta Chi somewhat later.

The Sigma Delta Chi Foundation, with which the awards have become associated, was founded in 1961 and supports the educational programs of the Society of Professional Journalists and serves the professional needs of journalists and students pursuing a career in journalism.

In 1942, Jacob Burck of the *Chicago Times* became the first recipient of a Sigma Delta Chi Award in editorial cartooning. The Sigma Delta Chi Awards cover print, radio, television, newsletters, photography, online, and research.

2008 Society of Professional Journalists' Sigma Delta Chi Award Winner

Chris Britt—*Springfield (IL) State Journal-Register*

Chris Britt was born in Phoenix, Arizona, and claims to have been given a diamondback rattlesnake to play with at the age of two. Having survived many venomous bites, he decided to begin inflicting pain on others and became an editorial cartoonist.

Now, as editorial cartoonist for the *State Journal-Register* in Springfield, Illinois, Britt's cartoons are syndicated by Creators News Service and carried in more than two hundred newspapers across the country.

Britt's cartoons have been published in *Newsweek*, *Newsweek Japan*, *Time*, *U.S. News and World Report*, the *New York Times*, the *Washington Post*, and *USA Today*. They have also been aired on CNN's *Inside Politics* and ABC's *Good Morning America*.

Named Cartoonist of the Year in 1994 by the National Press Foundation in Washington, D.C., Britt has also won press club awards in Texas, California, Washington State, and Illinois.

He has also worked for the *Arizona Business Gazette*, the *Sacramento Union*, the *Houston Post*, the *Tacoma (WA) News Tribune*, and the *Seattle Times*.

(For reprints, contact Chris Britt at the State Journal-Register*)*

Chris Britt Interview

Dean: Turn-of-the-century journalist Finley Peter Dunne is quoted as saying, "The job of the newspaper is to comfort the afflicted and afflict the comfortable." What do you see as the role of the editorial cartoonist?

Chris: I see the role of the editorial cartoonist as an opinion maker, not an entertainer. The cartoonist should stake out his territory and then defend it at all costs using his wit and strong graphics to drive his point home and draw the reader in. A few years before he passed away, I had breakfast with Bill Mauldin. I asked him what he thought of the state of editorial cartooning today. His reply was short and vintage Mauldin: " Too many gags and not enough guts." I think he was correct. I think you still see too many cartoons going for the easy gag.

Dean: With the continuing decline of newspaper readership, what do you believe the future holds for the fate of the editorial cartoonist?

Chris: As for the fate of the editorial cartoonist, I wish I knew. I do know that some very fine and powerful work is being produced right now. The Bush years really brought out some of the best work I had seen in years. I guess that happens when you have a criminally incompetent leader and a band of thugs running the country for eight years. It makes me angry to see the decline in our ranks. At a time when newspapers are trending more toward online content, it seems insane that more of them do not hire the very people (cartoonists) who would help them in their quest to bring eyeballs to the screen.

Dean: What do you feel distinguishes your work from that of your peers?

Chris: With my work, I do try to have something to say each morning. I want the readers to know exactly where I stand on the important issues. I also try to work hard on the visual and composition of the cartoon. I think my style has evolved to the point where many can look at my line work and know it is mine without having to see my name.

BRITT ©08
THE STATE JOURNAL-REGISTER
COPLEY NEWS SERVICE
3-19
WHITE
COLORED
NEW ORLEANS
WHERE DOES THE ANGER COME FROM?
FOX NEWS
24 hr. OBAMA MINISTER CHANNEL

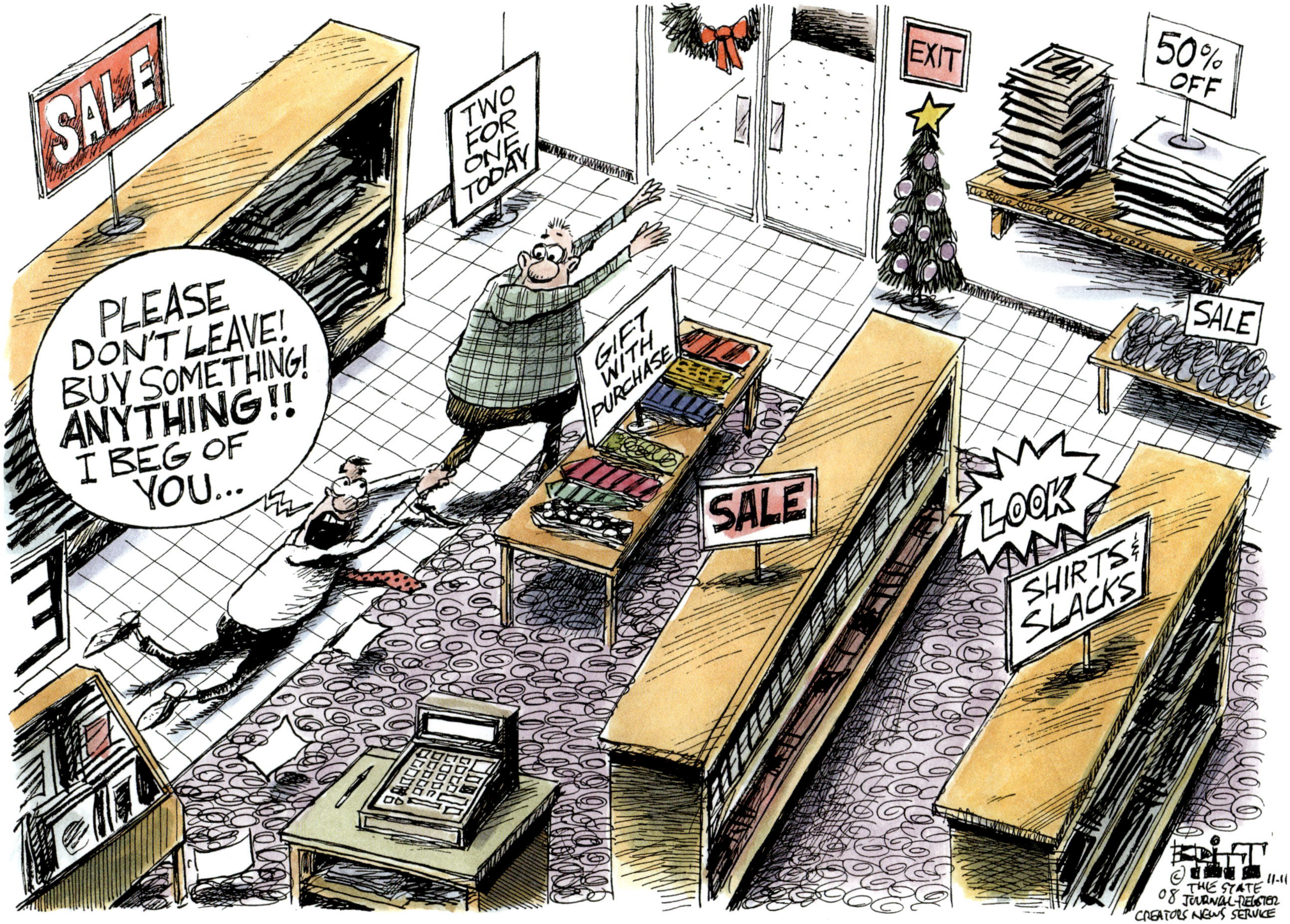

SALE
TWO FOR ONE TODAY
EXIT
50% OFF
PLEASE DON'T LEAVE! BUY SOMETHING! ANYTHING!! I BEG OF YOU...
GIFT WITH PURCHASE
SALE
SALE
LOOK
SHIRTS & SLACKS
BRITT
© 08 THE STATE JOURNAL-REGISTER CREATORS NEWS SERVICE
11-11

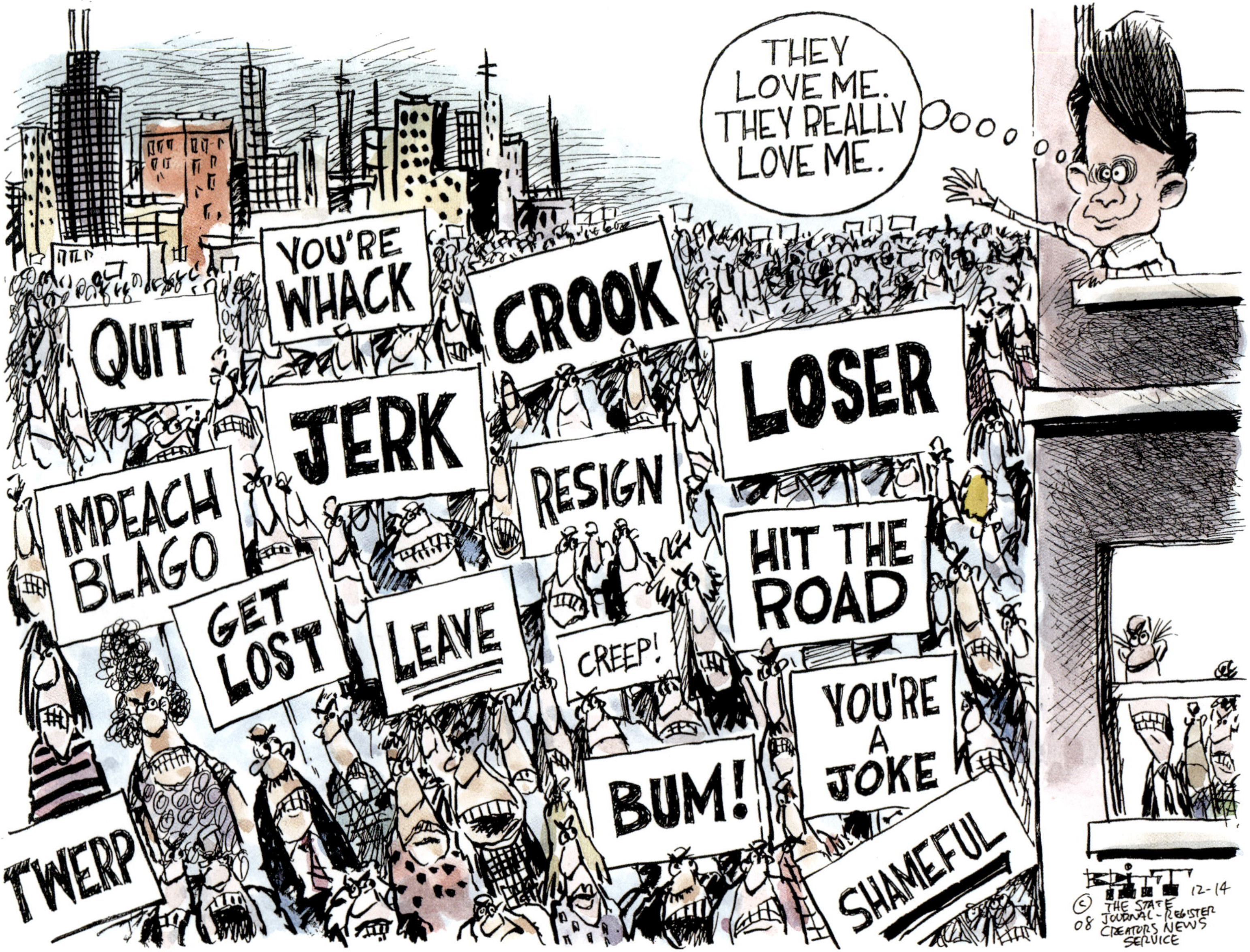
THEY LOVE ME. THEY REALLY LOVE ME.
YOU'RE WHACK
CROOK
QUIT
JERK
LOSER
IMPEACH BLAGO
RESIGN
HIT THE ROAD
GET LOST
LEAVE
CREEP!
YOU'RE A JOKE
BUM!
TWERP
SHAMEFUL
BRITT 12-14
© 08 THE STATE JOURNAL-REGISTER CREATORS NEWS SERVICE

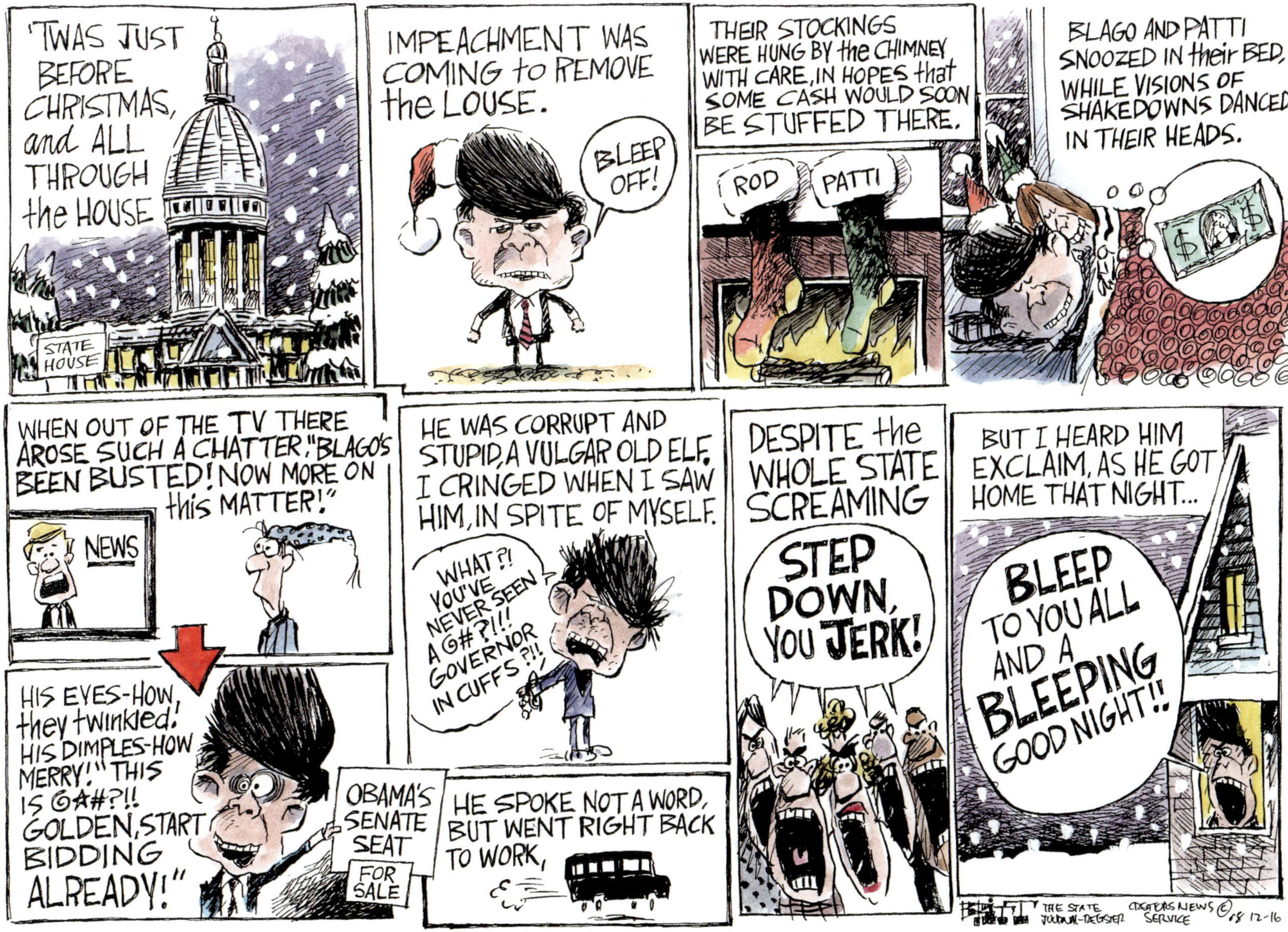
'TWAS JUST BEFORE CHRISTMAS, and ALL THROUGH the HOUSE
STATE HOUSE
IMPEACHMENT WAS COMING to REMOVE the LOUSE.
BLEEP OFF!
THEIR STOCKINGS WERE HUNG BY the CHIMNEY WITH CARE, IN HOPES that SOME CASH WOULD SOON BE STUFFED THERE.
ROD
PATTI
BLAGO AND PATTI SNOOZED IN their BED, WHILE VISIONS OF SHAKEDOWNS DANCED IN THEIR HEADS.
WHEN OUT OF THE TV THERE AROSE SUCH A CHATTER. "BLAGO'S BEEN BUSTED! NOW MORE ON this MATTER!"
NEWS
HIS EYES-HOW they twinkled! HIS DIMPLES-HOW MERRY! "THIS IS @*#?!! GOLDEN, START BIDDING ALREADY!"
OBAMA'S SENATE SEAT
FOR SALE
HE WAS CORRUPT AND STUPID, A VULGAR OLD ELF. I CRINGED WHEN I SAW HIM, IN SPITE OF MYSELF.
WHAT?! YOU'VE NEVER SEEN A @#?!!! GOVERNOR IN CUFFS?!!
HE SPOKE NOT A WORD, BUT WENT RIGHT BACK TO WORK,
DESPITE the WHOLE STATE SCREAMING
STEP DOWN, YOU JERK!
BUT I HEARD HIM EXCLAIM, AS HE GOT HOME THAT NIGHT...
BLEEP TO YOU ALL AND A BLEEPING GOOD NIGHT!!
THE STATE JOURNAL-REGISTER
CREATORS NEWS SERVICE ©'08 12-16

YOU CAN DUCK THE SHOES, BUT NOT THE BOOTS
U.S. TROOP DEATHS
BRITT
THE STATE JOURNAL-REGISTER
CREATORS NEWS SERVICE © 08 12-17

The Overseas Press Club's Thomas Nast Award

The founding tenets of the Overseas Press Club are to encourage the highest standards of professional integrity and skill in the reporting of news, help educate new generations of journalists, contribute to the freedom and independence of journalists and the press throughout the world, and work toward better communication and understanding among people. Since its founding in 1939 by a group of foreign correspondents in New York City, the OPC has awarded prizes for journalism.

Thomas Nast, considered to be the "Father of the Political Cartoon" in America, has given us such lasting icons as the Democratic Donkey, the Republican Elephant, and the Tammany Tiger. He is also generally regarded as having given us the commonly accepted versions of Uncle Sam and Santa Claus.

It is in the spirit with which Thomas Nast entertained and informed his readers that the Thomas Nast Award for editorial cartooning is presented. The award was first established and awarded in 1968 to Don Wright of the *Miami News*.

2008 Overseas Press Club's Thomas Nast Award—Citation

Steve Breen—*San Diego Union-Tribune*

In an amazing year, Steve Breen has won the Pulitzer Prize, the National Headliner Award, and the Thomas Nast Award.

As noted twice before, Breen is a Los Angeles native and University of California, Riverside graduate. Editorial cartoonist for the *San Diego Union-Tribune* since 2001, his work is nationally syndicated by Creators News Service and regularly appears in *USA Today*, the *New York Times*, and *Newsweek*.

Breen lives in San Diego with his wife and four children and in his spare time writes and illustrates children's books.

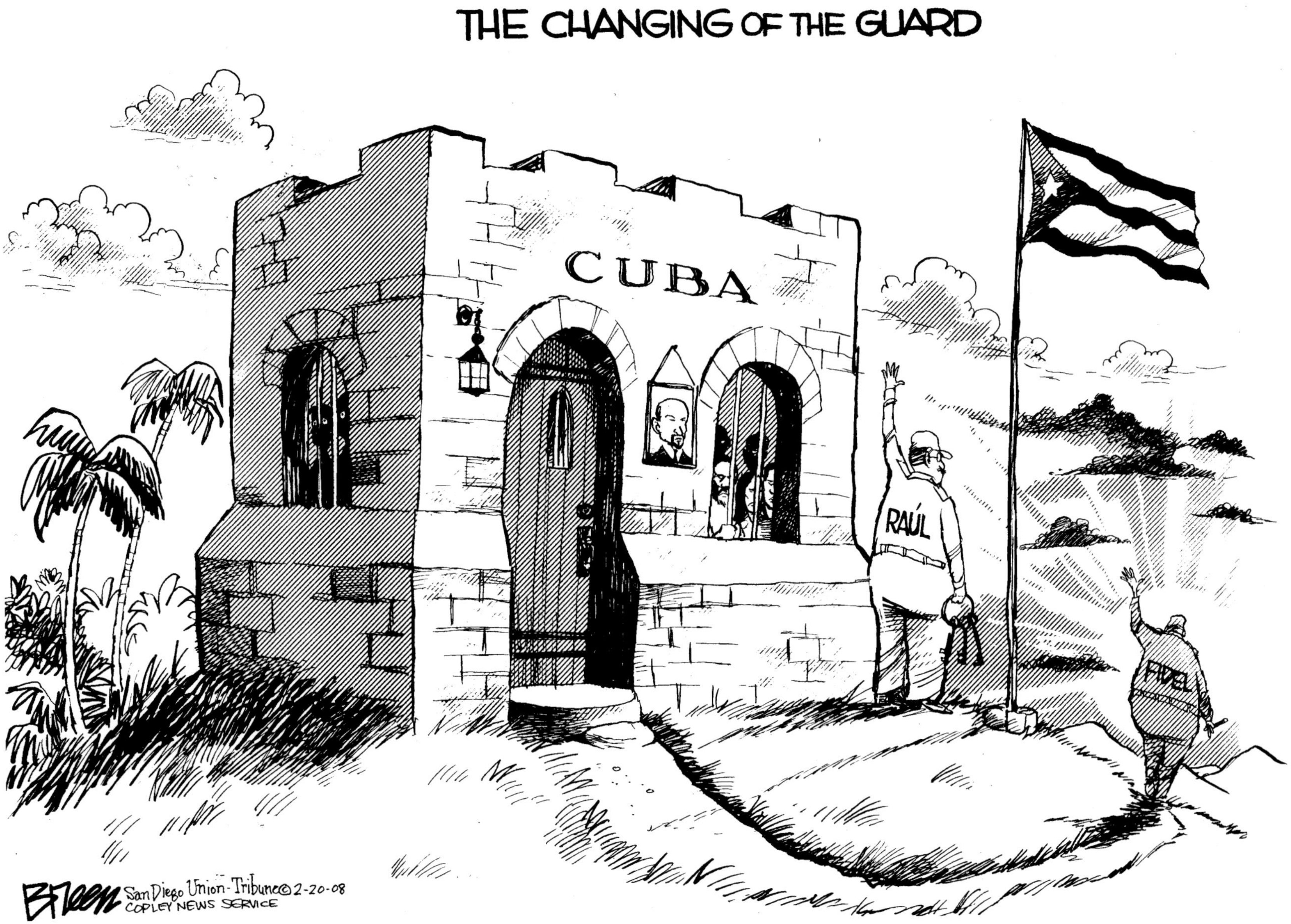
THE CHANGING OF THE GUARD
CUBA
RAÚL
FIDEL
Breen San Diego Union-Tribune © 2-20-08
COPLEY NEWS SERVICE

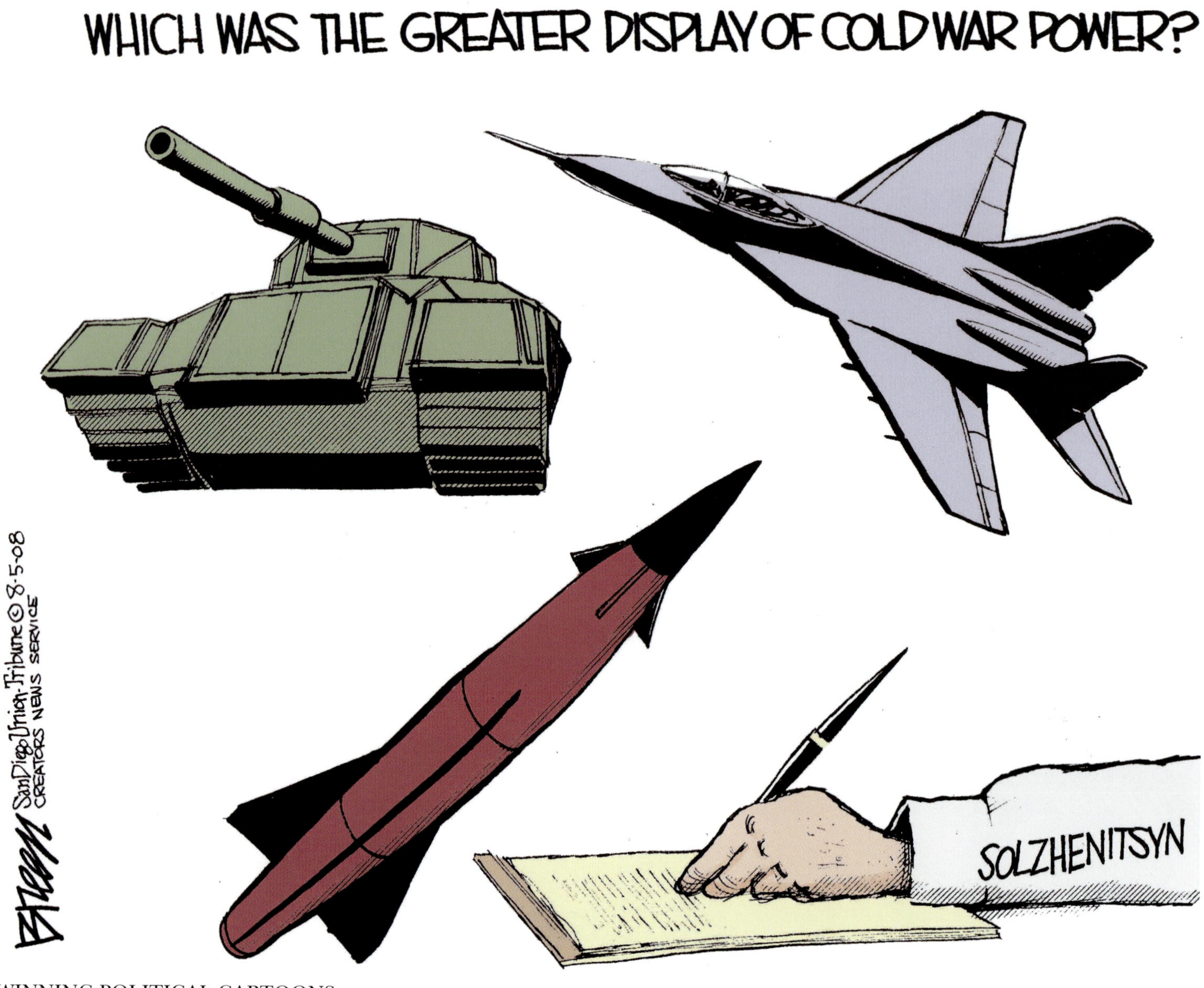
WHICH WAS THE GREATER DISPLAY OF COLD WAR POWER?
SOLZHENITSYN
SanDiegoUnion-Tribune © 8-5-08
CREATORS NEWS SERVICE

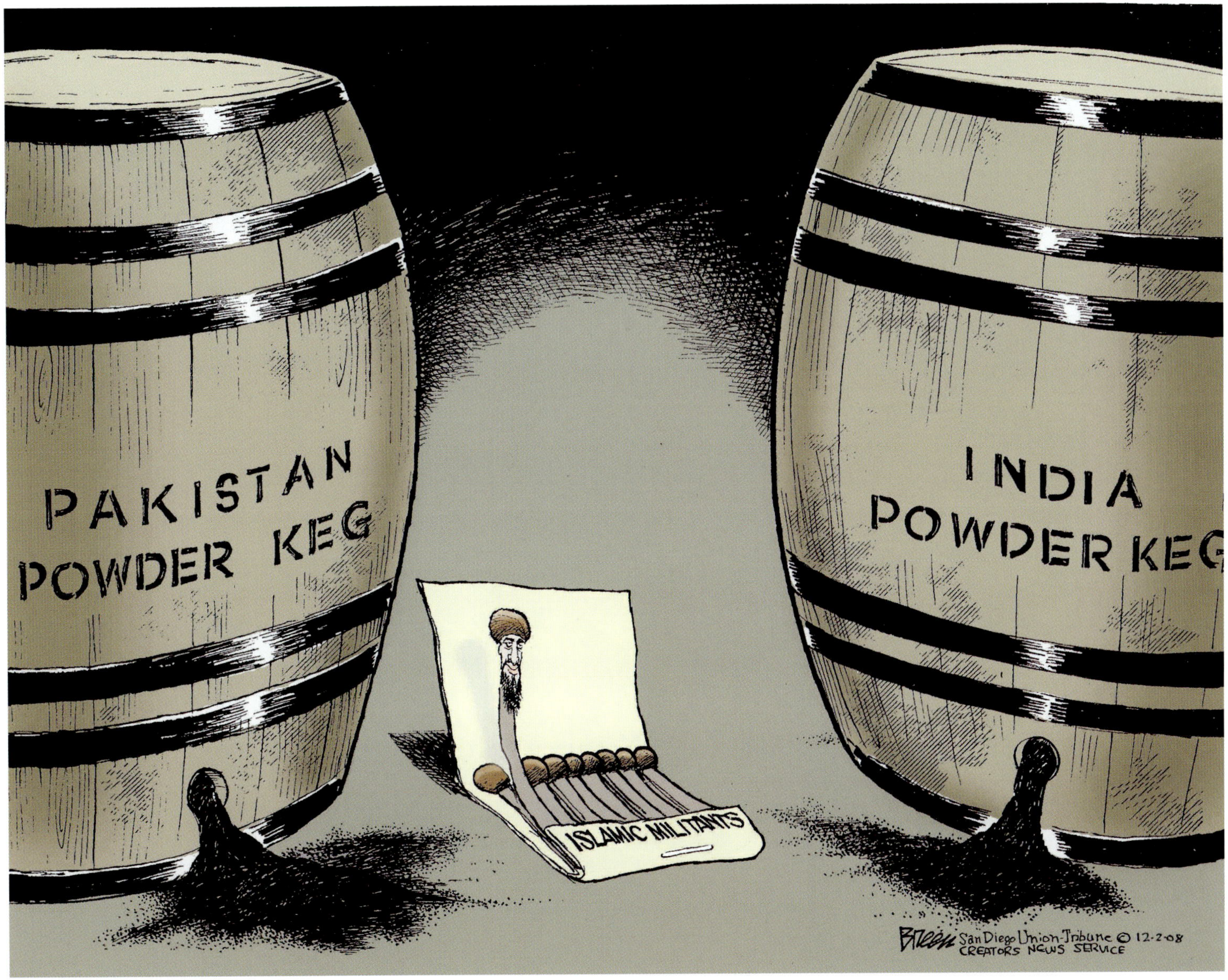
PAKISTAN
POWDER KEG
INDIA
POWDER KEG
ISLAMIC MILITANTS
Breen San Diego Union-Tribune © 12-2-08
CREATORS NEWS SERVICE

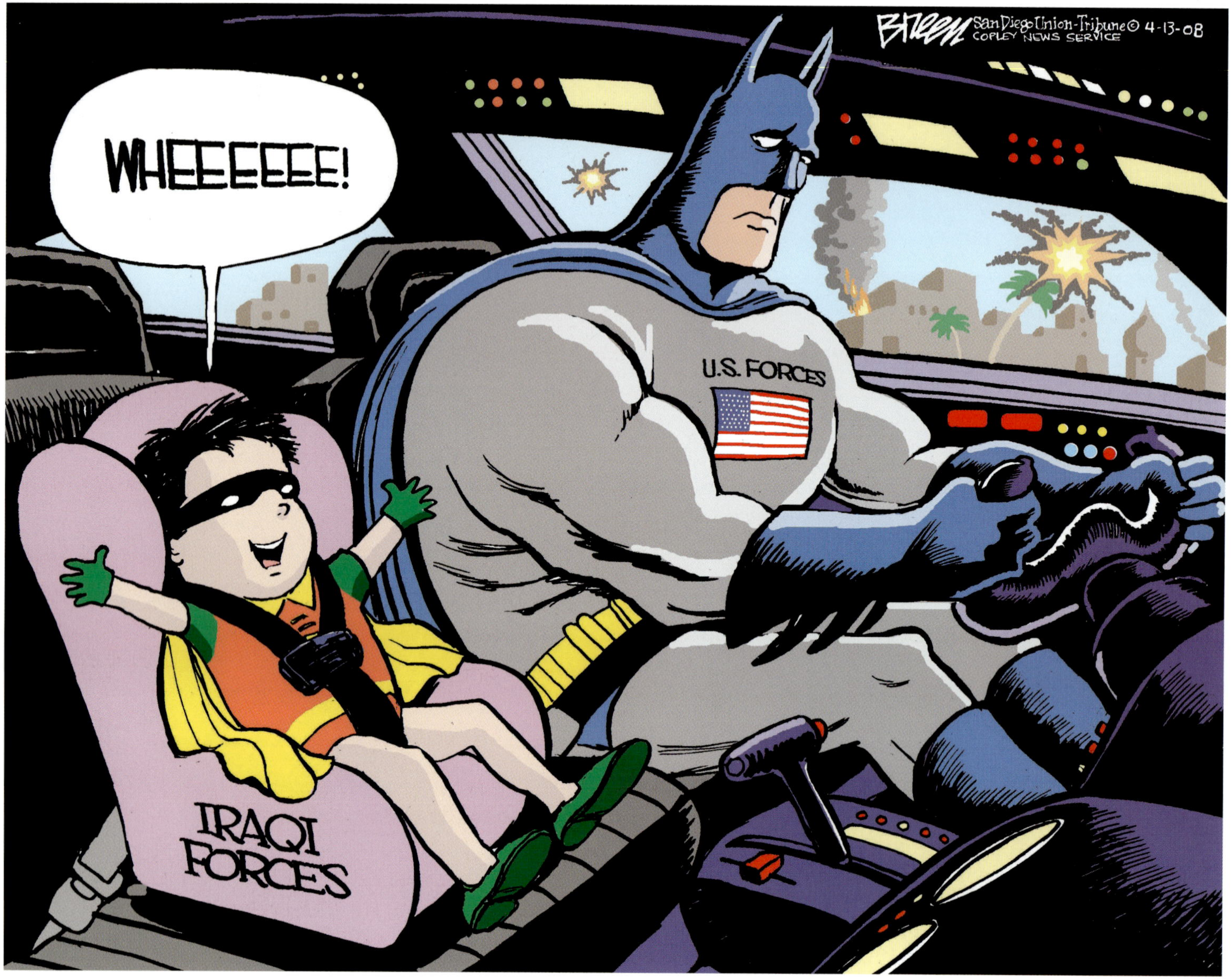
BREEN San Diego Union-Tribune © 4-13-08
COPLEY NEWS SERVICE
WHEEEEEEE!
U.S. FORCES
IRAQI FORCES

SADDAM SURE LOOKED PATHETIC HANGING FROM THAT NOOSE...
SanDiegoUnion-Tribune©
COPLEY NEWS SERVICE
1-05

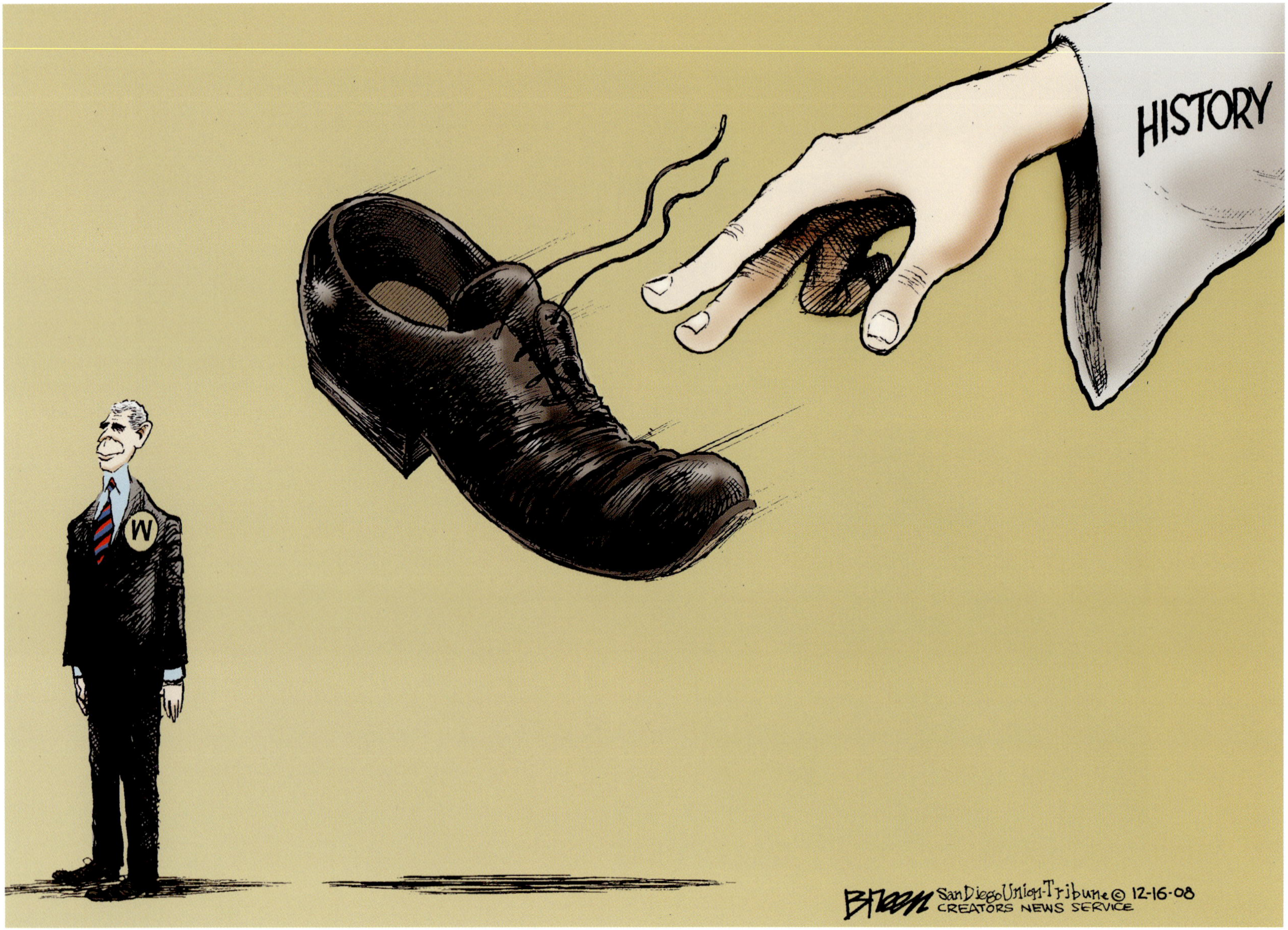
HISTORY
W
BREEN SanDiegoUnion-Tribune © 12-16-08
CREATORS NEWS SERVICE

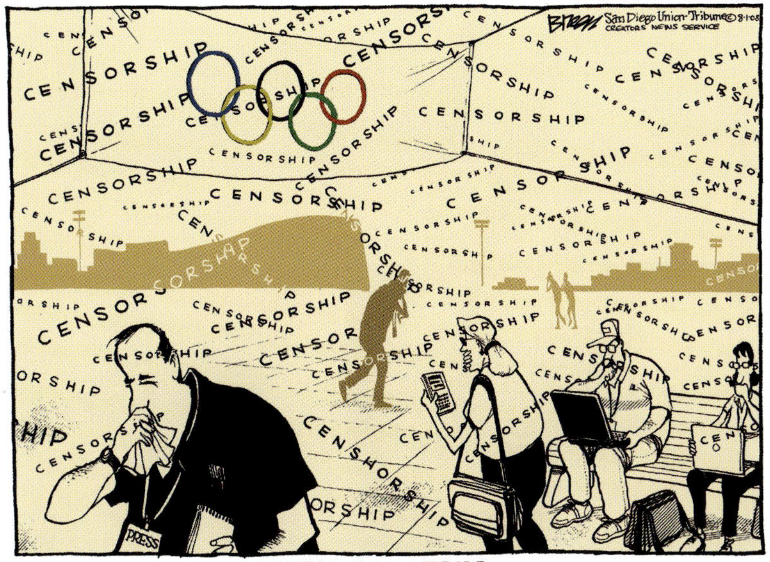
San Diego Union-Tribune © 8-1-08
CREATORS NEWS SERVICE
CENSORSHIP
PRESS
BEIJING POLLUTION

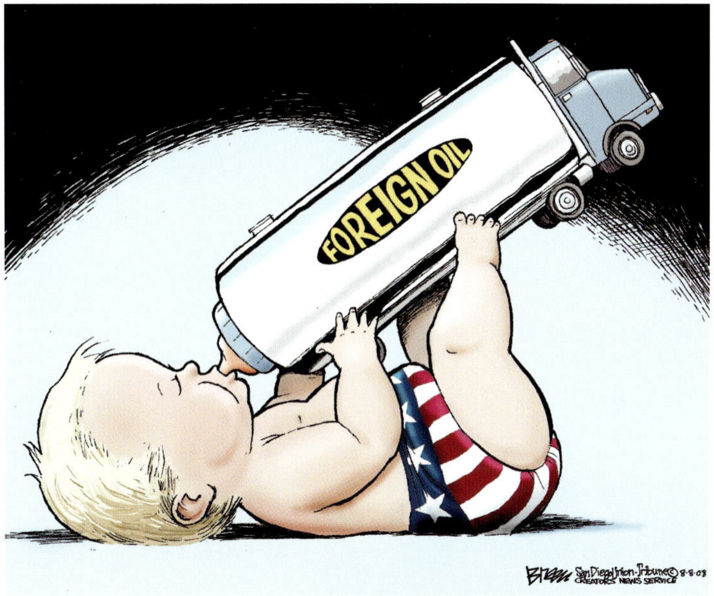
FOREIGN OIL
San Diego Union-Tribune © 8-8-08
CREATORS NEWS SERVICE

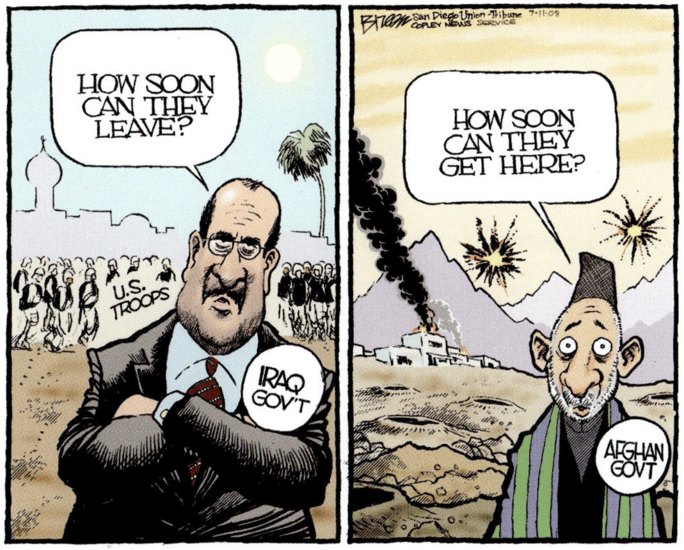
San Diego Union-Tribune 7-11-08
COPLEY NEWS SERVICE
HOW SOON CAN THEY LEAVE?
U.S. TROOPS
IRAQ GOV'T
HOW SOON CAN THEY GET HERE?
AFGHAN GOVT

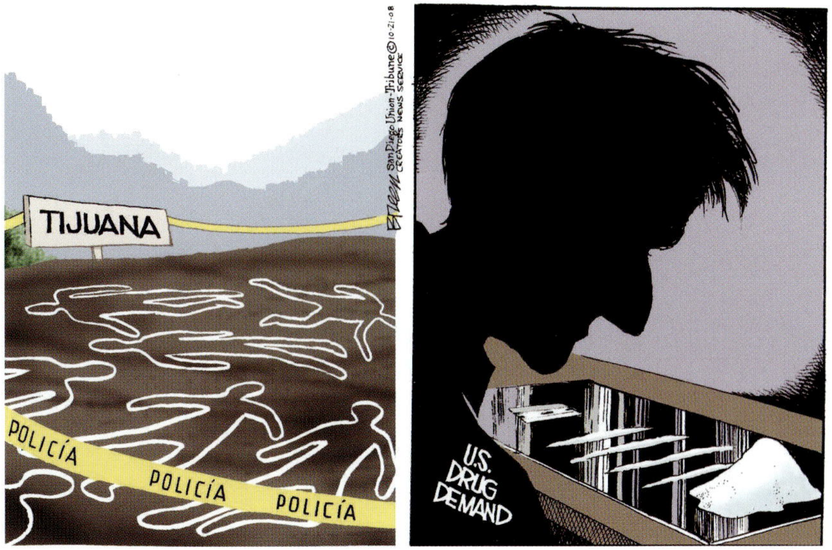
San Diego Union-Tribune © 10-21-08
CREATORS NEWS SERVICE
TIJUANA
POLICÍA
POLICÍA
POLICÍA
U.S. DRUG DEMAND

San Diego Union-Tribune © 4-5-08
COPLEY NEWS SERVICE
WE DON'T NEED A BORDER FENCE WITH MEXICO, JUST ECONOMIC CHARTS.
LAYOFFS
INFLATION
FORECLOSURES
FORGET IT... LET'S GO BACK.

I DITCHED MY MILITARY FATIGUES, PUT ON GLASSES, GREW A BEARD, BUT THEY **STILL** FOUND ME.
RADOVAN KARADZIC
San Diego Union-Tribune © 7-24-08
CREATORS NEWS SERVICE
...I WONDER WHAT TIPPED THEM OFF.

2008 Overseas Press Club's Thomas Nast Award—Citation

Kevin Kallaugher—Economist

Born March 23, 1955, in Norwalk, Connecticut, Kallaugher graduated from Harvard College with honors in visual and environmental studies in 1977. He then embarked on a bicycle tour of the British Isles, where he later joined the Brighton Basketball Club as a player and coach. After the club hit financial difficulties, Kallaugher drew caricatures of tourists in Trafalgar Square and on Brighton Pier. In March 1978, the *Economist* recruited him to become their first resident cartoonist in their 145-year history.

Kallaugher spent the next ten years working in London as a cartoonist for such publications as the *Observer*, the *Sunday Telegraph*, *Today*, and the *Mail on Sunday*. Returning to the U.S. in 1988, he joined the *Baltimore Sun* as its editorial cartoonist. Between 1988 and 2006, he drew more than four thousand cartoons for the *Sun* while continuing to draw two cartoons per week for the *Economist*.

KAL, as Kallaugher is also known, has won many of the top awards for his work including the Thomas Nast Award in 1999, 2002, and 2005. He has published five collections of his work. His newest, *KAL Draws Criticism: Editorial Cartoons by Kevin Kallaugher,* was published in June 2006. KAL's animation production company, Kaltoons LLC, is dedicated to creating 3-D animated political cartoons. He is a past president of the AAEC.

Kevin Kallaugher Interview

Dean: Turn-of-the-century journalist Finley Peter Dunne is quoted as saying, "The job of the newspaper is to comfort the afflicted and afflict the comfortable." What do you see as the role of the editorial cartoonist?

KAL: To entice, engage, challenge, cajole, and illuminate.

Dean: With the continuing decline of newspaper readership, what do you believe the future holds for the fate of the editorial cartoonist?

KAL: The web offers great new opportunities for graphic satire. The cartoonists of the twenty-first century will embrace the moving image and will reshape our ancient craft into a new powerful beast.

Dean: What do you feel distinguishes your work from that of your peers?

KAL: Just as each of us has unique handwriting so too does each artist have a distinct look. My visual influences are drawn from both sides of the Atlantic as I have spent much of my career in both Europe and the USA. My work carries traces from both areas.

Dean: Although the bulk of this book is dedicated to editorial contests in the U.S., the final section of this book deals with the international Lurie Award. How do you think U.S. cartoons differ from those of other countries?

KAL: Each country and culture has a unique visual history. Ours in the U.S. is affected by our fast-moving culture and easy way with words.

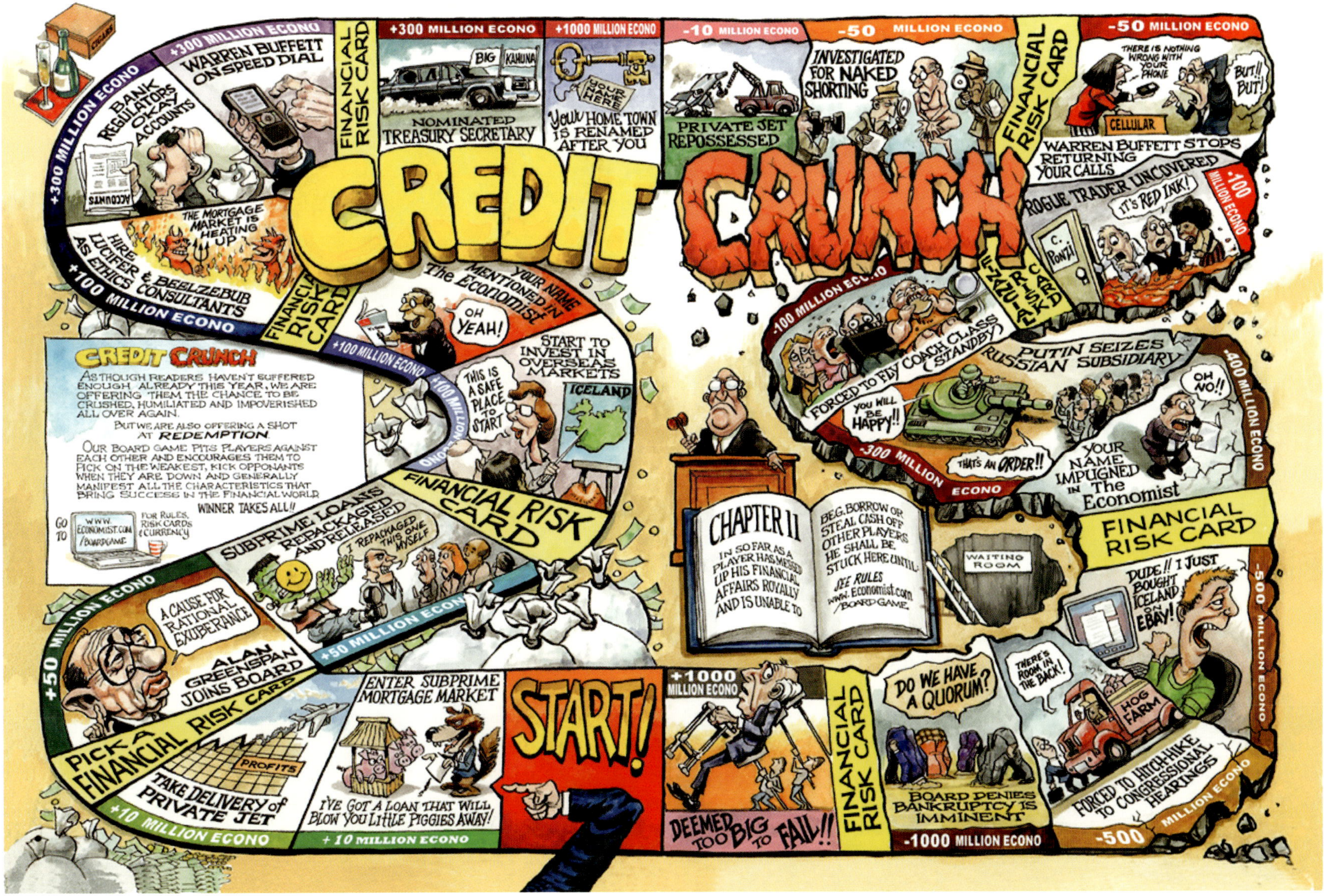
START!
ENTER SUBPRIME MORTGAGE MARKET
I'VE GOT A LOAN THAT WILL BLOW YOU LITTLE PIGGIES AWAY!
+10 MILLION ECONO
TAKE DELIVERY of PRIVATE JET
PROFITS
+10 MILLION ECONO
PICK A FINANCIAL RISK CARD
A CAUSE FOR RATIONAL EXUBERANCE
ALAN GREENSPAN JOINS BOARD
+50 MILLION ECONO
SUBPRIME LOANS REPACKAGED AND RELEASED
I REPACKAGED THIS ONE MYSELF
+50 MILLION ECONO
FINANCIAL RISK CARD
START TO INVEST IN OVERSEAS MARKETS
THIS IS A SAFE PLACE TO START
ICELAND
+100 MILLION ECONO
+100 MILLION ECONO
YOUR NAME MENTIONED IN The Economist
OH YEAH!
FINANCIAL RISK CARD
HIRE LUCIFER & BEELZEBUB AS ETHICS CONSULTANTS
THE MORTGAGE MARKET IS HEATING UP
+100 MILLION ECONO
BANK REGULATORS OKAY ACCOUNTS
ACCOUNTS
+300 MILLION ECONO
WARREN BUFFETT ON SPEED DIAL
+300 MILLION ECONO
FINANCIAL RISK CARD
+300 MILLION ECONO
BIG KAHUNA
NOMINATED TREASURY SECRETARY
+1000 MILLION ECONO
YOUR NAME HERE
YOUR HOME TOWN IS RENAMED AFTER YOU
CREDIT CRUNCH
-10 MILLION ECONO
PRIVATE JET REPOSSESSED
-50 MILLION ECONO
INVESTIGATED FOR NAKED SHORTING
FINANCIAL RISK CARD
-50 MILLION ECONO
THERE IS NOTHING WRONG WITH YOUR PHONE
BUT!! BUT!
CELLULAR
WARREN BUFFETT STOPS RETURNING YOUR CALLS
ROGUE TRADER UNCOVERED
IT'S RED INK!
C. PONZI
-100 MILLION ECONO
FINANCIAL RISK CARD
-100 MILLION ECONO
FORCED TO FLY COACH CLASS (STANDBY)
PUTIN SEIZES RUSSIAN SUBSIDIARY
YOU WILL BE HAPPY!!
THAT'S AN ORDER!!
-300 MILLION ECONO
-400 MILLION ECONO
OH NO!!
YOUR NAME IMPUGNED IN The Economist
FINANCIAL RISK CARD
CHAPTER 11
IN SO FAR AS A PLAYER HAS MESSED UP HIS FINANCIAL AFFAIRS ROYALLY AND IS UNABLE TO
BEG, BORROW OR STEAL CASH OFF OTHER PLAYERS HE SHALL BE STUCK HERE UNTIL...
SEE RULES www.economist.com/BOARDGAME
WAITING ROOM
-500 MILLION ECONO
DUDE!! I JUST BOUGHT ICELAND ON EBAY!
THERE'S ROOM IN THE BACK!
HOG FARM
FORCED TO HITCH-HIKE TO CONGRESSIONAL HEARINGS
-500 MILLION ECONO
DO WE HAVE A QUORUM?
BOARD DENIES BANKRUPTCY IS IMMINENT
-1000 MILLION ECONO
FINANCIAL RISK CARD
+1000 MILLION ECONO
DEEMED TOO BIG TO FAIL!!
CREDIT CRUNCH
AS THOUGH READERS HAVEN'T SUFFERED ENOUGH ALREADY THIS YEAR, WE ARE OFFERING THEM THE CHANCE TO BE CRUSHED, HUMILIATED AND IMPOVERISHED ALL OVER AGAIN.
BUT WE ARE ALSO OFFERING A SHOT AT REDEMPTION.
OUR BOARD GAME PITS PLAYERS AGAINST EACH OTHER AND ENCOURAGES THEM TO PICK ON THE WEAKEST, KICK OPPONANTS WHEN THEY ARE DOWN AND GENERALLY MANIFEST ALL THE CHARACTERISTICS THAT BRING SUCCESS IN THE FINANCIAL WORLD.
WINNER TAKES ALL!!
GO TO WWW.ECONOMIST.COM/BOARDGAME
FOR RULES, RISK CARDS & CURRENCY

CAPITALISM IS DEAD!
SOUVENIRS
MERCHANDISE
I THINK I'VE FOUND A GROWTH MARKET...
CAPITALISM IS DEAD!!
$15.00
2 for $25.00
DEAD!
R.I.P
DEAD!
TEE SHIRTS
MUGS
CAPITALISM
CAPITALISM
CAPITALISM IS
INVEST IN CAPITALISM IS DEAD GO TO OUR WEBSITE
CAPITALISM IS DEAD!.COM
$40
SIGN UP FOR OUR NEWSLETTER
CAPITA IS DEA
CAPITALISM IS DEAD!
CAPITALISM CAPITALISM IS DEAD BUTTONS
CAPITA IS DEAD
KAL 2008
The Economist

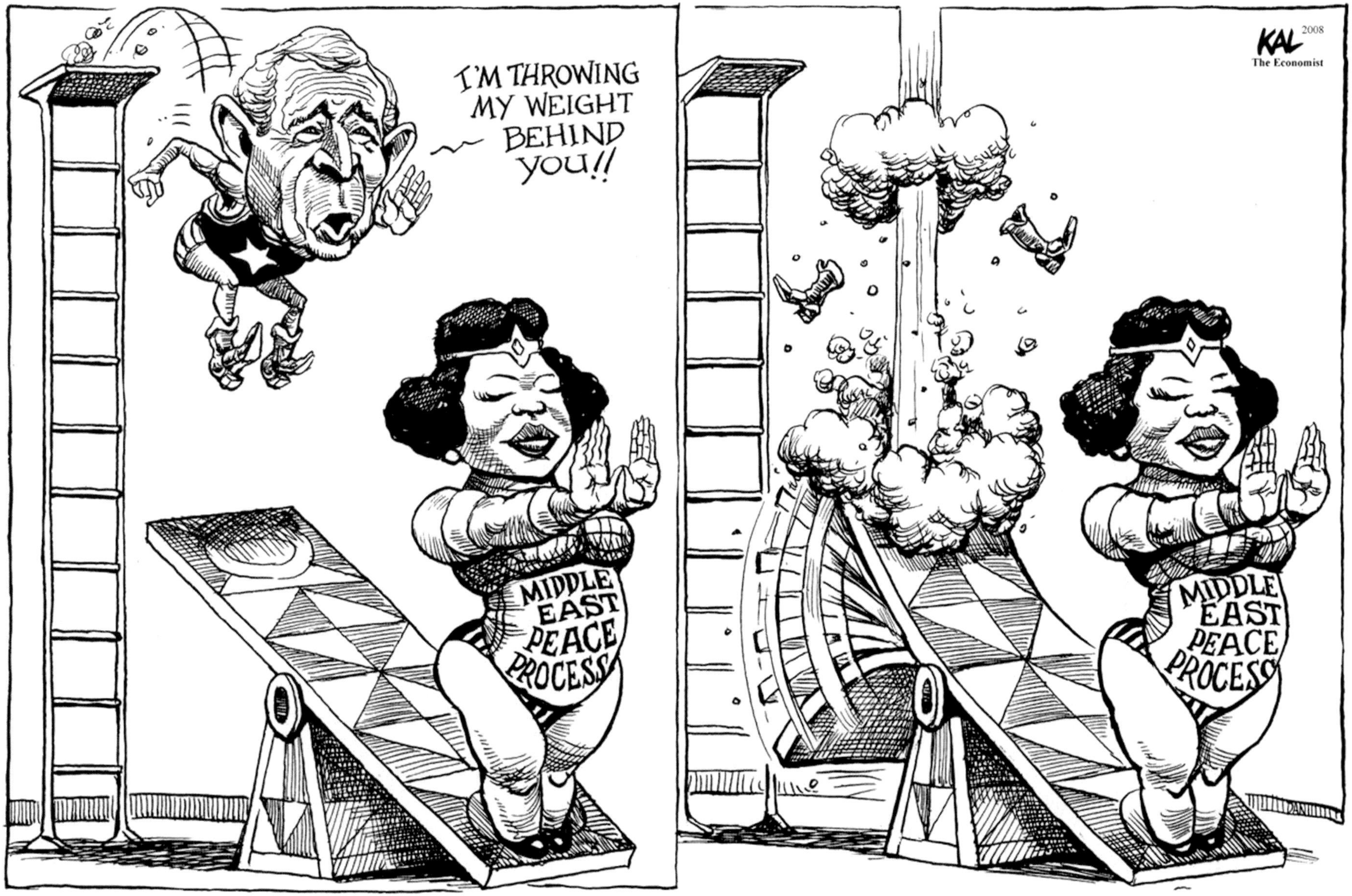
I'M THROWING
MY WEIGHT
BEHIND
YOU!!
MIDDLE
EAST
PEACE
PROCESS
KAL
2008
The Economist
MIDDLE
EAST
PEACE
PROCESS

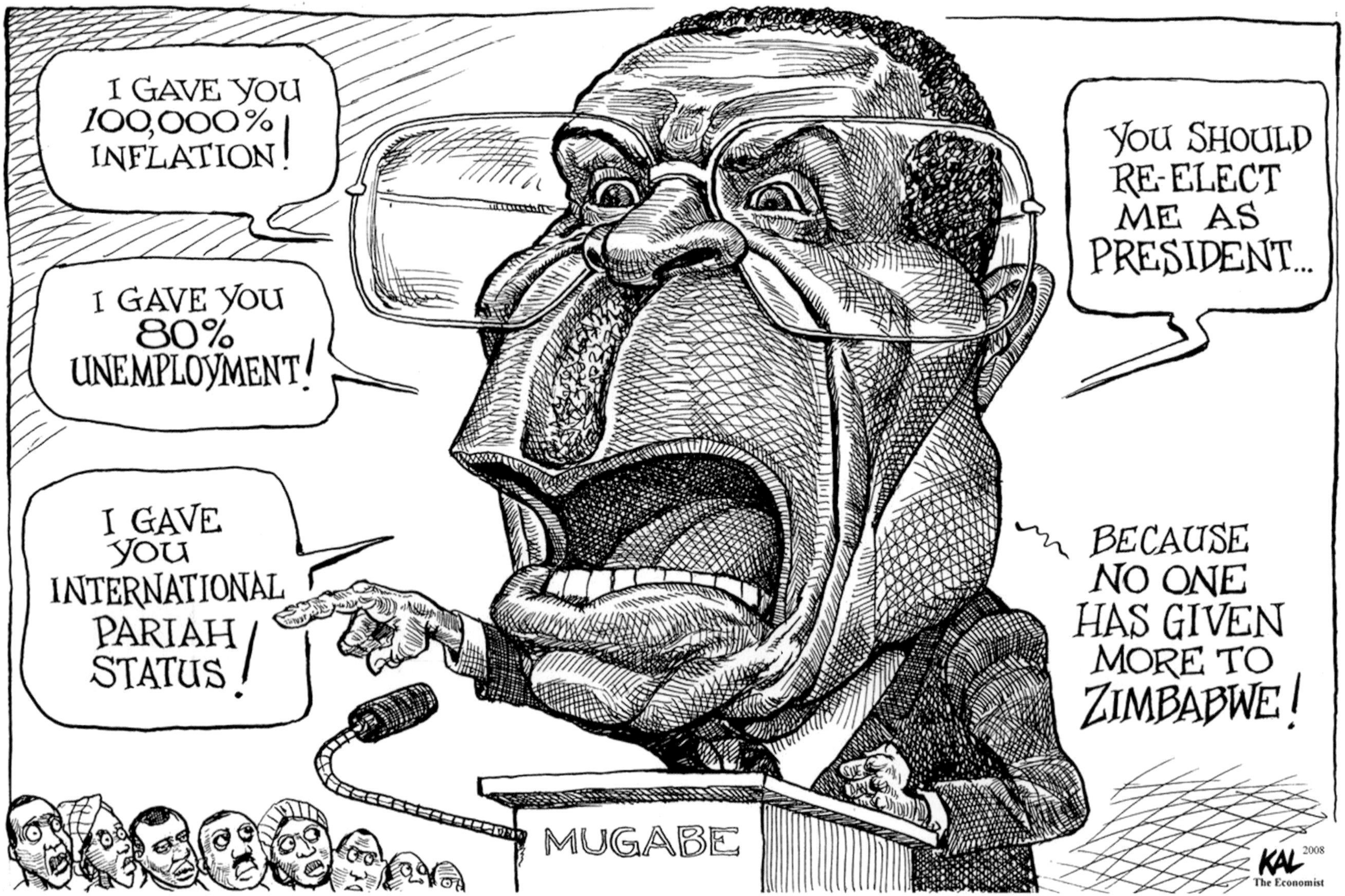

I GAVE YOU 100,000% INFLATION!
I GAVE YOU 80% UNEMPLOYMENT!
I GAVE YOU INTERNATIONAL PARIAH STATUS!
YOU SHOULD RE-ELECT ME AS PRESIDENT...
BECAUSE NO ONE HAS GIVEN MORE TO ZIMBABWE!
MUGABE
KAL 2008
The Economist

The Economist, March 22, 2008

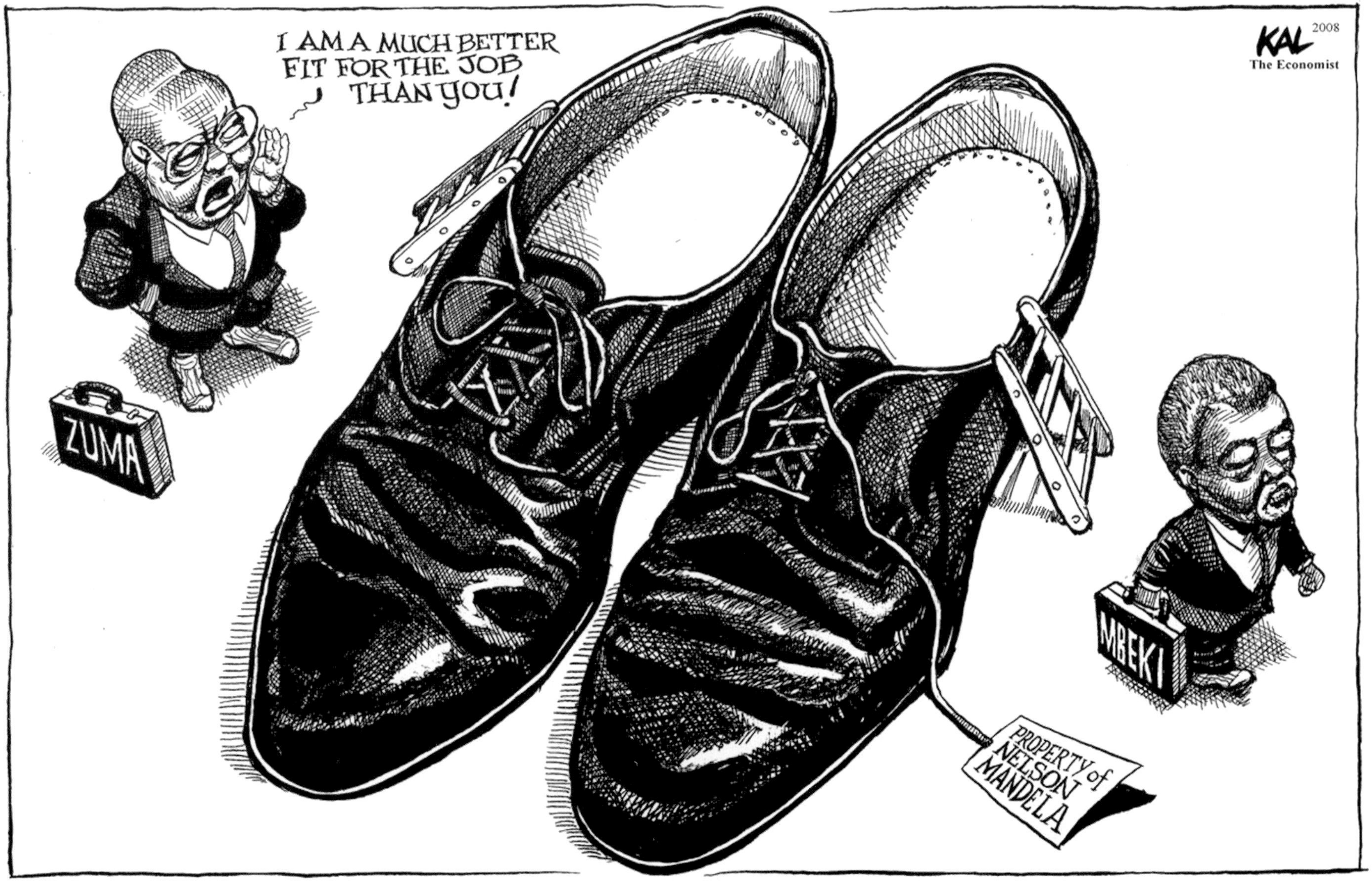
I AM A MUCH BETTER FIT FOR THE JOB THAN YOU!
KAL 2008
The Economist
ZUMA
MBEKI
PROPERTY of NELSON MANDELA

The Scripps Howard National Journalism Award

Since 1953, the Scripps Howard Foundation has recognized the best work in journalism through the National Journalism Awards. The Scripps Howard Foundation is the corporate foundation of the E. W. Scripps Company. Its mission is to advance the cause of a free press through support of excellence in journalism, quality journalism education, and professional development. The foundation's support of sound educational programs, strong families, vital social services, enriching arts and culture, and inclusive civic affairs, with a special commitment to the communities, in which Scripps does business, helps build healthy communities and improves the quality of life.

The awards recognize excellence in editorial cartooning as well as sixteen other categories, including editorial writing, human interest writing, environmental and public service reporting, investigative reporting, business/economics reporting, commentary, photojournalism, radio and television journalism, college cartooning, and Web reporting. The awards also honor distinguished service to journalism education and the First Amendment.

The first National Journalism Award for editorial cartooning, not awarded until 1990, was won by Signe Wilkinson, working for the *Philadelphia Daily News*.

2008 Scripps Howard National Journalism Award Winner

Mike Luckovich—*Atlanta Journal-Constitution*

As editorial cartoonist for the *Atlanta Journal-Constitution*, Mike Luckovich has won two Pulitzer Prizes (1995, 2006), the Overseas Press Club's Thomas Nast Award (1989, 1993, 2006), the Robert F. Kennedy Journalism Award (1994), the Society of Professional Journalists' Sigma Delta Chi Award (2005), as well as winning the National Headliner Award in 1992, 2006, and 2007, making two years in a row.

A Seattle native, Luckovich earned a bachelor's degree in political science from the University of Washington. He freelanced for a time with local papers in Washington while working as a traveling salesman to pay his bills.

After working for the *New Orleans Times-Picayune* from 1984 to 1989, Luckovich joined the *Atlanta Journal-Constitution* in 1989. Creators Syndicate distributes his cartoons nationally.

(Editor's note: Mr. Luckovich was unavailable for an interview)

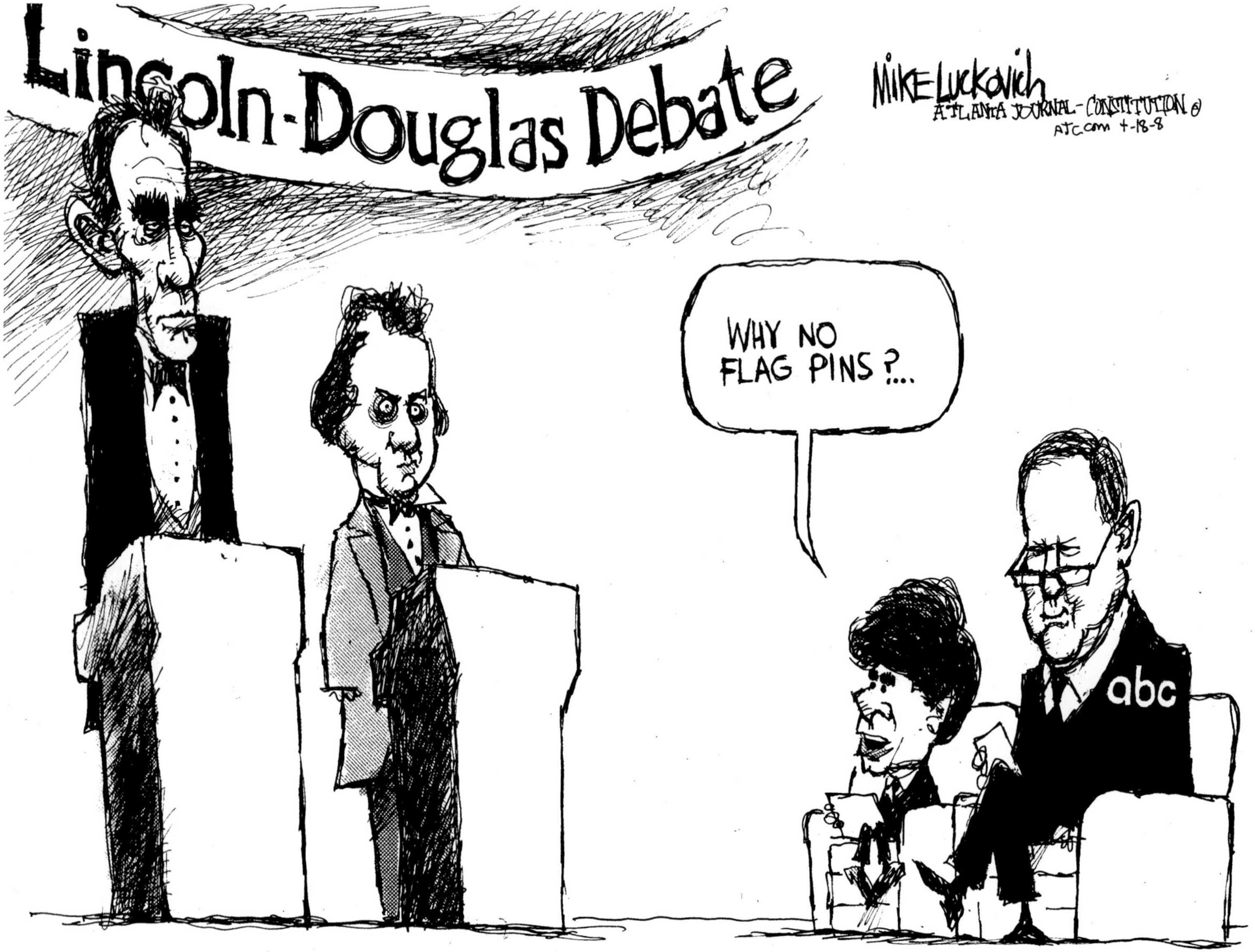
Lincoln-Douglas Debate
MIKE LUCKOVICH
ATLANTA JOURNAL-CONSTITUTION
WHY NO FLAG PINS ?...
abc

By permission of Mike Luckovich and Creators Syndicate, Inc.

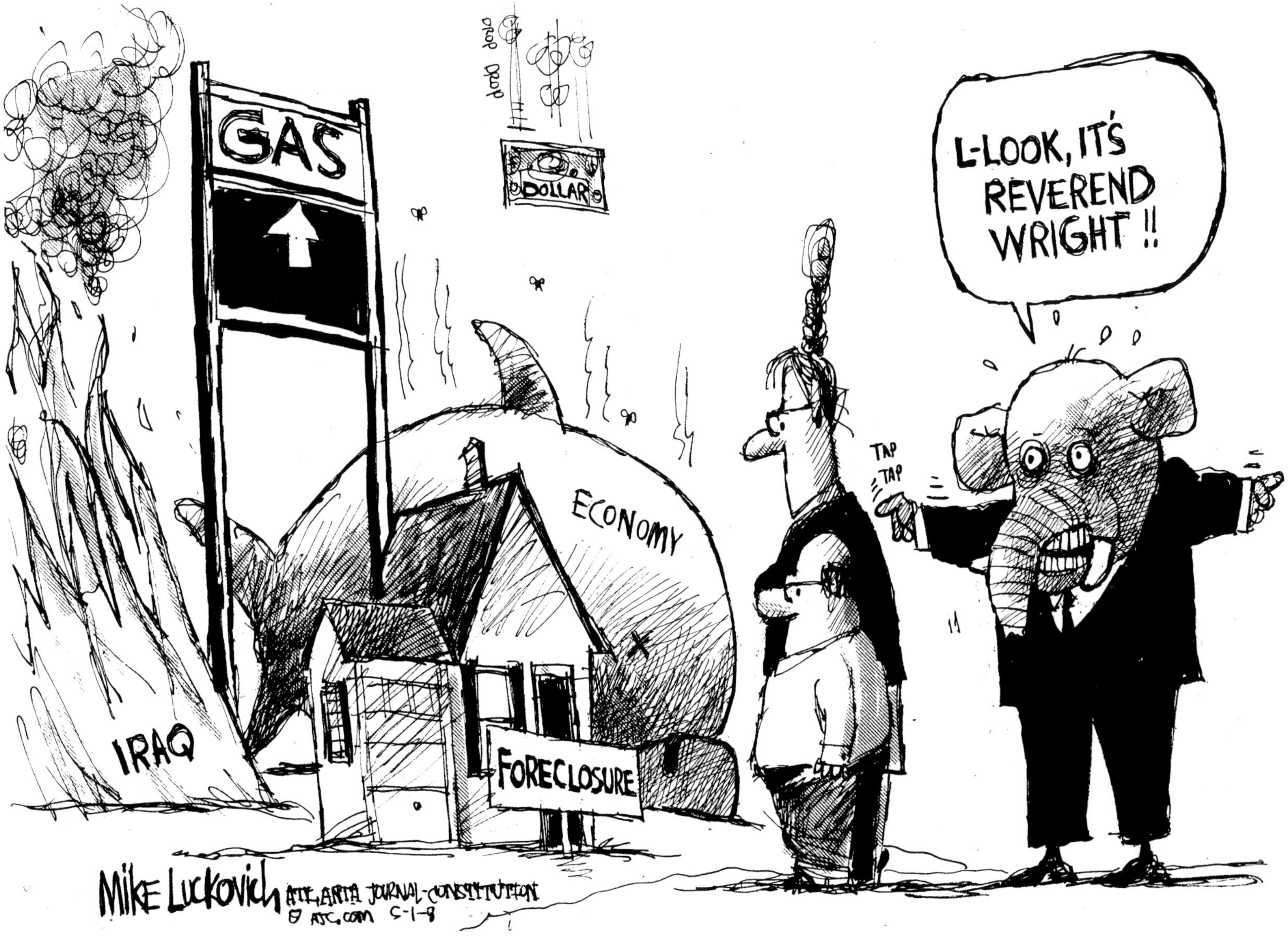
GAS
DOLLAR
ECONOMY
IRAQ
FORECLOSURE
TAP TAP
L-LOOK, IT'S REVEREND WRIGHT !!
MIKE LUCKOVICH

By permission of Mike Luckovich and Creators Syndicate, Inc.

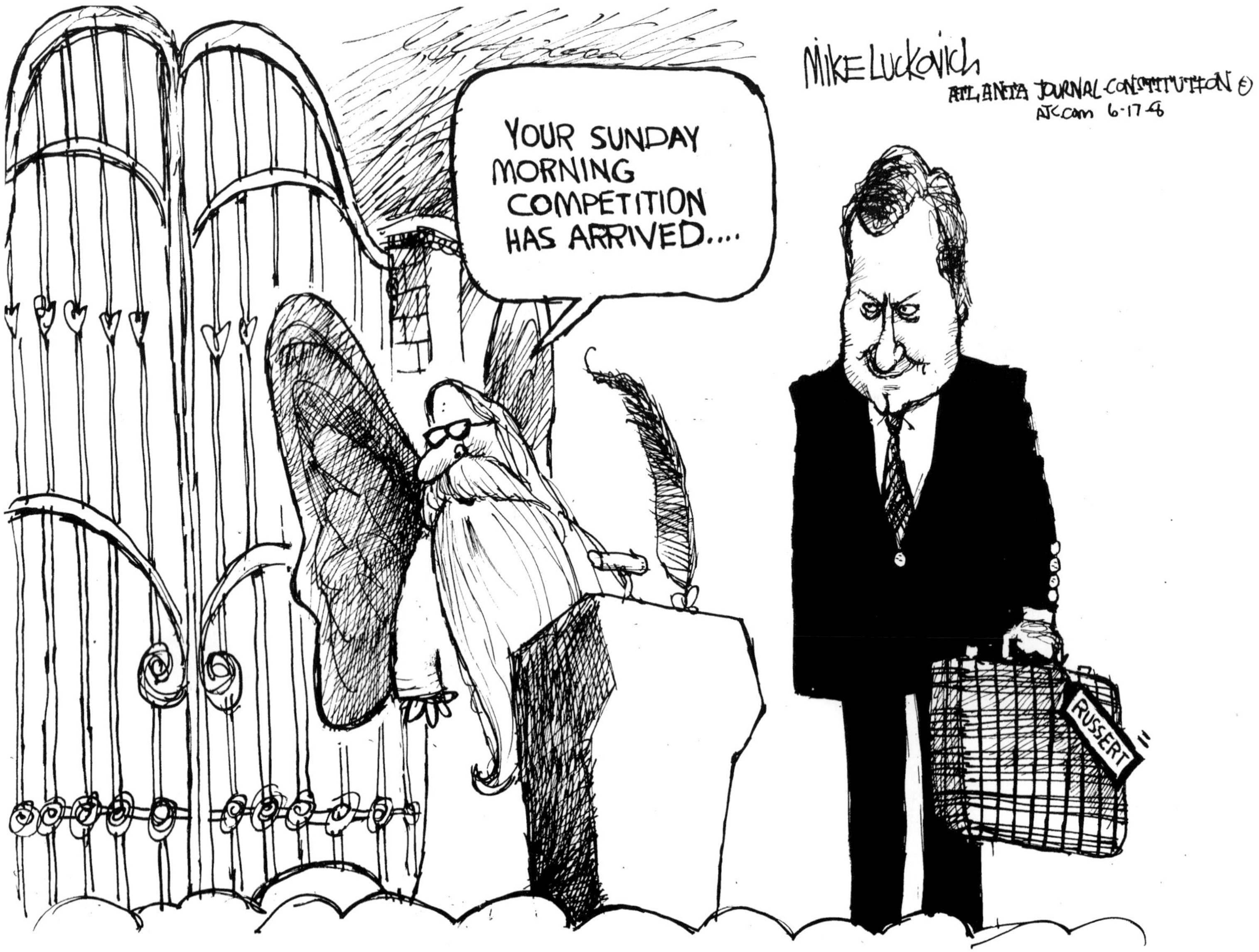
YOUR SUNDAY MORNING COMPETITION HAS ARRIVED....
MIKE LUCKOVICH
ATLANTA JOURNAL-CONSTITUTION
RUSSERT

By permission of Mike Luckovich and Creators Syndicate, Inc.

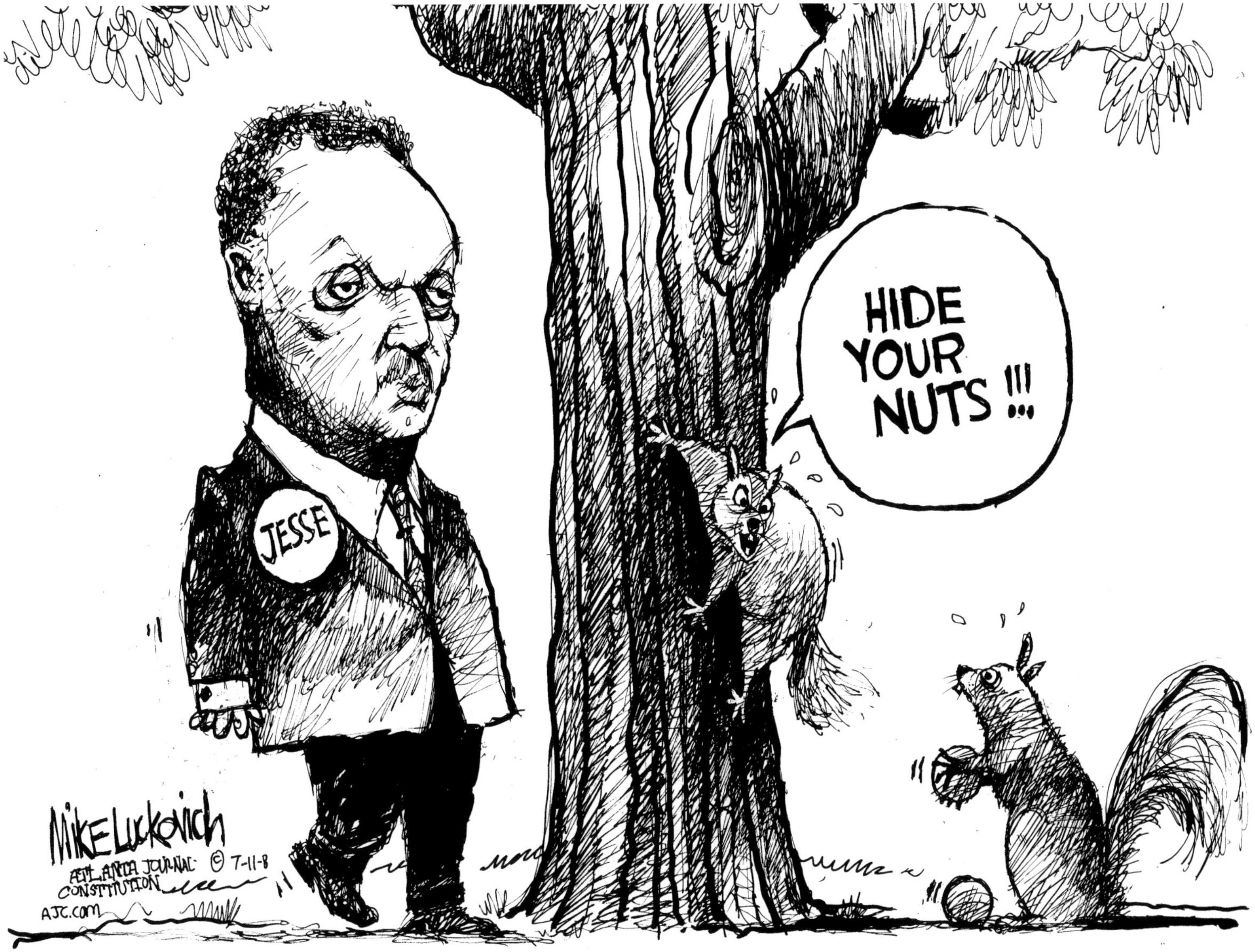
JESSE
HIDE YOUR NUTS !!!
MikeLuckovich
ATLANTA JOURNAL CONSTITUTION © 7-11-8
AJC.COM

By permission of Mike Luckovich and Creators Syndicate, Inc.

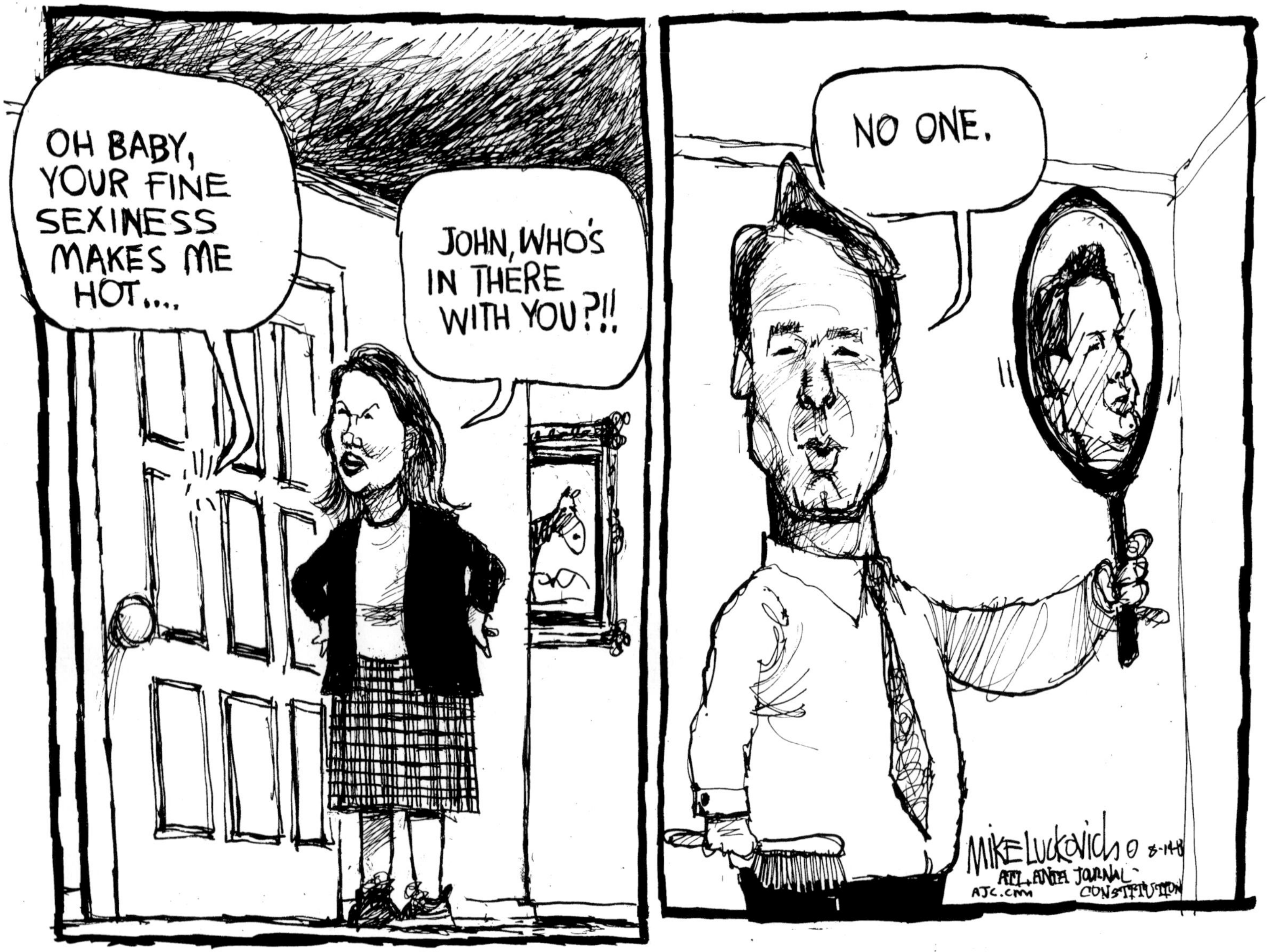
OH BABY, YOUR FINE SEXINESS MAKES ME HOT....
JOHN, WHO'S IN THERE WITH YOU?!!
NO ONE.
MIKE LUCKOVICH © 8-14-08
ATLANTA JOURNAL CONSTITUTION
AJC.COM

By permission of Mike Luckovich and Creators Syndicate, Inc.

By permission of Mike Luckovich and Creators Syndicate, Inc.

The Scripps Howard National Journalism Award

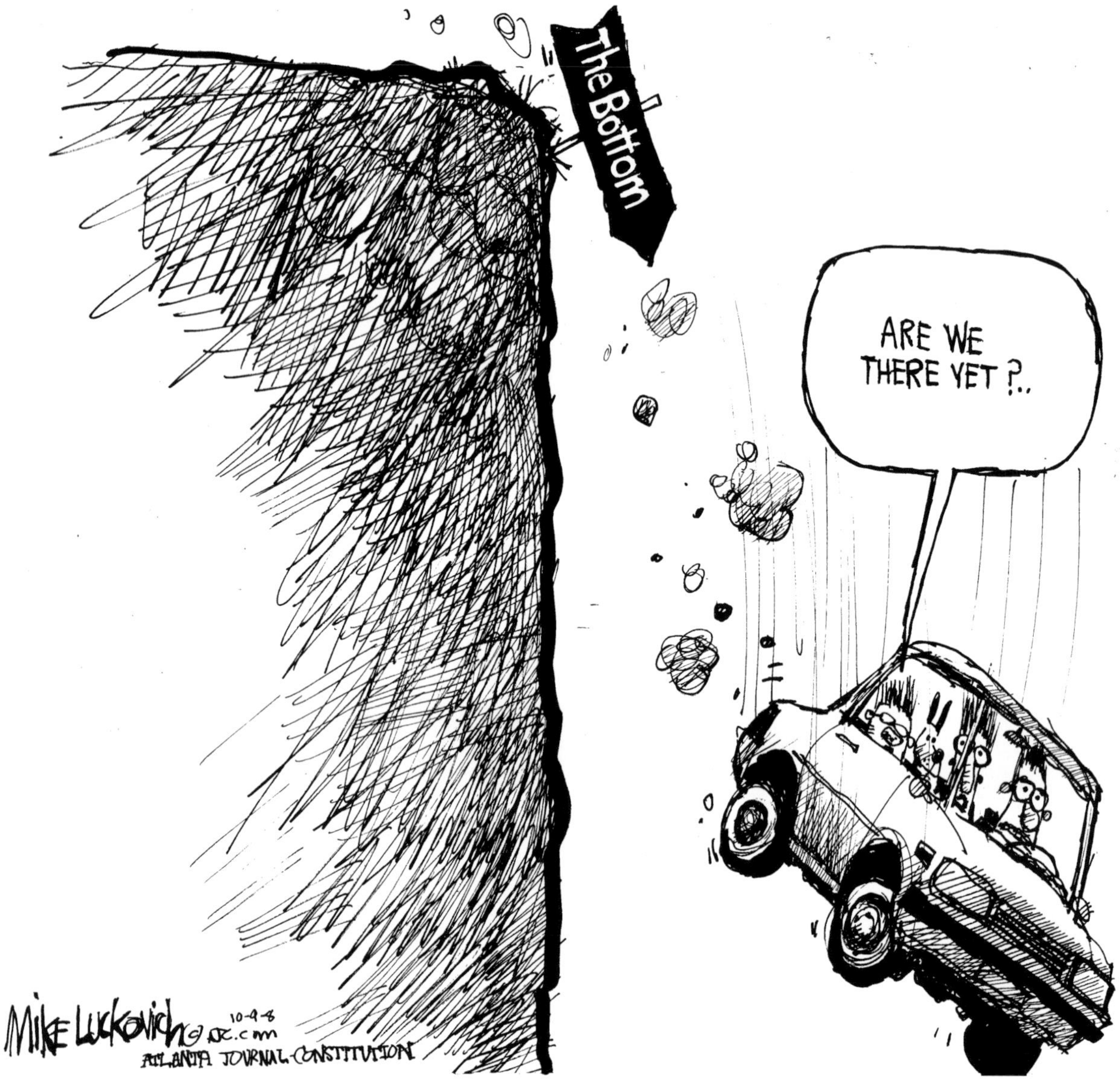
The Bottom
ARE WE THERE YET ?..
Mike Luckovich 10-4-8 @ajc.com
ATLANTA JOURNAL-CONSTITUTION

By permission of Mike Luckovich and Creators Syndicate, Inc.

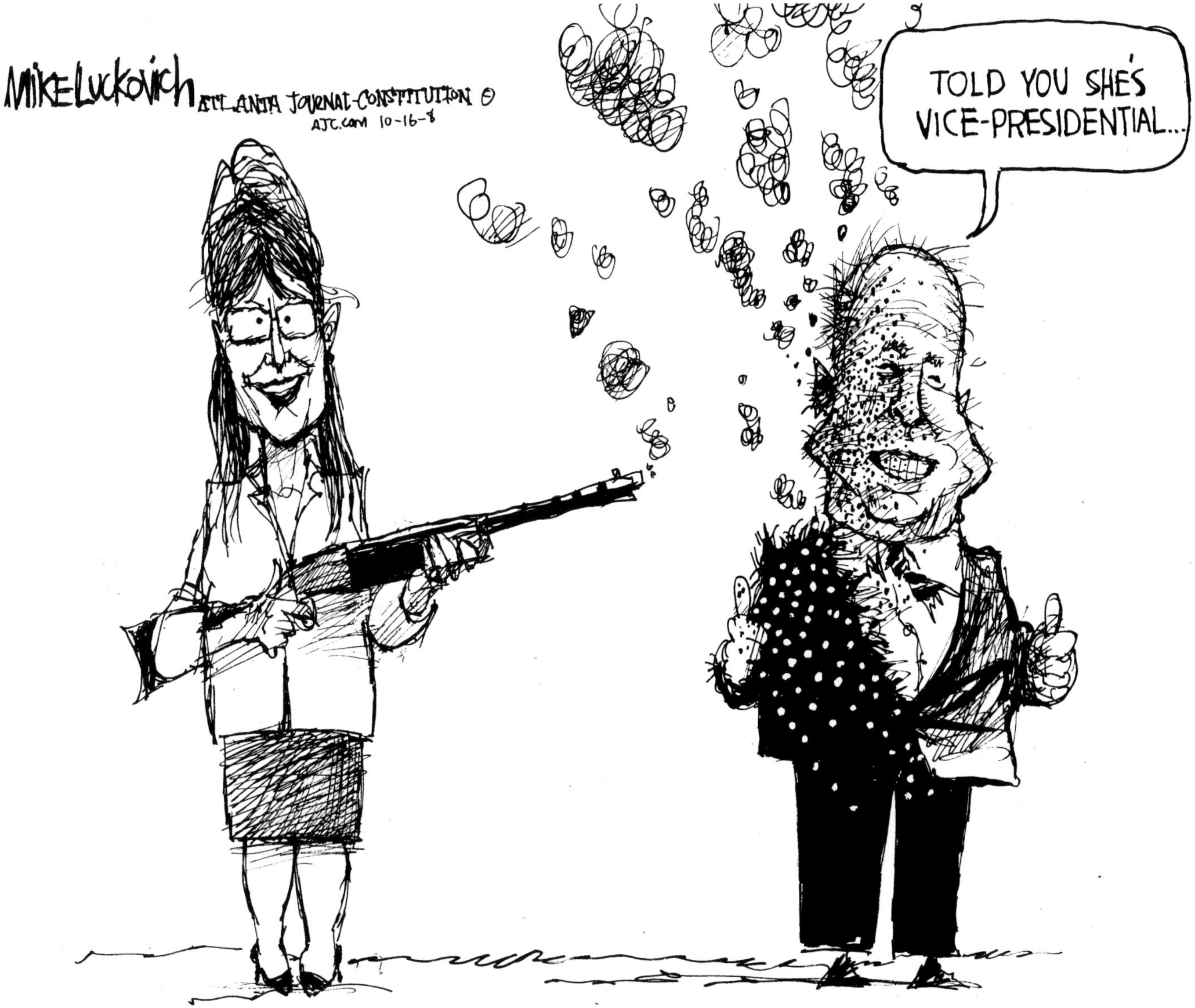
MIKE LUCKOVICH ATLANTA JOURNAL-CONSTITUTION ©
AJC.com 10-16-8
TOLD YOU SHE'S VICE-PRESIDENTIAL...

By permission of Mike Luckovich and Creators Syndicate, Inc.

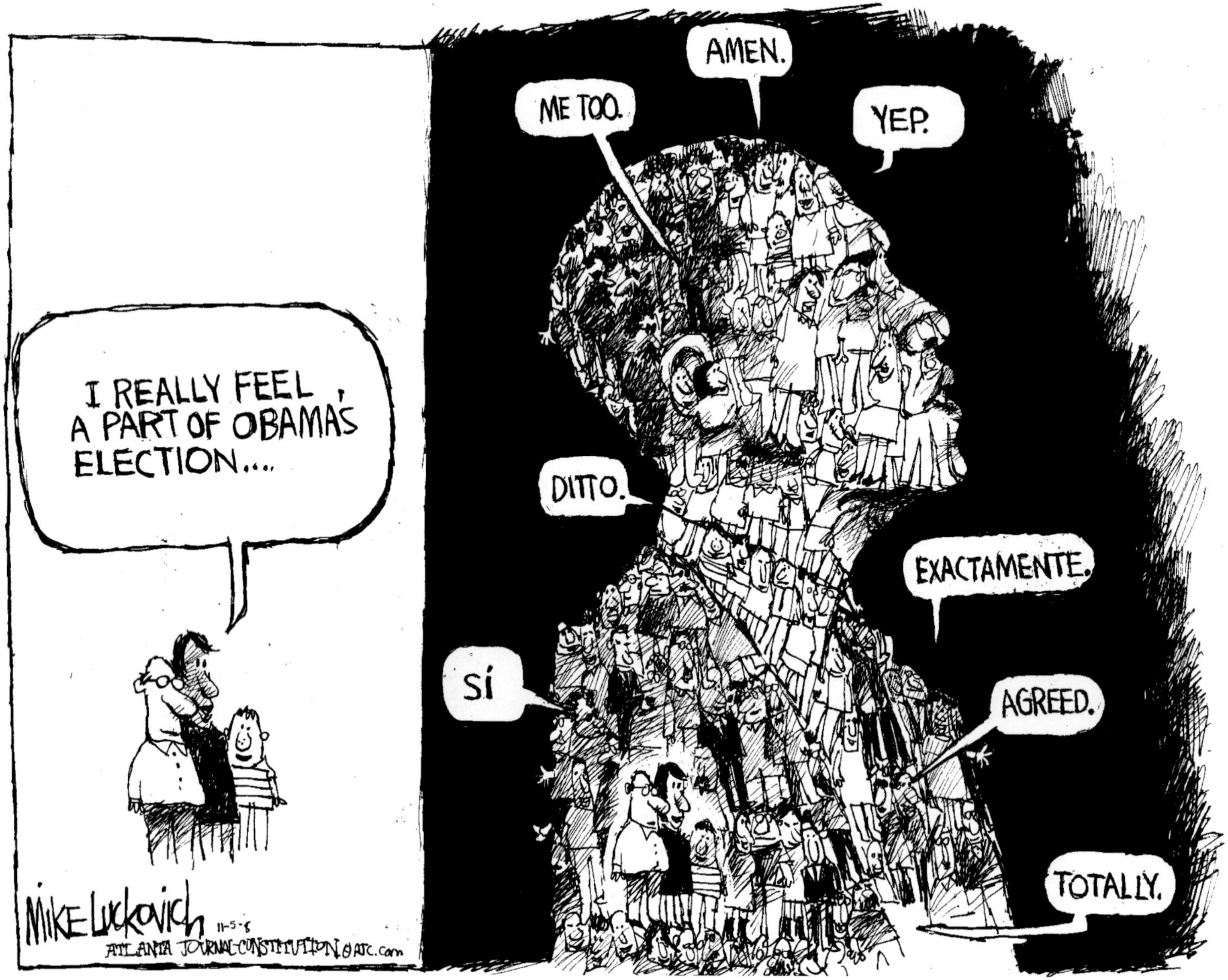
I REALLY FEEL A PART OF OBAMA'S ELECTION....
AMEN.
ME TOO.
YEP.
DITTO.
EXACTAMENTE.
SÍ
AGREED.
TOTALLY.
MIKE LUCKOVICH 11-5-8
ATLANTA JOURNAL-CONSTITUTION @AJC.com

By permission of Mike Luckovich and Creators Syndicate, Inc.

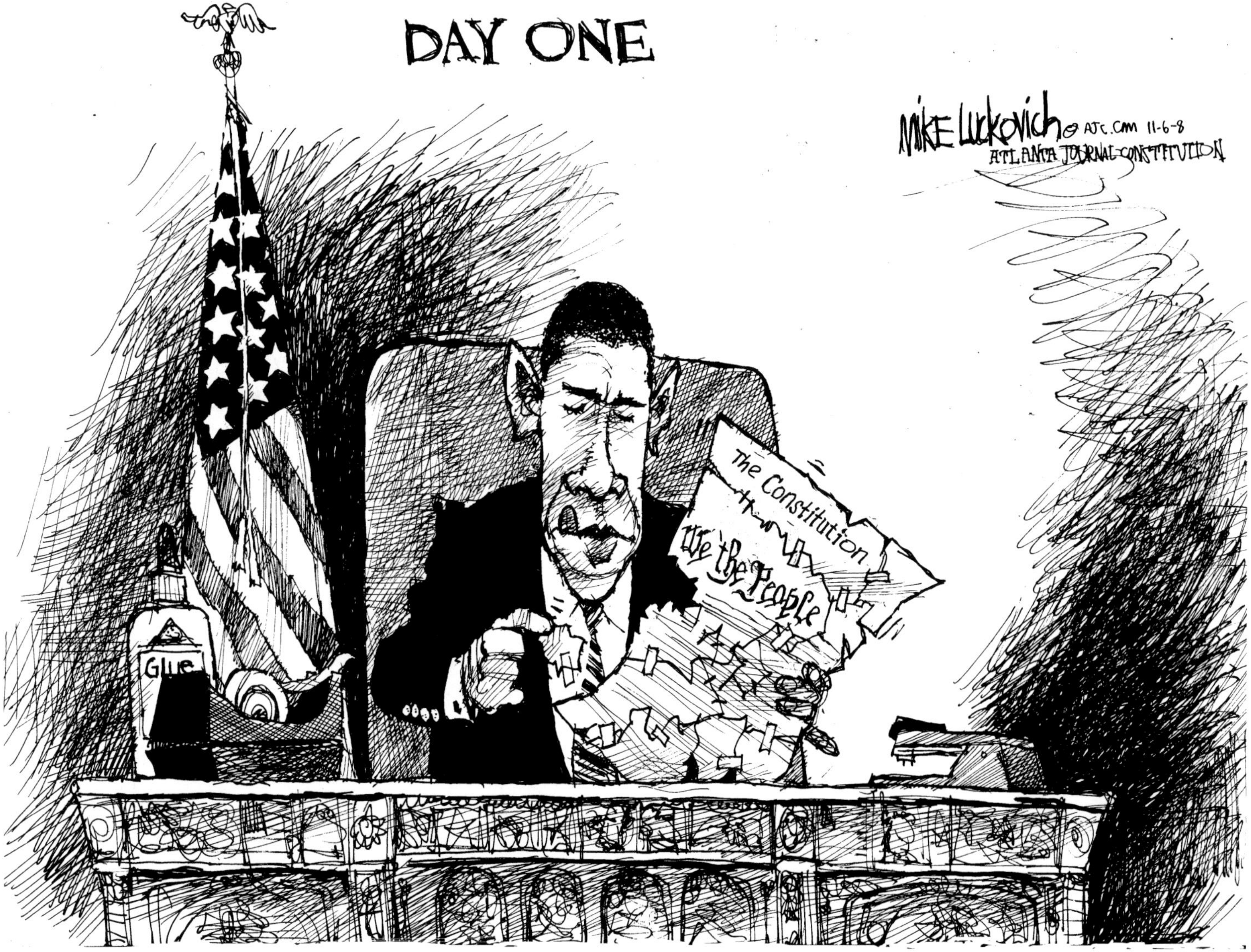
DAY ONE
MIKE LUCKOVICH © AJC.COM 11-6-8
ATLANTA JOURNAL-CONSTITUTION
The Constitution
We the People
GLUE

By permission of Mike Luckovich and Creators Syndicate, Inc.
(This cartoon was also entered in the John Fischetti Award contest)

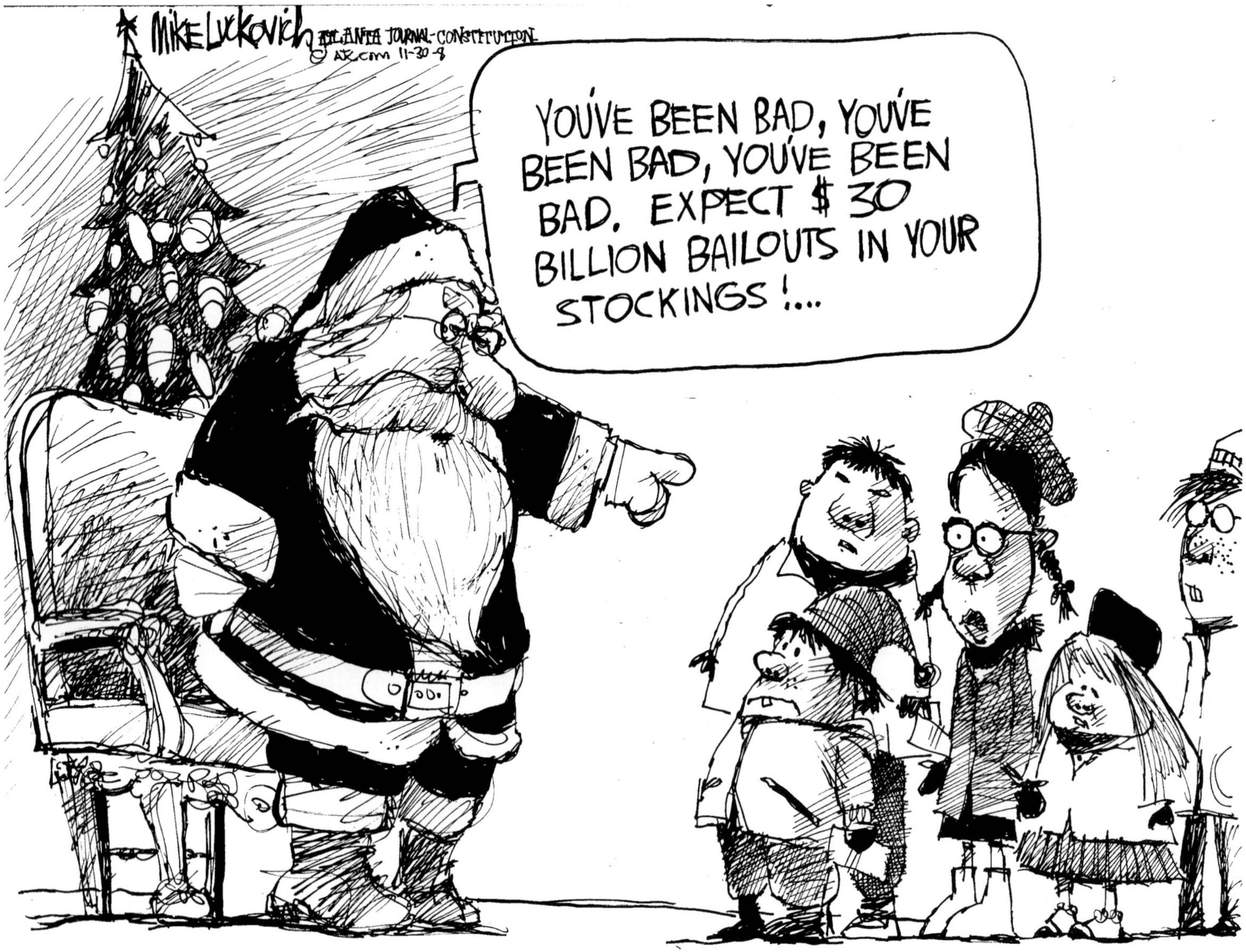
MIKE LUCKOVICH ATLANTA JOURNAL-CONSTITUTION
YOU'VE BEEN BAD, YOU'VE BEEN BAD, YOU'VE BEEN BAD. EXPECT $30 BILLION BAILOUTS IN YOUR STOCKINGS!...

By permission of Mike Luckovich and Creators Syndicate, Inc.

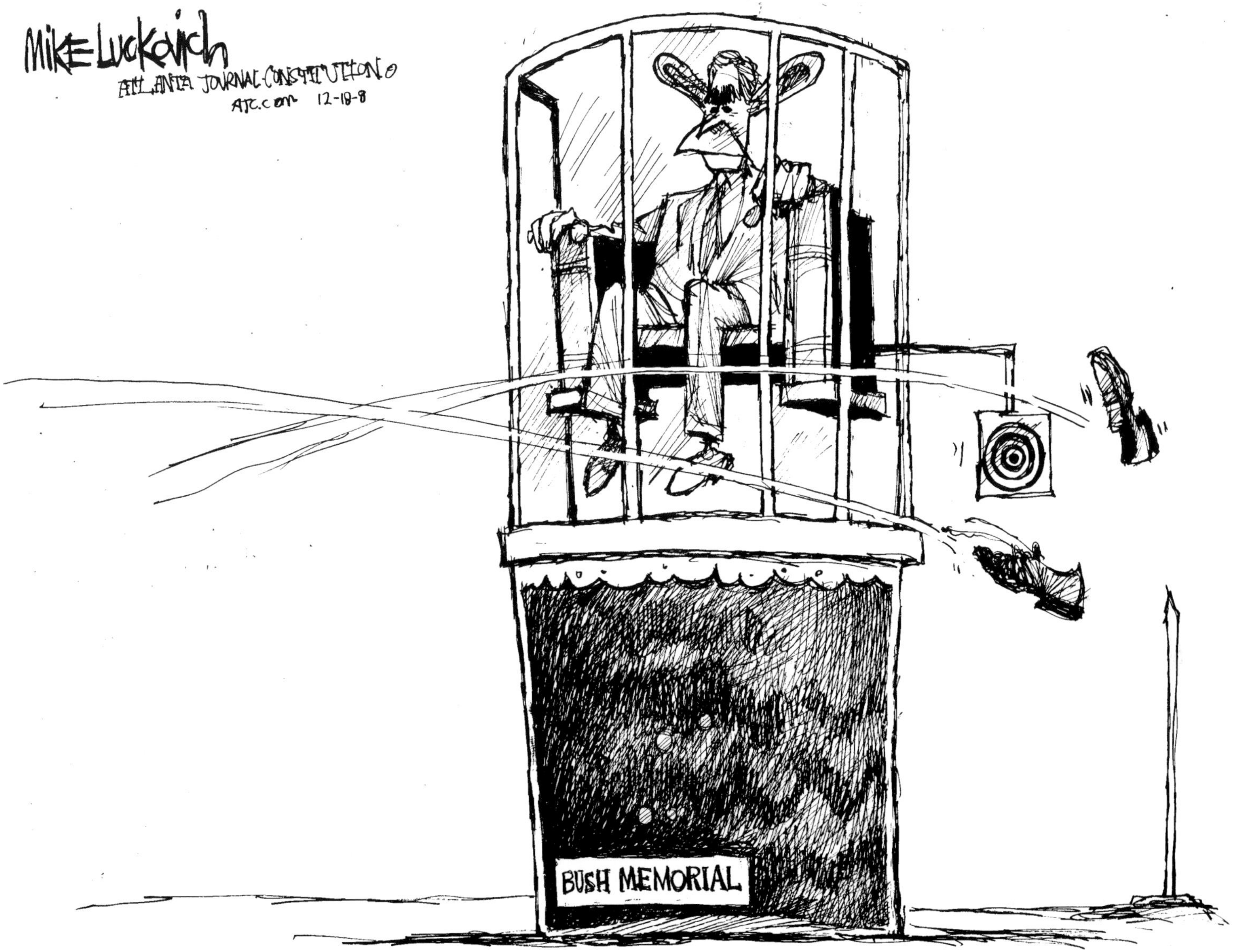

MIKE LUCKOVICH
ATLANTA JOURNAL-CONSTITUTION
AJC.com 12-18-8
BUSH MEMORIAL

By permission of Mike Luckovich and Creators Syndicate, Inc.

2008 Scripps Howard National Journalism Award Finalist

Don Asmussen—*San Francisco Chronicle*

Don Asmussen, the creator of *Bad Reporter*, a twice-weekly strip syndicated by Universal Press Syndicate, has worked at the *San Francisco Chronicle*, the *Detroit News*, the *San Diego Union-Tribune*, and *Portland Press Herald*.

His work has been profiled in *Communication Arts* and *Step-by-Step Magazine* and on Poynter.org. He had a regular strip in *Time* magazine from 1997 to 2002 and is the creator of the weekly Web animation *Like, News* and the strip *The Hero Santon* for *Mad* magazine and Salon.com.

Don Asmussen
BAD REPORTER
The LIES behind the TRUTH, and the TRUTH behind those LIES that are behind that TRUTH.
The Chronicle
IBM'S DEEP BLUE REMEMBERS BOBBY FISCHER AS 'ALL TOO HUMAN'
'COMPLETELY PACKAGED IN FLESHY MEMBRANE,' RECLUSIVE CHESS-PLAYING COMPUTER RECALLS OF LEGEND
Deep Blue suggests Fischer's humanness may have led to his death.
Deep Blue, like Fischer, ran from the spotlight.
First Black or Female President?
The GOP has a similar historic choice ...
The New York Times
WEDNESDAY, JANUARY 23, 2008
ANALYSIS: POSSIBILITY OF BEING COUNTRY'S FIRST BEIGE PRESIDENT WEIGHING HEAVILY ON ROMNEY
UNSPOKEN DISTRUST OF TANS STILL AMERICA'S DIRTY LITTLE SECRET
Did the breakthrough of actor George Hamilton mean absolutely nothing?
Will skin tone sway voters in 2008?
Yahoo Cuts Hundreds
What possibly went wrong?
LAID-OFF YAHOO WORKER USES GOOGLE MAPS® TO FIND EXIT
Google
'IT JUST WORKED QUICKER AND THEY WANTED ME OUT FAST,' EMBARRASSED EX-EMPLOYEE EXPLAINS
© 2008 Don Asmussen/Universal Press Syndicate dasmussen@sfchronicle.com
Send LOVE and HATE e-mails to dasmussen@sfchronicle.com

Don Asmussen
BAD REPORTER
The LIES behind the TRUTH, and the TRUTH behind those LIES that are behind that TRUTH.
The Chronicle
NASA CONFIRMS MYSTERIOUS IMAGE ON MARS IS DISENCHANTED BLACK FEMALE VOTER
'SHE JUST WANTS CLINTON AND OBAMA TO LEAVE HER ALONE,' FAMILY SAYS
Hillary ads are scheduled to run on Mars next week.
Mars image transmitted last week is of hiding voter.
Infamous 'Face on Mars' Explained
Scientists downplay an alien presence ...
The New York Times
FRIDAY, JANUARY 25, 2008
NASA: MYSTERIOUS 'CLINTON POUT' ON MARS ONLY A ROCK FORMATION
MARS NOT ACTUALLY BUMMED, SCIENTISTS CONFIRM
But NASA has no explanation for why the planet is getting redder as Nov. approaches.
Magnified image suggests an unhappy Bill.
Latest Cheney Pic Stuns
More unexplained phenomena!
NASA: MYSTERIOUS FORMATION TRANSMITTED FROM CHENEY'S HEAD 'NOT A SMILE'
'MOST LIKELY CARVED BY HIGH WINDS,' SCIENTISTS GUESS
Magnification reveals rock bed, not smile.
© 2008 Don Asmussen/Universal Press Syndicate dasmussen@sfchronicle.com
Send LOVE and HATE e-mails to dasmussen@sfchronicle.com

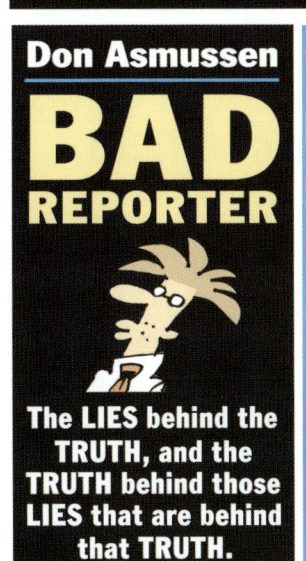

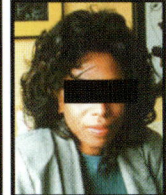

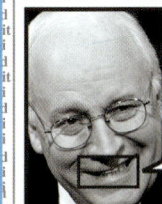

Don Asmussen: BAD REPORTER

The LIES behind the TRUTH, and the TRUTH behind those LIES that are behind that TRUTH.

The Chronicle
AL QAEDA CLOSES FOR THREE HOURS TO RETRAIN TERRORISTS

QUICK EXPANSION WORLDWIDE CAUSES LOSS OF THAT PERSONAL TERROR TOUCH

New Venti IED formula is demonstrated.

AL QAEDA: DOMINATION • FEAR • TERROR • SERVICE

Al-Zawahiri sends trainers to all al Qaeda sites.

Presidential Campaign Gets Dirtier
A blindsided McCain is the victim this time...

The New York Times — FRIDAY, FEBRUARY 29, 2008 — $1.00

CLINTON: NOT BEHIND PIC OF McCAIN AT TRADITIONAL OOMPA LOOMPA CEREMONY

TINY TERROR GROUP KNOWN FOR TORTURING GREEDY CHILDREN

Dems plant subtle fear that McCain may turn our kids into huge blueberries.

Obama's pic pales in comparison to McCain's.

Front-Line Celebrity
A famous soldier is revealed

ARMY REVEALS PRINCE HAS BEEN ON AFGHANISTAN FRONT LINE FOR THREE MONTHS

INSISTS HE WOULD DIE FOR U

Prince alerts soldiers to incoming missile.

Send LOVE and HATE e-mails to dasmussen@sfchronicle.com

Don Asmussen: BAD REPORTER

The LIES behind the TRUTH, and the TRUTH behind those LIES that are behind that TRUTH.

The Chronicle
CALL GIRL CLIENTS 1-8 RECORD CHARITY SINGLE FOR SPITZER FUND

HOPEFUL, PLAINTIVE 'THAT'S WHAT FRIENDS ARE FOR' HITS STORES TUESDAY

Plans for a live concert simulcast are nixed when the johns realize their wives might watch it.

Proof that every john can make a difference.

Nancy Pelosi Calls for China Protest
But will the White House listen to her?

The New York Times — WEDNESDAY, APRIL 2, 2008 — $1.00

BUSH REMAINS SILENT ON 2008 OLYMPIC SYNCHRONIZED WATERBOARDING CATEGORY

PRESIDENT HAS ALWAYS DISMISSED WIMPY GIRLIE COMPETITION AS 'NOT REALLY TORTURE'

Reports surface of secret water-curling.

Perfect leg sync won for U.S. in '04.

Congress Targets Big Oil
Is bulk caused by big profits?

BIG OIL TELLS CONGRESS THAT SUPPLIER ONLY INJECTED IT WITH FLAXSEED OIL

ALSO BALKS AT NEW TEST TO DISTINGUISH CRUDE OIL FROM FLAXSEED OIL

McNamee, ExxonMobil building at hearing.

Send LOVE and HATE e-mails to dasmussen@sfchronicle.com

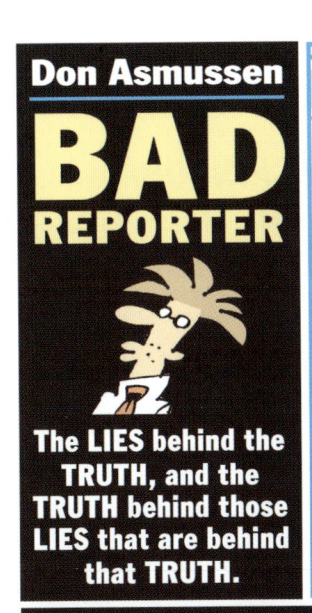

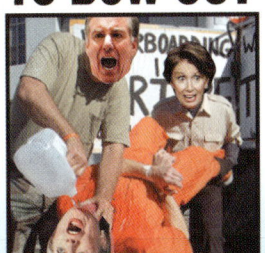

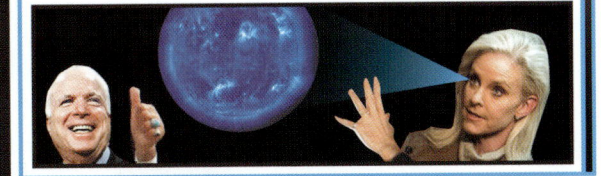

Don Asmussen
BAD REPORTER
The LIES behind the TRUTH, and the TRUTH behind those LIES that are behind that TRUTH.
The Chronicle
HOPEFUL 3-YEAR-OLD DREAMS OF SEEING FIRST WHITE PRESIDENT ELECTED IN HIS LIFETIME
YOUNGSTER REFUSES TO LET ENTIRE LIFE OF REVERSE RACISM DESTROY HOPE FOR HIS PEOPLE
Can Hillary's new strategy reach these disenfranchised people, or will Obama bring more status quo?
Clinton Still Holding Tough
A test of wills is tearing apart a party ...
The New York Times
FRIDAY, MAY 9, 2008
PICS LEAK OF DEMS PRESSURING HILLARY TO BOW OUT OF RACE
HOWARD DEAN PLEADS FOR ATTORNEY GENERAL TO LOOSEN POLITICAL PRESSURING RESTRICTIONS
Reader poll: If country is at stake, should waterboarding a candidate be allowed?
Hillary Strategy Shift
Opens up to alternatives ...
PUTIN NAMED PM OF RUSSIA — CLINTON STILL INSISTING SHE HAS SHOT
RUSSIANS STUNNED AS RADIOACTIVE POLONIUM 210 ONLY SEEMS TO ENERGIZE HER
© 2008 Don Asmussen/Universal Press Syndicate dasmussen@sfchronicle.com
Send LOVE and HATE e-mails to dasmussen@sfchronicle.com

Don Asmussen
BAD REPORTER
The LIES behind the TRUTH, and the TRUTH behind those LIES that are behind that TRUTH.
The Chronicle
McCAIN PLEDGES WIFE'S DEMEANOR WILL SLOW GLOBAL WARMING
FRIENDS SAY THEY'VE SEEN CINDY'S ICEY STARE FREEZE THE SUN FOR UP TO 3 HOURS
GOP Goes (Non-Money) Green?
Is a conservative wooing independents?
The New York Times
WEDNESDAY, MAY 14, 2008
BODY LANGUAGE EXPERTS SAY McCAIN'S HUG WITH EARTH APPEARED AWKWARD
CYNICS SAY 3RD PLANET IS ALL ABOUT THE SPIN
Earth denies it's angry that Dems act as if everything revolves around the sun.
A hug — but will the earth campaign for McCain?
Clinton's Last Stand
She pulls out all the stops
HILLARY QUESTIONS VOTER VOTEABILITY IN NATIONAL ELECTION
CAN MAN BELOW FIND HIS LOCAL VOTING STATION UNDER THE INTENSE, UNFORGIVING GLARE OF A NATIONAL ELECTION?
Hillary: different voters must be picked.
© 2008 Don Asmussen/Universal Press Syndicate dasmussen@sfchronicle.com
Send LOVE and HATE e-mails to dasmussen@sfchronicle.com

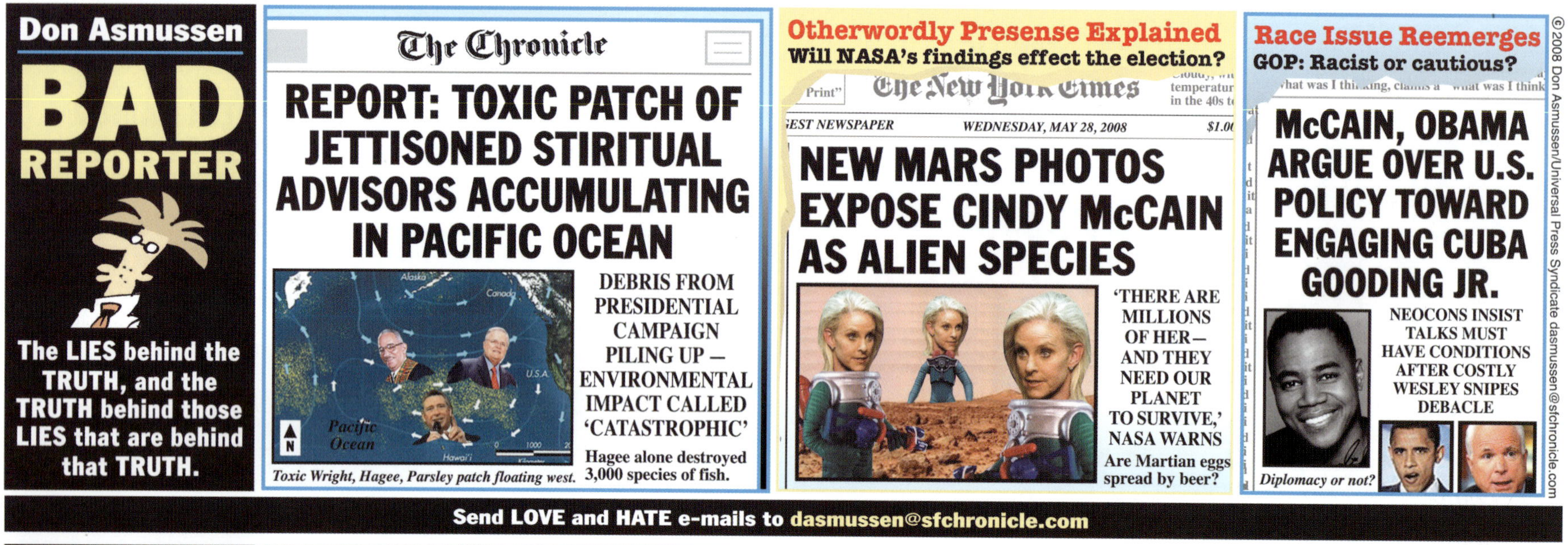
Don Asmussen
BAD REPORTER
The LIES behind the TRUTH, and the TRUTH behind those LIES that are behind that TRUTH.
The Chronicle
REPORT: TOXIC PATCH OF JETTISONED STIRITUAL ADVISORS ACCUMULATING IN PACIFIC OCEAN
Alaska
Canada
U.S.A.
Pacific Ocean
Hawai'i
N
DEBRIS FROM PRESIDENTIAL CAMPAIGN PILING UP — ENVIRONMENTAL IMPACT CALLED 'CATASTROPHIC'
Toxic Wright, Hagee, Parsley patch floating west.
Hagee alone destroyed 3,000 species of fish.
Otherwordly Presense Explained
Will NASA's findings effect the election?
The New York Times
WEDNESDAY, MAY 28, 2008
NEW MARS PHOTOS EXPOSE CINDY McCAIN AS ALIEN SPECIES
'THERE ARE MILLIONS OF HER— AND THEY NEED OUR PLANET TO SURVIVE,' NASA WARNS
Are Martian eggs spread by beer?
Race Issue Reemerges
GOP: Racist or cautious?
McCAIN, OBAMA ARGUE OVER U.S. POLICY TOWARD ENGAGING CUBA GOODING JR.
NEOCONS INSIST TALKS MUST HAVE CONDITIONS AFTER COSTLY WESLEY SNIPES DEBACLE
Diplomacy or not?
© 2008 Don Asmussen/Universal Press Syndicate dasmussen@sfchronicle.com
Send LOVE and HATE e-mails to dasmussen@sfchronicle.com

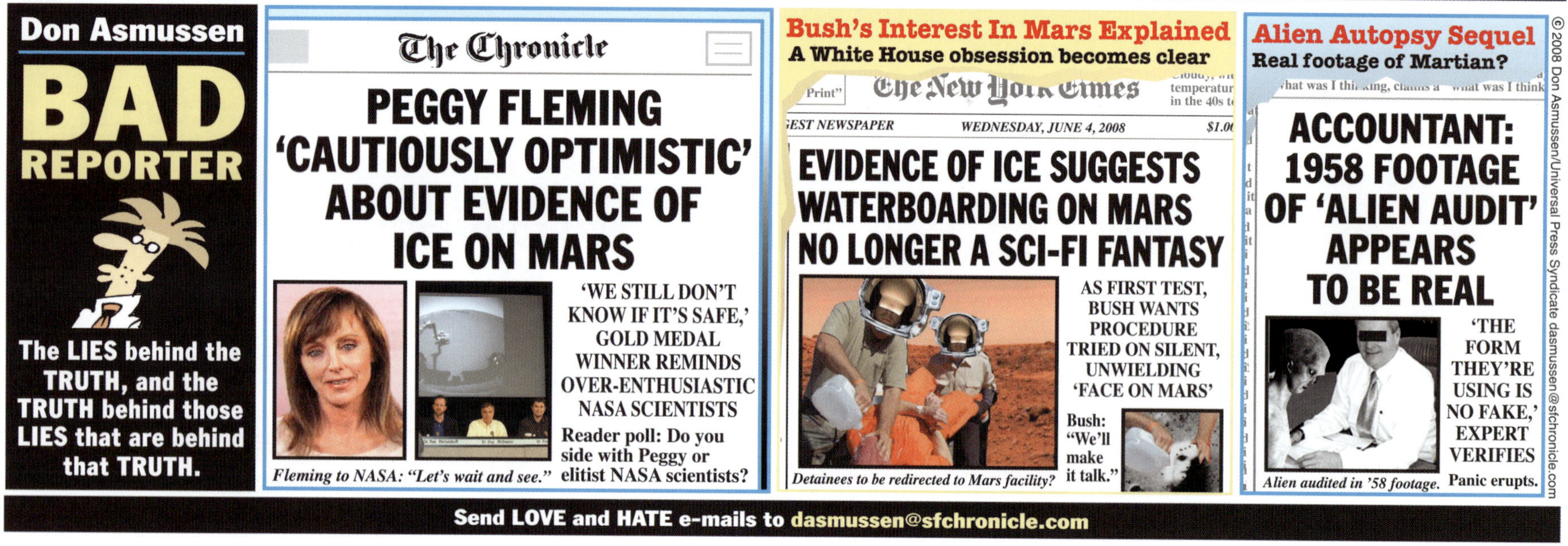
Don Asmussen
BAD REPORTER
The LIES behind the TRUTH, and the TRUTH behind those LIES that are behind that TRUTH.
The Chronicle
PEGGY FLEMING 'CAUTIOUSLY OPTIMISTIC' ABOUT EVIDENCE OF ICE ON MARS
'WE STILL DON'T KNOW IF IT'S SAFE,' GOLD MEDAL WINNER REMINDS OVER-ENTHUSIASTIC NASA SCIENTISTS
Fleming to NASA: "Let's wait and see."
Reader poll: Do you side with Peggy or elitist NASA scientists?
Bush's Interest In Mars Explained
A White House obsession becomes clear
The New York Times
WEDNESDAY, JUNE 4, 2008
EVIDENCE OF ICE SUGGESTS WATERBOARDING ON MARS NO LONGER A SCI-FI FANTASY
AS FIRST TEST, BUSH WANTS PROCEDURE TRIED ON SILENT, UNWIELDING 'FACE ON MARS'
Bush: "We'll make it talk."
Detainees to be redirected to Mars facility?
Alien Autopsy Sequel
Real footage of Martian?
ACCOUNTANT: 1958 FOOTAGE OF 'ALIEN AUDIT' APPEARS TO BE REAL
'THE FORM THEY'RE USING IS NO FAKE,' EXPERT VERIFIES
Alien audited in '58 footage.
Panic erupts.
© 2008 Don Asmussen/Universal Press Syndicate dasmussen@sfchronicle.com
Send LOVE and HATE e-mails to dasmussen@sfchronicle.com

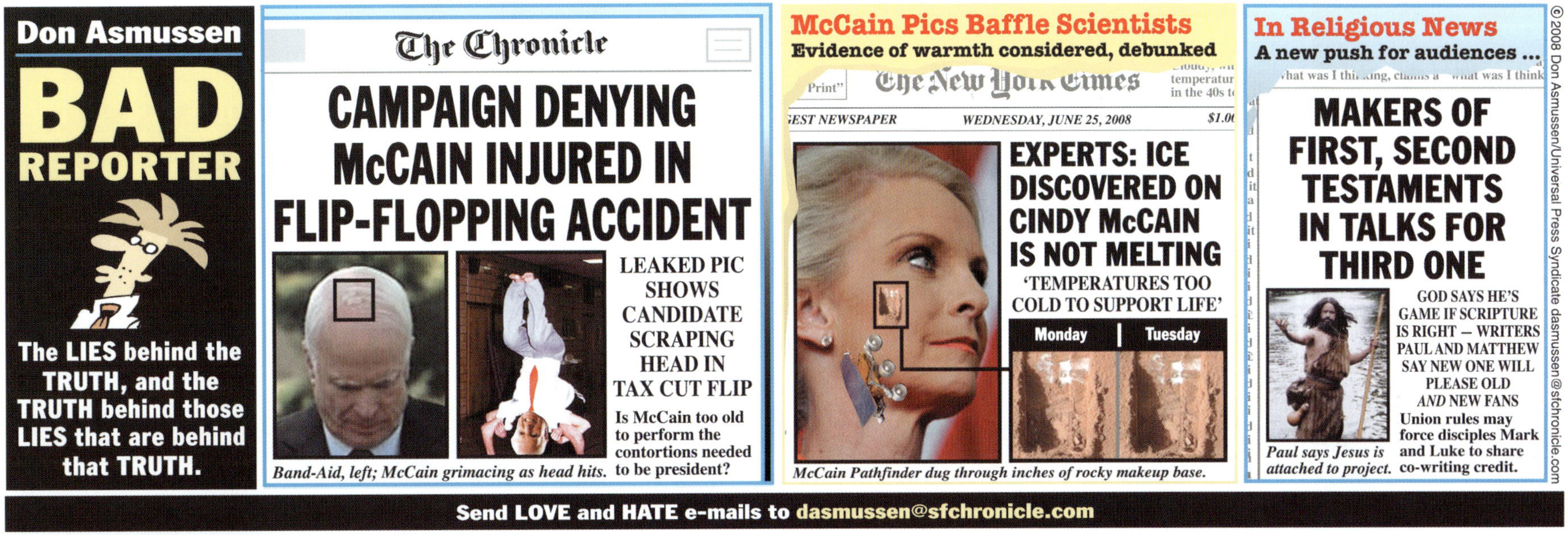

Don Asmussen: BAD REPORTER

The LIES behind the TRUTH, and the TRUTH behind those LIES that are behind that TRUTH.

The Chronicle

CAMPAIGN DENYING McCAIN INJURED IN FLIP-FLOPPING ACCIDENT

LEAKED PIC SHOWS CANDIDATE SCRAPING HEAD IN TAX CUT FLIP

Is McCain too old to perform the contortions needed to be president?

Band-Aid, left; McCain grimacing as head hits.

McCain Pics Baffle Scientists
Evidence of warmth considered, debunked

The New York Times — WEDNESDAY, JUNE 25, 2008

EXPERTS: ICE DISCOVERED ON CINDY McCAIN IS NOT MELTING

'TEMPERATURES TOO COLD TO SUPPORT LIFE'

Monday | Tuesday

McCain Pathfinder dug through inches of rocky makeup base.

In Religious News
A new push for audiences ...

MAKERS OF FIRST, SECOND TESTAMENTS IN TALKS FOR THIRD ONE

GOD SAYS HE'S GAME IF SCRIPTURE IS RIGHT — WRITERS PAUL AND MATTHEW SAY NEW ONE WILL PLEASE OLD *AND* NEW FANS

Union rules may force disciples Mark and Luke to share co-writing credit.

Paul says Jesus is attached to project.

Send LOVE and HATE e-mails to dasmussen@sfchronicle.com

Don Asmussen: BAD REPORTER

The LIES behind the TRUTH, and the TRUTH behind those LIES that are behind that TRUTH.

The Chronicle

GOD RUMORED TO BE ON OBAMA'S V.P. SHORT LIST

'HEAVILY DISGUISED' DEITY PHOTOGRAPHED MEETING WITH DEM CANDIDATE ON MONDAY

Experts agrees that God speaking at the Dem convention could trump Leiberman's GOP speech.

Obama met man in heaven Monday. Was it God?

More Unpatriotic Leaders Exposed
The latest is America-hater is a shocker ...

The New York Times — WEDNESDAY, JULY 1, 2008

'PATRIOTIC' UNCLE SAM PHOTOGRAPH REVEALS NO FLAG PIN ON LAPEL

'ARROGANT' NATIONAL ICON FAILS TO PAY TRIBUTE TO U.S. TROOPS' SACRIFICES

Aloof Uncle to all had no problem recruiting the same young men he now ignores.

He hates America.

Cell Phones in Cars
California battles terror!

NEW SLEEPER CELL PHONE LAW BANS TERRORISTS FROM IGNITING BOMBS WITH HAND HELDS

DEADLY PLOTS CAN ONLY BE EXECUTED ON HEADSETS

ILLEGAL AS OF JULY 1!

Send LOVE and HATE e-mails to dasmussen@sfchronicle.com

The Scripps Howard National Journalism Award

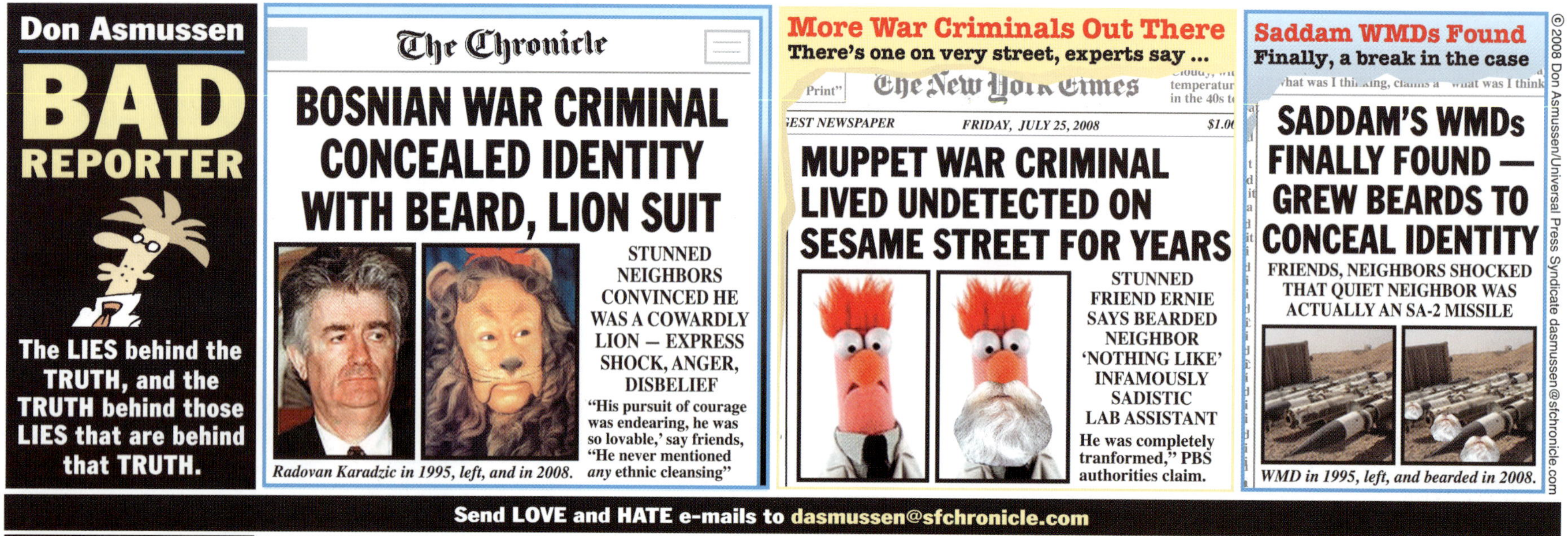
Don Asmussen
BAD REPORTER
The LIES behind the TRUTH, and the TRUTH behind those LIES that are behind that TRUTH.
The Chronicle
BOSNIAN WAR CRIMINAL CONCEALED IDENTITY WITH BEARD, LION SUIT
STUNNED NEIGHBORS CONVINCED HE WAS A COWARDLY LION — EXPRESS SHOCK, ANGER, DISBELIEF
"His pursuit of courage was endearing, he was so lovable,' say friends, "He never mentioned any ethnic cleansing"
Radovan Karadzic in 1995, left, and in 2008.
More War Criminals Out There
There's one on very street, experts say ...
The New York Times
FRIDAY, JULY 25, 2008
MUPPET WAR CRIMINAL LIVED UNDETECTED ON SESAME STREET FOR YEARS
STUNNED FRIEND ERNIE SAYS BEARDED NEIGHBOR 'NOTHING LIKE' INFAMOUSLY SADISTIC LAB ASSISTANT
He was completely tranformed," PBS authorities claim.
Saddam WMDs Found
Finally, a break in the case
SADDAM'S WMDs FINALLY FOUND — GREW BEARDS TO CONCEAL IDENTITY
FRIENDS, NEIGHBORS SHOCKED THAT QUIET NEIGHBOR WAS ACTUALLY AN SA-2 MISSILE
WMD in 1995, left, and bearded in 2008.
Send LOVE and HATE e-mails to dasmussen@sfchronicle.com
© 2008 Don Asmussen/Universal Press Syndicate dasmussen@sfchronicle.com

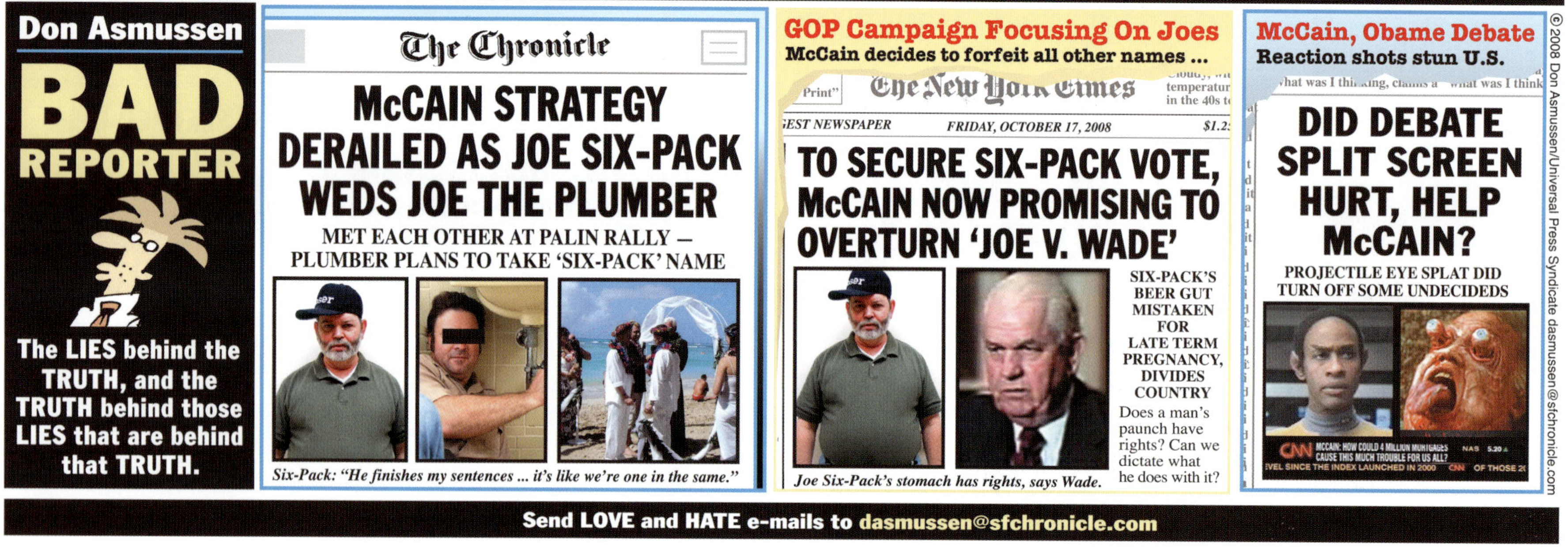
Don Asmussen
BAD REPORTER
The LIES behind the TRUTH, and the TRUTH behind those LIES that are behind that TRUTH.
The Chronicle
McCAIN STRATEGY DERAILED AS JOE SIX-PACK WEDS JOE THE PLUMBER
MET EACH OTHER AT PALIN RALLY — PLUMBER PLANS TO TAKE 'SIX-PACK' NAME
Six-Pack: "He finishes my sentences ... it's like we're one in the same."
GOP Campaign Focusing On Joes
McCain decides to forfeit all other names ...
The New York Times
FRIDAY, OCTOBER 17, 2008
TO SECURE SIX-PACK VOTE, McCAIN NOW PROMISING TO OVERTURN 'JOE V. WADE'
SIX-PACK'S BEER GUT MISTAKEN FOR LATE TERM PREGNANCY, DIVIDES COUNTRY
Does a man's paunch have rights? Can we dictate what he does with it?
Joe Six-Pack's stomach has rights, says Wade.
McCain, Obame Debate
Reaction shots stun U.S.
DID DEBATE SPLIT SCREEN HURT, HELP McCAIN?
PROJECTILE EYE SPLAT DID TURN OFF SOME UNDECIDEDS
Send LOVE and HATE e-mails to dasmussen@sfchronicle.com
© 2008 Don Asmussen/Universal Press Syndicate dasmussen@sfchronicle.com

2008 Scripps Howard National Journalism Award Finalist

Alexander Hunter—*Washington Times*

Born in Long Beach, California, in 1960, Alexander Hunter and his two younger brothers began drawing from the time they could hold pencils and received their art education at home from their parents, both gifted artists. The young Mr. Hunter struck out on his own in pursuit of life as a "fine artist." This means in no particular order, he traveled, worked at some odd jobs, and didn't go to college.

During the past twenty-seven years, Hunter has worked (often concurrently) as an illustrator, political cartoonist, graphic designer, and art director for various sections of the *Washington Times*. He's won many accolades along the way, and his supervisor and coworkers seem to like him.

Hunter's Big Picture is now in it's fourteenth month of publication, featured Sundays in the *Washington Times*. In some respects, its form hearkens back to the full-page political cartoons and Sunday comics pages of the early twentieth century, presenting not only funny, color-filled pictures and lot of words, but sometimes very LARGE funny, color-filled pictures and lots of words.

(Editor's note: In order to do Mr. Hunter's unique approach to editorial cartooning justice, it was necessary to split what were originally full-page cartoons into three sections. Owing to that, this is not his full entry. Apologies to Mr. Hunter for this necessary perversion of his art.)

Alexander Hunter Interview

Dean: Turn-of-the-century journalist Finley Peter Dunne is quoted as saying, "The job of the newspaper is to comfort the afflicted and afflict the comfortable." What do you see as the role of the editorial cartoonist?

Alexander: The editorial cartoonist serves at least three roles, to three constituencies:

A. To the readers, he(or she) is a stalwart servant, a secular preacher, a Calphurnian cut-up, laying bare the heart of a public situation in a way that gives emotional and intellectual relief by reiterating what is "right" and what is "wrong," saying and showing what "somebody ought to be saying and showing" about whatever's (or whoever's) going on. Sadly, most of us poor screevers fail to offer much more than what is "Right" or what is "Left" or a shallow joke. I don't believe that a political cartoonist is called to be simply a clown. Great cartoonists, like great preachers, bring a gospel transcending party or culture or race, illuminating moral poles that bracket a larger sphere than Planet Mirth. Then again, sometimes, the greatest relief for man is found in manslaughter, sorry, man's laughter. Sometimes if we don't laugh, we cry. Diffusing anger or pain with humor can be a great service in itself.

B. To the subjects (or targets as the case may be) of his (or her) work, the cartoonist is a mirror, a funhouse mirror, but a mirror nonetheless. Political cartoonists don't have to seek and destroy the personage in their sights, just the hubris and mendacity that's leading the personage to disaster. Holding feet to fire is fine. Better to enter the kingdom without feet than lose the whole magilla.

C. To their own publication, the political cartoonist is an important bellweather of editorial integrity and standards, a canary in the coal mine, gauging what the editor's and publisher's actual gas emissions are. From the saga of Beaverbrook and Low to the *New York Post* and Sean Delonas, what cartoon a paper will actually run, and with what revisions, often plumbs with tiny candle the dark inward parts of the editorial machine.

There's a lot of pith and vinegar in Dunne's fourteen words, but it can be said that people sometimes find themselves afflicted because they are headed in some wrong direction, and sometimes the comfort we see others enjoying is the gracious fruit of righteous life. I believe things are often subtler than we surmise. Being loaded for bear with a Menkenesque indignation often as not hides juvenile blind spots and bigotries that will eventually bear itself out in the work.

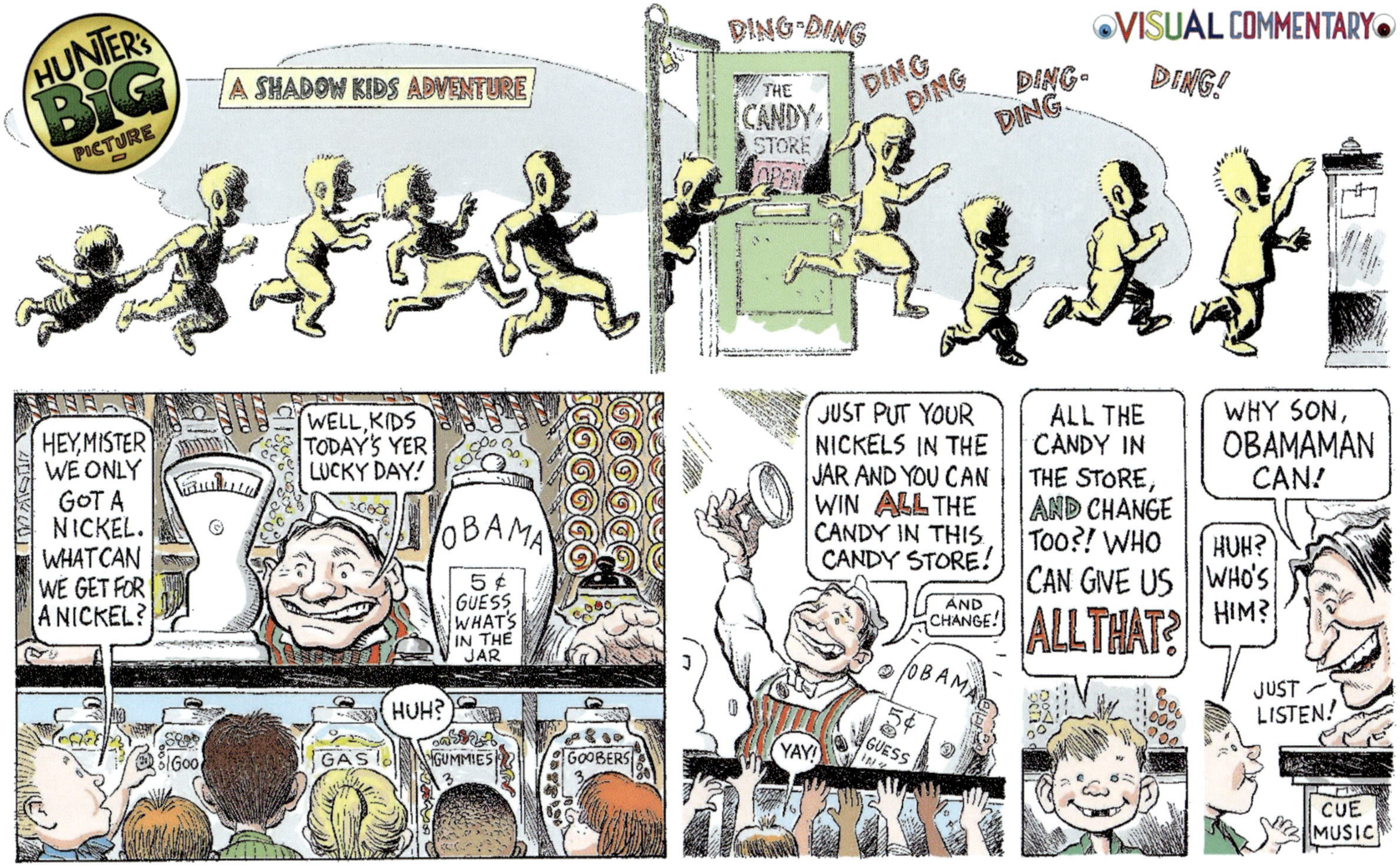
HUNTER'S BIG PICTURE
A SHADOW KIDS ADVENTURE
VISUAL COMMENTARY
DING-DING
THE CANDY STORE
OPEN
DING DING
DING-DING
DING!
HEY, MISTER WE ONLY GOT A NICKEL. WHAT CAN WE GET FOR A NICKEL?
WELL, KIDS TODAY'S YER LUCKY DAY!
OBAMA
5¢ GUESS WHAT'S IN THE JAR
HUH?
GOO
GAS
GUMMIES 3
GOOBERS 3
JUST PUT YOUR NICKELS IN THE JAR AND YOU CAN WIN ALL THE CANDY IN THIS CANDY STORE!
AND CHANGE!
YAY!
OBAMA
5¢ GUESS
ALL THE CANDY IN THE STORE, AND CHANGE TOO?! WHO CAN GIVE US ALL THAT?
WHY SON, OBAMAMAN CAN!
HUH? WHO'S HIM?
JUST LISTEN!
CUE MUSIC

WHO CAN TAKE A SUNRISE...
WHO CAN TAKE A SUNRISE
Obama?
SPRINKLE IT WITH DEW...
SPIZT
Eau de 400 years
SMOTHER IT WITH OPRAH
AND A MIRACLE OR TWO...
OBAMAMAN,
OBAMAMAN CAN!
OBAMAMAN CAN 'CAUSE HE KEEPS IT KINDA VAGUE AND MAKES HIS WORDS TASTE GOOD...
MAKES HIS WORDS TASTE GOOD
SWOON SECTION
WHO CAN MAKE THE RAINBOW COALITION SIGH, SAYS WE'LL ALL GET COLLEGE AND A BIGGER PIECE OF PIE...
OBAMAMAN!
OBAMAMAN CAN! OBAMAMAN CAN CAUSE HE KEEPS IT KINDA VAGUE AND MAKES HIS WORDS TASTE GOOD!!!
TAKE ME TO THE BRIDGE!
BARAK OBAMA MAKES...
GROOVY
EVERYTHING HE BAKES MYSTIFYING YET DELICIOUS, TALK ABOUT YOUR CHERISHED WISHES... AND HE NEVER COMES OFF VICIOUS...
-OOOH! -AAAH! -YAY!
OH POO!
WHO CAN TAKE TOMORROW...
DIP IT IN YOUR DREAMS...
HOPE

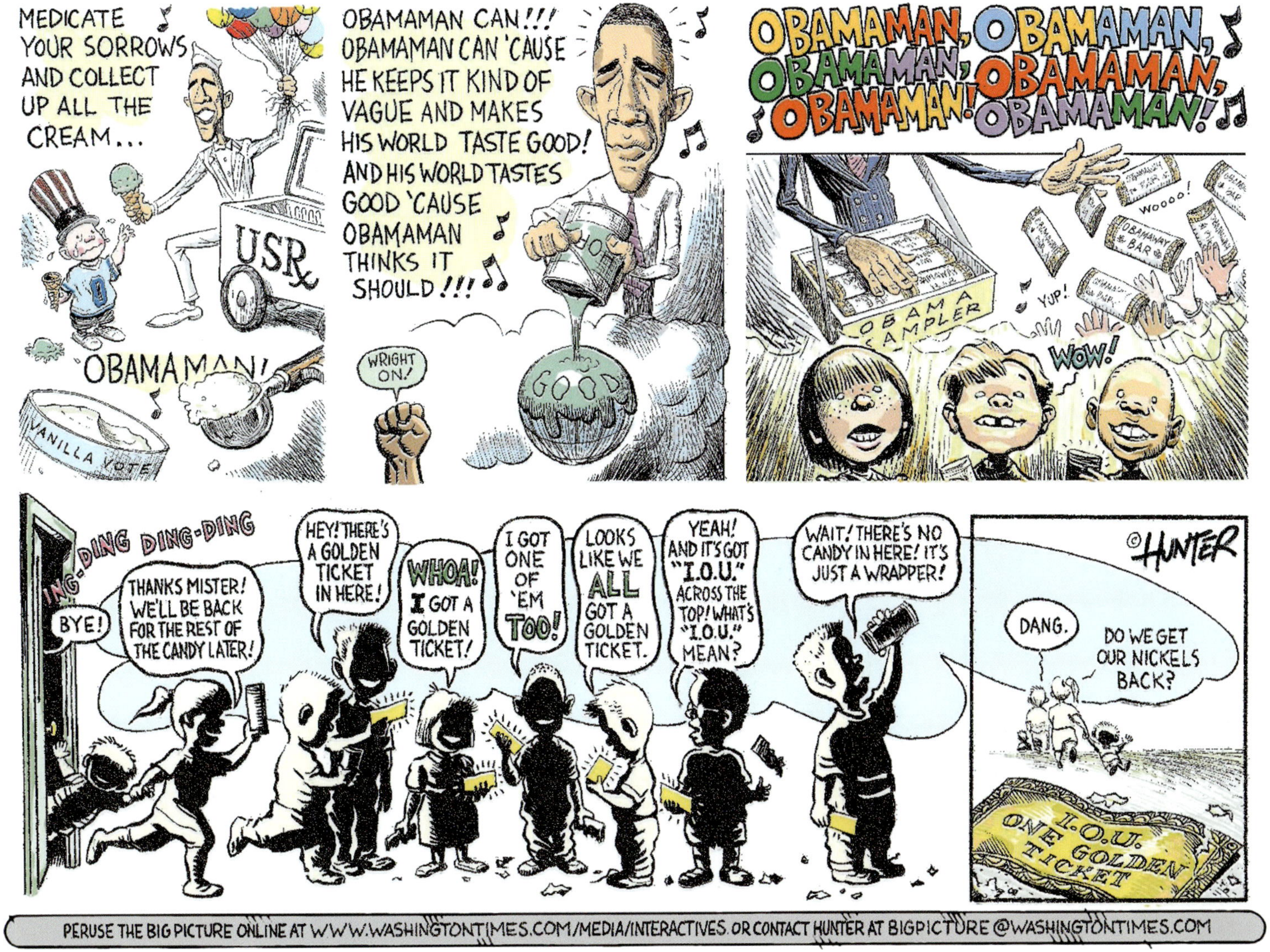
MEDICATE YOUR SORROWS AND COLLECT UP ALL THE CREAM...
USRx
"OBAMAMAN!"
VANILLA VOTE
OBAMAMAN CAN!!! OBAMAMAN CAN 'CAUSE HE KEEPS IT KIND OF VAGUE AND MAKES HIS WORLD TASTE GOOD! AND HIS WORLD TASTES GOOD 'CAUSE OBAMAMAN THINKS IT SHOULD!!!
WRIGHT ON!
GOOD
OBAMAMAN, OBAMAMAN, OBAMAMAN, OBAMAMAN, OBAMAMAN! OBAMAMAN!
OBAMA SAMPLER
WOOOO!
OBAMAWAY BAR
YUP!
WOW!
ING-DING DING-DING
BYE!
THANKS MISTER! WE'LL BE BACK FOR THE REST OF THE CANDY LATER!
HEY! THERE'S A GOLDEN TICKET IN HERE!
WHOA! I GOT A GOLDEN TICKET!
I GOT ONE OF 'EM TOO!
LOOKS LIKE WE ALL GOT A GOLDEN TICKET.
YEAH! AND IT'S GOT "I.O.U." ACROSS THE TOP! WHAT'S "I.O.U." MEAN?
WAIT! THERE'S NO CANDY IN HERE! IT'S JUST A WRAPPER!
© HUNTER
DANG.
DO WE GET OUR NICKELS BACK?
I.O.U. ONE GOLDEN TICKET
PERUSE THE BIG PICTURE ONLINE AT WWW.WASHINGTONTIMES.COM/MEDIA/INTERACTIVES. OR CONTACT HUNTER AT BIGPICTURE@WASHINGTONTIMES.COM

CRUDE AWAKENING
Part One
TEXOCON
REGULAR SUPER DIESEL
GRAB YOUR ANKLES
WITH ENERGY COSTS SKYROCKETING, THE LASER SHARP AMERICAN MIND CUTS TO THE HEART OF THINGS AND ASKS: "WHO DO WE BLAME FOR HIGH GAS PRICES?"
IS IT:
A. SOME OPEC GUY
B. THE EXXON TIGER
C. ERNEST P. STATIONOWNER
D. THE 'THERE WILL BE BLOOD' GUY
E. W. OF COURSE
SINCE FORTY PERCENT OF THOSE QUESTIONED ANSWERED 'D,' WE CALLED IN AN EXPERT TO EXPLORE THE ISSUE A LITTLE MORE DEEPLY.
¡HOLA YANQUIS! YO SOY HUGO CHAVEZ, SEÑOR ROJO. ¿CÓMO ESTÁN USTEDES?
WHEN 'LA VISIÓN GRANDE' ASKED ME TO 'SPLAIN' TO YOU THE BIG WORLD OF OIL, I JUMPED AT THE CHANCE "BECAUSE," I SAID, "MIS AMIGOS IN LOS ESTADOS UNIDOS NEED ALL THE HELP THEY CAN GET!"
AND DON'T YOU WORRY! I'LL BE SPEAKING VERY SIMPLE INGLES SO YOU GRINGOS CAN UNDERSTAND.
ASSISTING ME IS MY RESEARCH TEAM, THE CHAVEZ CHICAS! AND SO ¡VAMONOS AMIGOS! LET'S GO!
LAS MAS LINDAS
BOOM CHICKA BOOM CHICKA
CHICKA BOOM BADA BOOM CHIC
FIRST OF ALL, LET'S LOOK AT A FIVE DOLLAR GALLON OF GASOLINA... OKAY, YOU CAN STOP LOOKING AT IT NOW.
BUT SERIOUSLY, AMIGOS, HERE IS THE SIMPLE *BREAKDOWN:
16% ALL TAXES .80¢
GASOLINE
$5.00 CHEAP
54% COST OF OIL $2.70
30% REFINING DISTRIBUTION MARKETING $1.50
*APRIL 2008 CRS REPORT
HUNTER'S BIG PICTURE
WHERE CAN YOU CUT COST?
NOT REFINING: GRINGOLANDIA IS USING 9 MILLION BARRELS OF GAS A DAY. YANQUIS HAVEN'T BUILT A NEW REFINERY FOR 30 YEARS. THE ONES YOU HAVE ARE, HOW YOU SAY, "MAXXED OUT." YOU IMPORT GASOLINA NOW JUST TO KEEP UP! IN SUMMER, YOU HAVE TO SUPER-REFINE BECAUSE OF CLEAN AIR LAWS. POBRECITOS!
HEY! IT'S SO TIGHT, IF A TOILET CLOGS UP IN ELIZABETH OR SOMEONE SNEEZES WRONG DOWN IN MOBILE, GAS JUMPS... TEN CENTS A GALLON.
fig.1
GASOLINE
DIESEL
JET
SUMMER BLEND
BENGAL TRADER COFFEE
ALL THIS FOR $1.50
WITH 9¢ PROFIT!
BEEP BEEP
YO, WHAT'S THE HOLDUP?
GAS

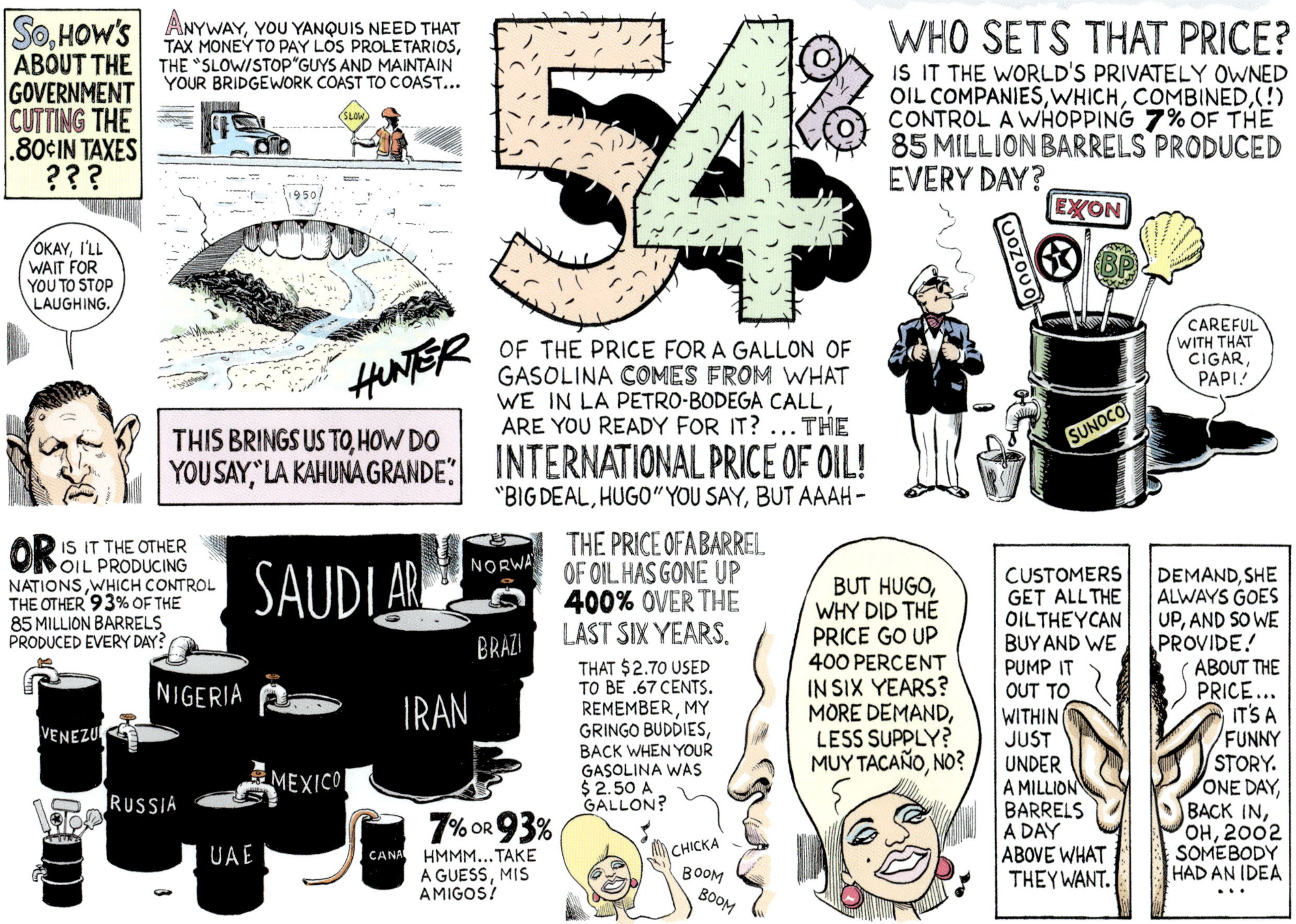

SO, HOW'S ABOUT THE GOVERNMENT CUTTING THE .80¢ IN TAXES ???
OKAY, I'LL WAIT FOR YOU TO STOP LAUGHING.
ANYWAY, YOU YANQUIS NEED THAT TAX MONEY TO PAY LOS PROLETARIOS, THE "SLOW/STOP" GUYS AND MAINTAIN YOUR BRIDGEWORK COAST TO COAST...
SLOW
1950
HUNTER
THIS BRINGS US TO, HOW DO YOU SAY, "LA KAHUNA GRANDE."
54%
OF THE PRICE FOR A GALLON OF GASOLINA COMES FROM WHAT WE IN LA PETRO-BODEGA CALL, ARE YOU READY FOR IT? ... THE
INTERNATIONAL PRICE OF OIL!
"BIG DEAL, HUGO" YOU SAY, BUT AAAH-
WHO SETS THAT PRICE?
IS IT THE WORLD'S PRIVATELY OWNED OIL COMPANIES, WHICH, COMBINED, (!) CONTROL A WHOPPING 7% OF THE 85 MILLION BARRELS PRODUCED EVERY DAY?
EXXON
CONOCO
BP
SUNOCO
CAREFUL WITH THAT CIGAR, PAPI!
OR IS IT THE OTHER OIL PRODUCING NATIONS, WHICH CONTROL THE OTHER 93% OF THE 85 MILLION BARRELS PRODUCED EVERY DAY?
SAUDI AR
NORWA
BRAZI
NIGERIA
IRAN
VENEZU
RUSSIA
MEXICO
UAE
CANA
7% OR 93%
HMMM... TAKE A GUESS, MIS AMIGOS!
THE PRICE OF A BARREL OF OIL HAS GONE UP 400% OVER THE LAST SIX YEARS.
THAT $2.70 USED TO BE .67 CENTS. REMEMBER, MY GRINGO BUDDIES, BACK WHEN YOUR GASOLINA WAS $2.50 A GALLON?
CHICKA BOOM BOOM
BUT HUGO, WHY DID THE PRICE GO UP 400 PERCENT IN SIX YEARS? MORE DEMAND, LESS SUPPLY? MUY TACAÑO, NO?
CUSTOMERS GET ALL THE OIL THEY CAN BUY AND WE PUMP IT OUT TO WITHIN JUST UNDER A MILLION BARRELS A DAY ABOVE WHAT THEY WANT.
DEMAND, SHE ALWAYS GOES UP, AND SO WE PROVIDE!
ABOUT THE PRICE... IT'S A FUNNY STORY. ONE DAY, BACK IN, OH, 2002 SOMEBODY HAD AN IDEA ...

HEY! LET'S RAISE THE PRICE TO 50 DOLLARS A BARREL AND SEE WHAT HAPPENS!
ARE YOU MAD?
WE'LL LOSE OUR BURNOOSES!
I THINK IT'S "BURNEESE."
OPEC 2002
AND SO ON UNTIL
HEY! LET'S RAISE THE PRICE TO 100 DOLLARS A BARREL AND SEE WHAT HAPPENS!
ARE YOU INSANE?
BUT THE AMERICANS NEED THAT OIL!
IT'S ALMOST IMMORAL.
OPEC 2007
OPEC 2007
AHAHAHAHAHAHAH
AHAH HAH HAHAH
HOOO HEE HEE HEE H
HAH!
NYUK!
HEE HEE
SNORT!
OPEC 2007
ON THAT HAPPY NOTE, WE SAY "ADIOS" FOR NOW. JOIN ME, HUGO CHAVEZ, HERE AGAIN WHEN WE ASK, "WHY DO THE YANQUIS KEEP PAYING SO MUCH?" IN OUR NEXT EXCITING CHAPTER:
"OILS WELL THAT ENDS WELL" OR "THE DRILL OF IT ALL"

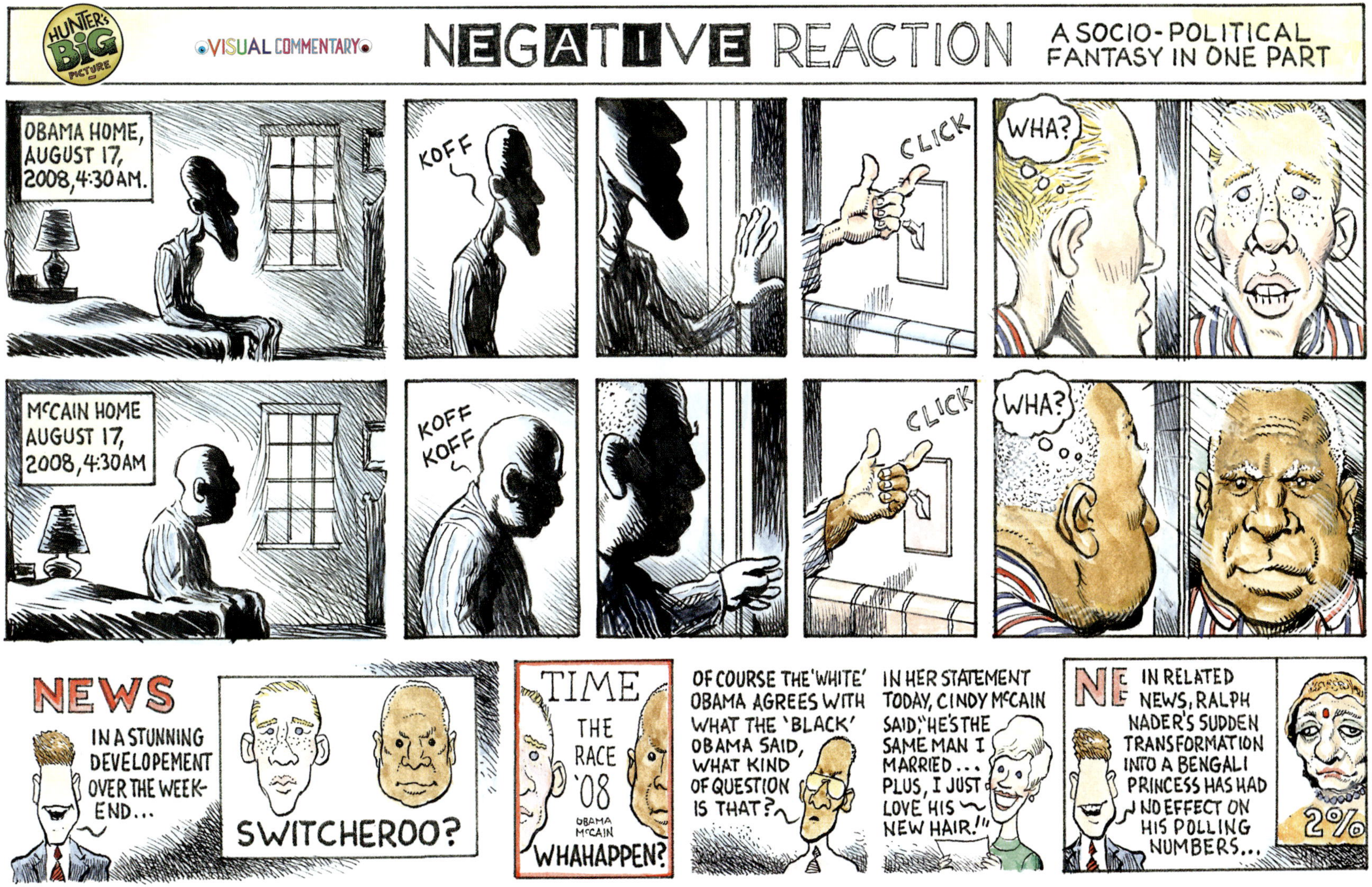
HUNTER'S BIG PICTURE
VISUAL COMMENTARY
NEGATIVE REACTION
A SOCIO-POLITICAL FANTASY IN ONE PART
OBAMA HOME, AUGUST 17, 2008, 4:30 AM.
KOFF
CLICK
WHA?
McCAIN HOME AUGUST 17, 2008, 4:30 AM
KOFF KOFF
CLICK
WHA?
NEWS
IN A STUNNING DEVELOPEMENT OVER THE WEEK-END...
SWITCHEROO?
TIME
THE RACE '08
OBAMA McCAIN
WHAHAPPEN?
OF COURSE THE 'WHITE' OBAMA AGREES WITH WHAT THE 'BLACK' OBAMA SAID, WHAT KIND OF QUESTION IS THAT?
IN HER STATEMENT TODAY, CINDY McCAIN SAID, "HE'S THE SAME MAN I MARRIED... PLUS, I JUST LOVE HIS NEW HAIR!"
NE
IN RELATED NEWS, RALPH NADER'S SUDDEN TRANSFORMATION INTO A BENGALI PRINCESS HAS HAD NO EFFECT ON HIS POLLING NUMBERS...
2%

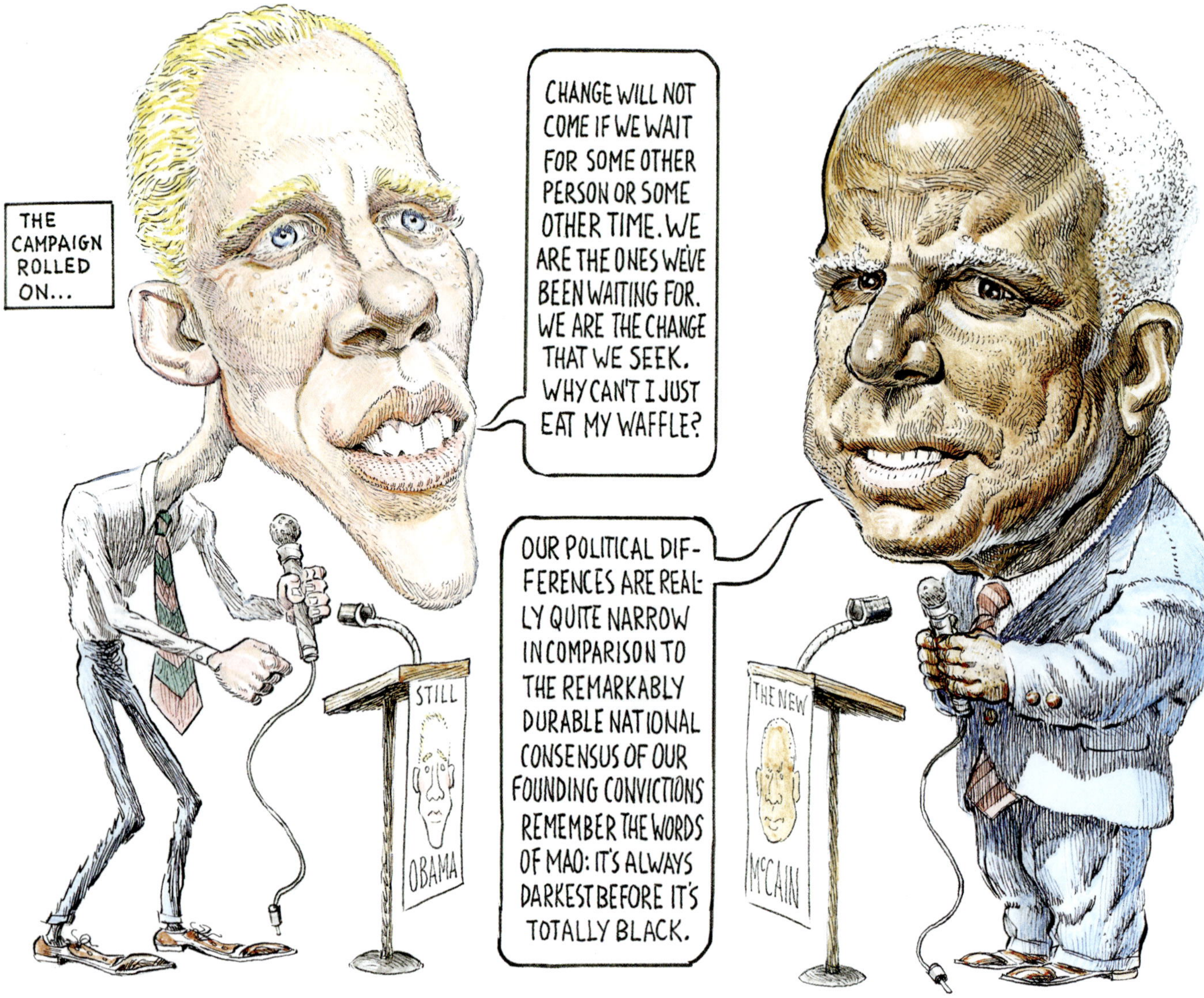
THE CAMPAIGN ROLLED ON...
CHANGE WILL NOT COME IF WE WAIT FOR SOME OTHER PERSON OR SOME OTHER TIME. WE ARE THE ONES WE'VE BEEN WAITING FOR. WE ARE THE CHANGE THAT WE SEEK. WHY CAN'T I JUST EAT MY WAFFLE?
OUR POLITICAL DIFFERENCES ARE REALLY QUITE NARROW IN COMPARISON TO THE REMARKABLY DURABLE NATIONAL CONSENSUS OF OUR FOUNDING CONVICTIONS REMEMBER THE WORDS OF MAO: IT'S ALWAYS DARKEST BEFORE IT'S TOTALLY BLACK.
STILL
OBAMA
THE NEW
McCAIN

AND THE PEOPLE WERE MUCH ASTONISHED...
AND
HOW DOES THIS MAKE YOU FEEL?
I DON'T KNOW, I WANT CHANGE AND...YEAH. IT'S JUST, HE SEEMS A LITTLE LESS...WELL, SINCERE TO ME NOW...
NBS
WILL THIS CHANGE YOUR VOTE?
LOOK, I HAVE NO PROBLEM WITH A BLACK MAN IN THE WHITEHOUSE... JUST NOT THAT BLACK MAN.
NBS
DOES THIS MAKE YOU ANGRY?
HEY, I HEARD SOMEONE SAY HE HOPED FOR A DAY WHEN A PERSON IS JUDGED NOT BY THE COLOR OF THEIR SKIN, BUT BY THE CONTENT OF THEIR CHARACTER. I'M JUST SAYIN'.
NBS
THEN
OBAMA HOME, AUG 24, 2008, 4:30 AM
KOFF
CLICK
OH COME ON!
McCAIN HOME, AUG 24, 2008, 4:30 AM
KOFF KOFF
CLICK
OH COME ON!
JOIN US FOR OUR NEXT EXCITING EPISODE: 'ENTER THE DRAGONS' OR 'McCAIN GETS REAL GOOD AT MATH!'

The National Cartoonist Society's Reuben Award

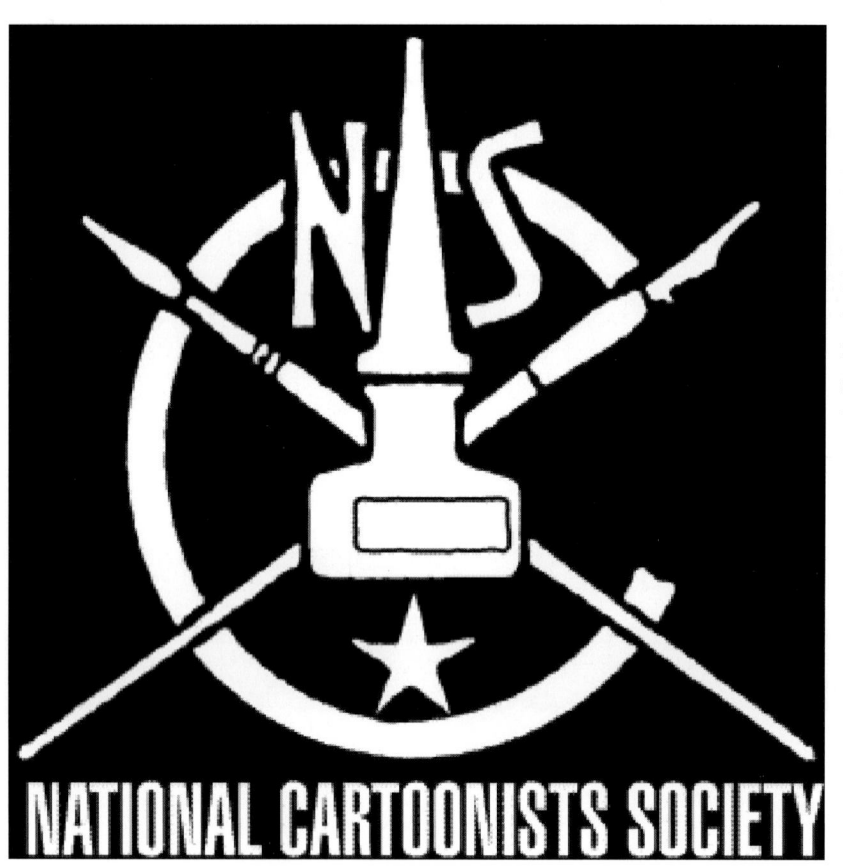

The Reuben is awarded by the National Cartoonist Society each year to recognize outstanding achievements in the world of cartooning. The National Cartoonists Society came into being during a dinner designed for the occasion in New York in 1946. Rube Goldberg was the organization's first president and namesake. The Reuben Award was first introduced in 1954.

Editorial cartoons is one of thirteen divisions in which Reubens are awarded. The Reuben is one of a number of awards that is cartoon-specific in its consideration, but the only one in this volume that awards all manner of cartoons and illustration, from strips to magazine gag cartoons to book, magazine, and magazine feature illustrations to greeting cards to television animation and as such is unique. For the purpose of this book, only the Editorial Cartoon Division is represented.

2008 National Cartoonist Society's Reuben Award Winner

Michael Ramirez—*Investor's Business Daily*

"An editorial cartoon is not just a funny picture," says internationally known editorial cartoonist Michael Ramirez. "It is a powerful instrument of journalism, sometimes sharp and refined, its message cutting quickly to the point, and other times, blunt and overpowering, seizing the readers' attention with its dark imagery."

Ramirez is a two-time recipient of the prestigious Pulitzer Prize in 1994 and 2008 and a three-time Sigma Delta Chi Award winner. He is a senior editor and the editorial cartoonist for *Investor's Business Daily*. Ramirez is a Lincoln Fellow, an honorary member of Pi Sigma Alpha National Political Science Honor Society, and has won almost every journalism award in addition to the prestigious UC Irvine Medal from the University of California, Irvine, and the H. L. Mencken Award. He is the author of *Everyone Has the Right to My Opinion*.

Michael Ramirez Interview

Dean: Turn-of-the-century journalist Finley Peter Dunne is quoted as saying, "The job of the newspaper is to comfort the afflicted and afflict the comfortable." What do you see as the role of the editorial cartoonist?

Michael: Editorial cartooning is about justice not afflicting the comfortable. It is an extension of journalism, or what the beltway calls the fourth branch of governance. My approach to the job is to research and read about an issue to understand its complexity in order to sufficiently determine what the long-term consequences are of these issues. It is neither Republican nor Democrat nor is it defined through some broad philosophical filter, but rather simply determining what is right or wrong through the structure of our constitutional and founding principles.

Dean: With the continuing decline of newspaper readership, what do you believe the future holds for the fate of the editorial cartoonist?

Michael: You can't really talk about editorial cartooning without talking about the newspaper industry as a whole. They are very much interconnected. I believe newspapers are at a crossroads very much like radio was at the advent of television. There will be a convergence of our media interwoven into the Internet. Through newspaper failures and the consolidation of our industry, there will continue to be a decline in editorial cartoonists for a while, but there will be a broader spectrum of available outlets in other areas, especially the Internet and cable television. I believe there will be a resurrection of print media, but generationally the erosion of those subscriptions will continue while Internet subscriptions will grow.

The medium itself will undergo changes such as the advancement of color now and possible incorporation of better animation in the future. However, the nature of the beast should remain unchanged. That is to say, editorial cartoons should remain an art form that makes substantive statements rather than humorous anecdotes about politics or current events.

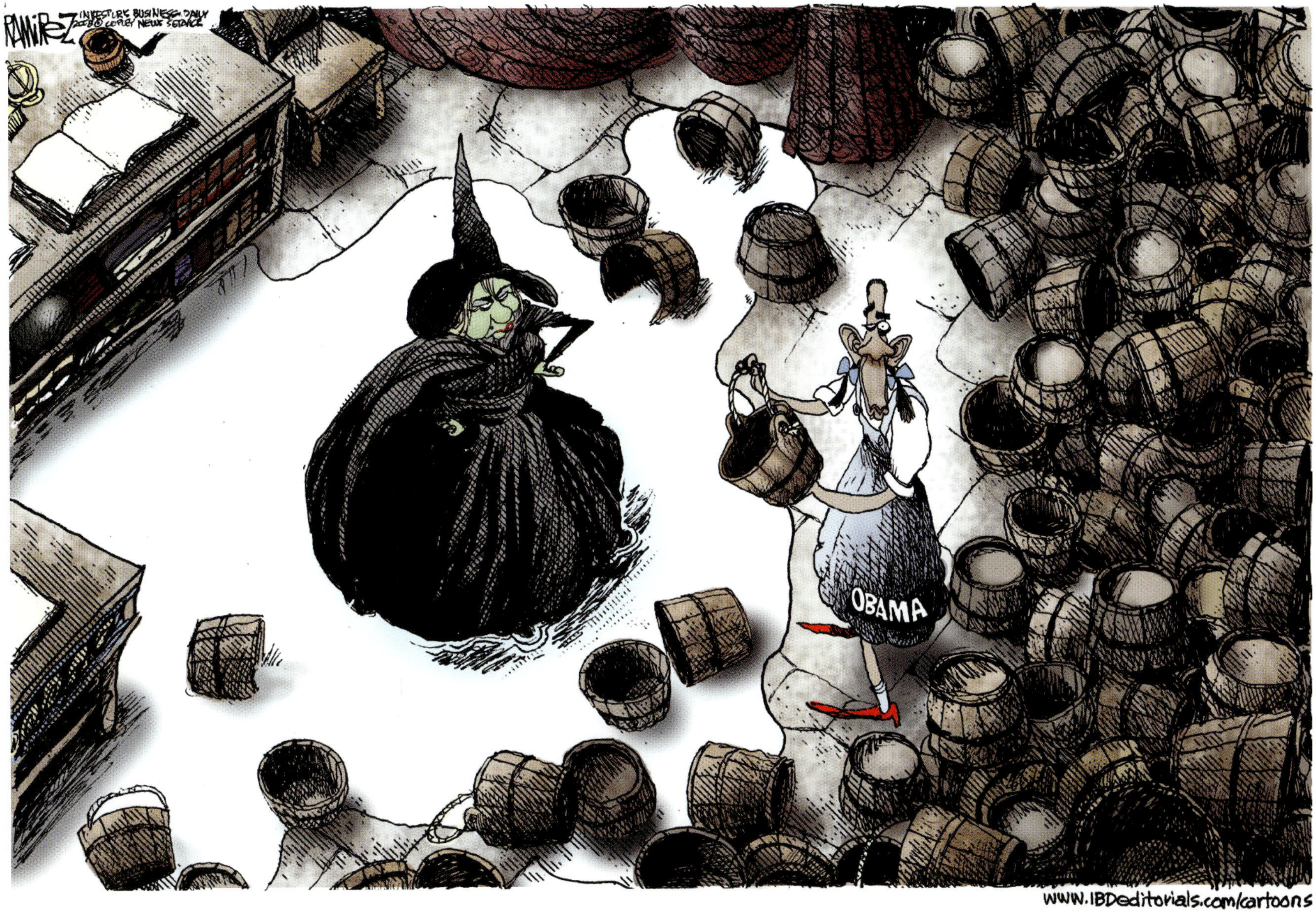
RAMIREZ
INVESTOR'S BUSINESS DAILY
2008 © COPLEY NEWS SERVICE
OBAMA
WWW.IBDeditorials.com/cartoons

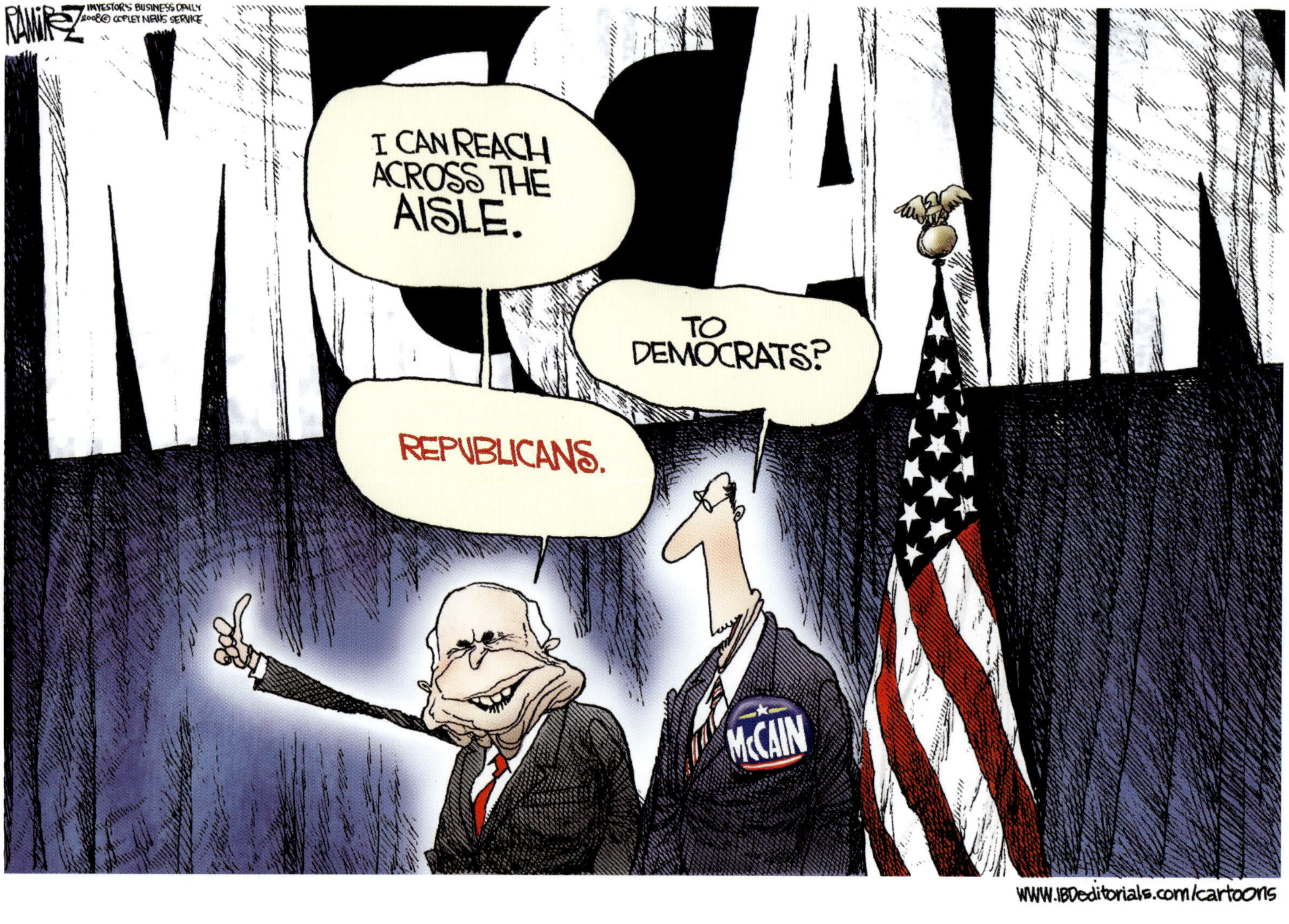
RAMIREZ INVESTOR'S BUSINESS DAILY 2008 © COPLEY NEWS SERVICE
McCAIN
I CAN REACH ACROSS THE AISLE.
TO DEMOCRATS?
REPUBLICANS.
McCAIN
WWW.IBDeditorials.com/cartoons

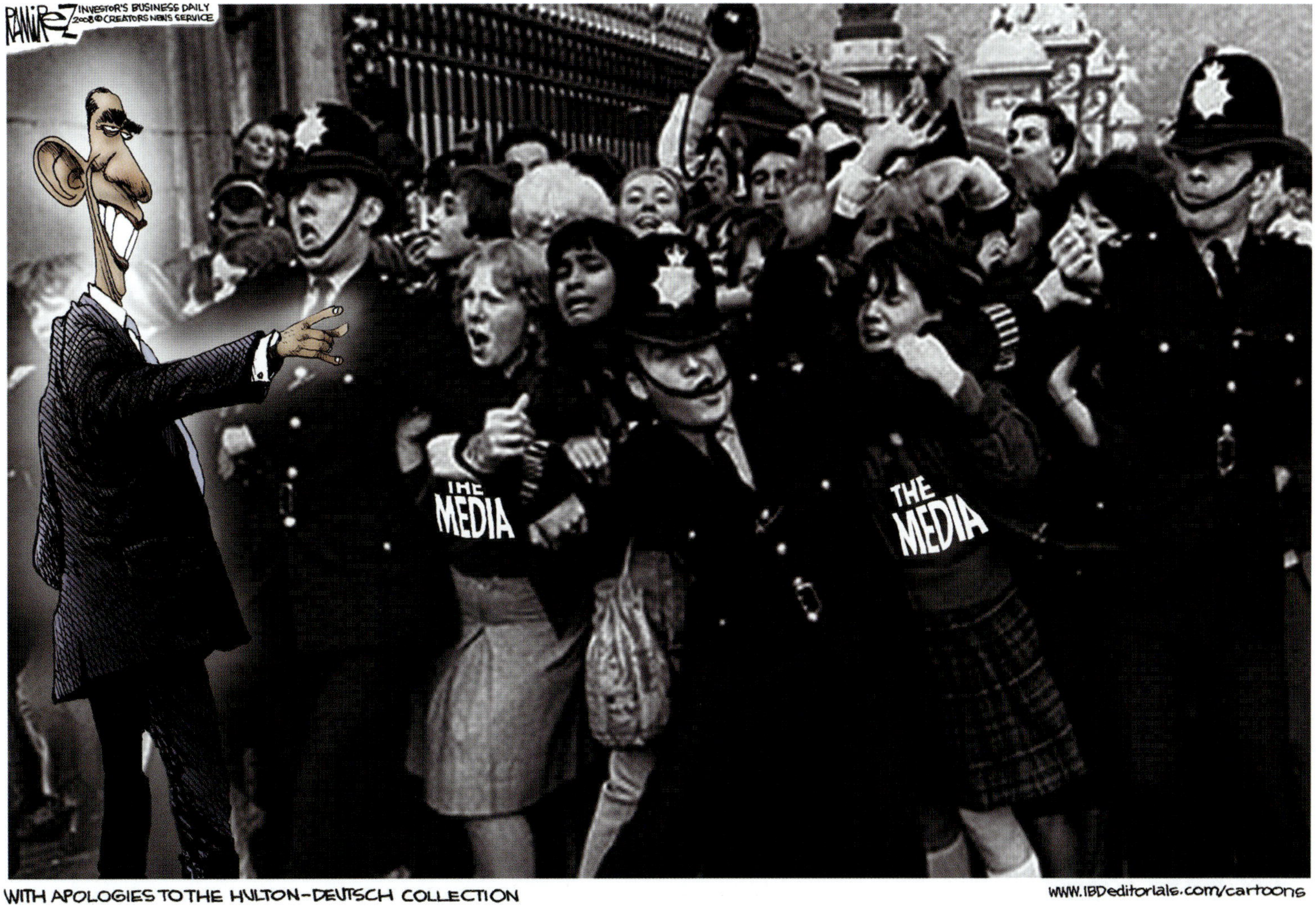
RAMIREZ
INVESTOR'S BUSINESS DAILY
2008 © CREATORS NEWS SERVICE
THE MEDIA
THE MEDIA
WITH APOLOGIES TO THE HULTON-DEUTSCH COLLECTION
WWW.IBDeditorials.com/cartoons

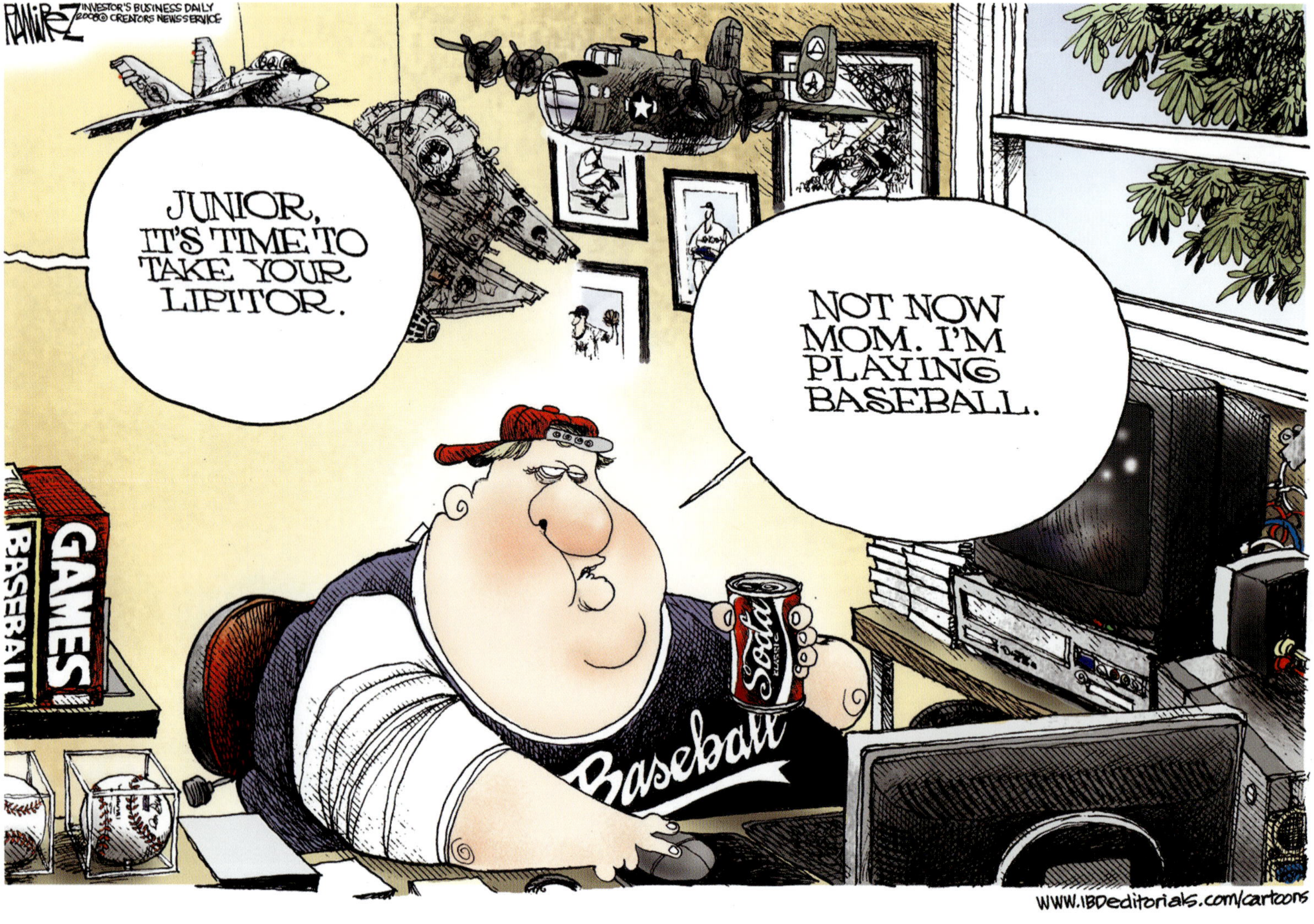
RAMIREZ INVESTOR'S BUSINESS DAILY 2008© CREATORS NEWS SERVICE
JUNIOR, IT'S TIME TO TAKE YOUR LIPITOR.
NOT NOW MOM. I'M PLAYING BASEBALL.
GAMES
BASEBALL
Soda
Baseball
WWW.IBDeditorials.com/cartoons

RAMIREZ
INVESTOR'S BUSINESS DAILY
2008 © COPLEY NEWS SERVICE
WWW.IBDeditorials.com/cartoons

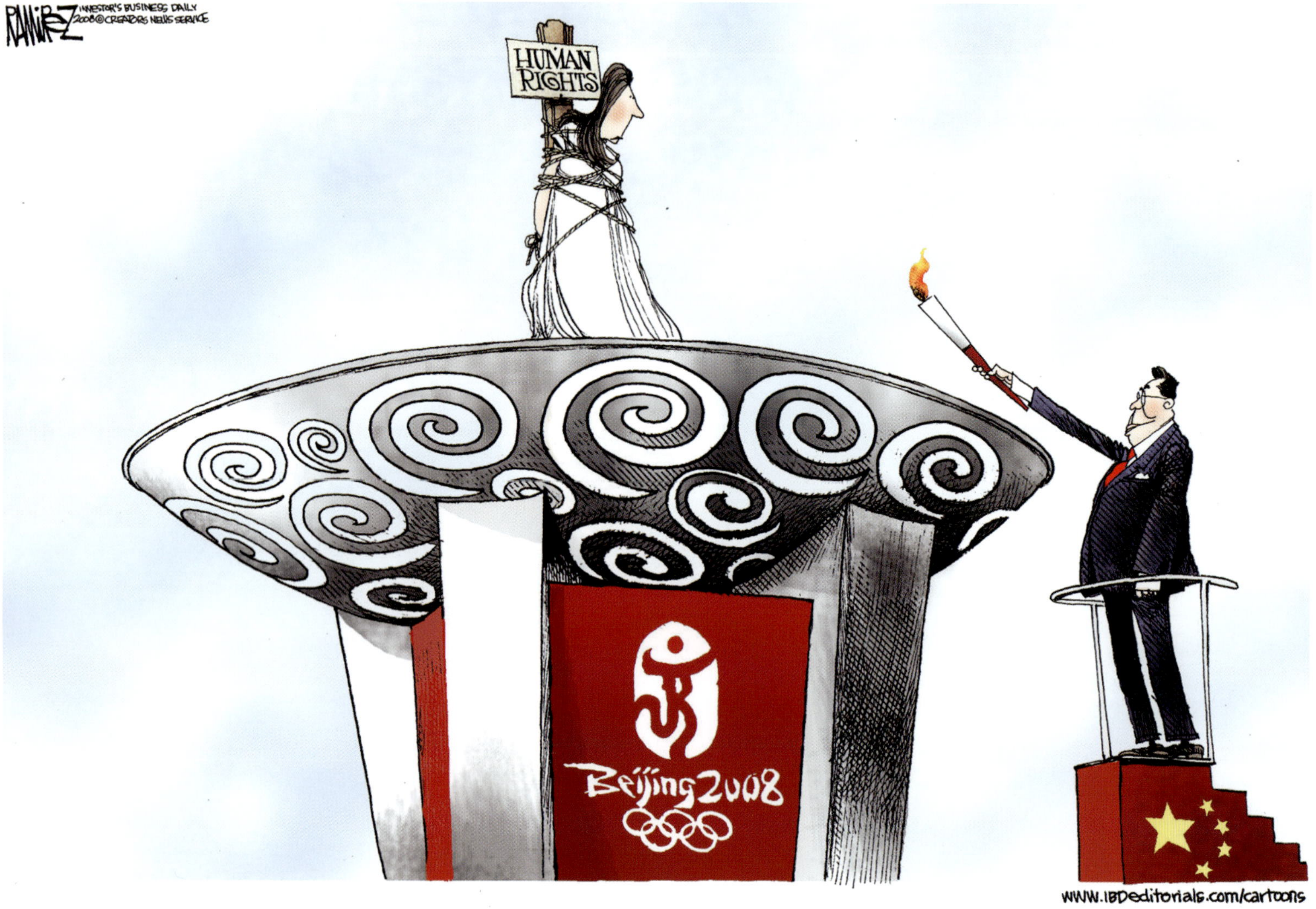
RAMIREZ
INVESTOR'S BUSINESS DAILY
2008 © CREATORS NEWS SERVICE
HUMAN RIGHTS
Beijing 2008
WWW.IBDeditorials.com/cartoons

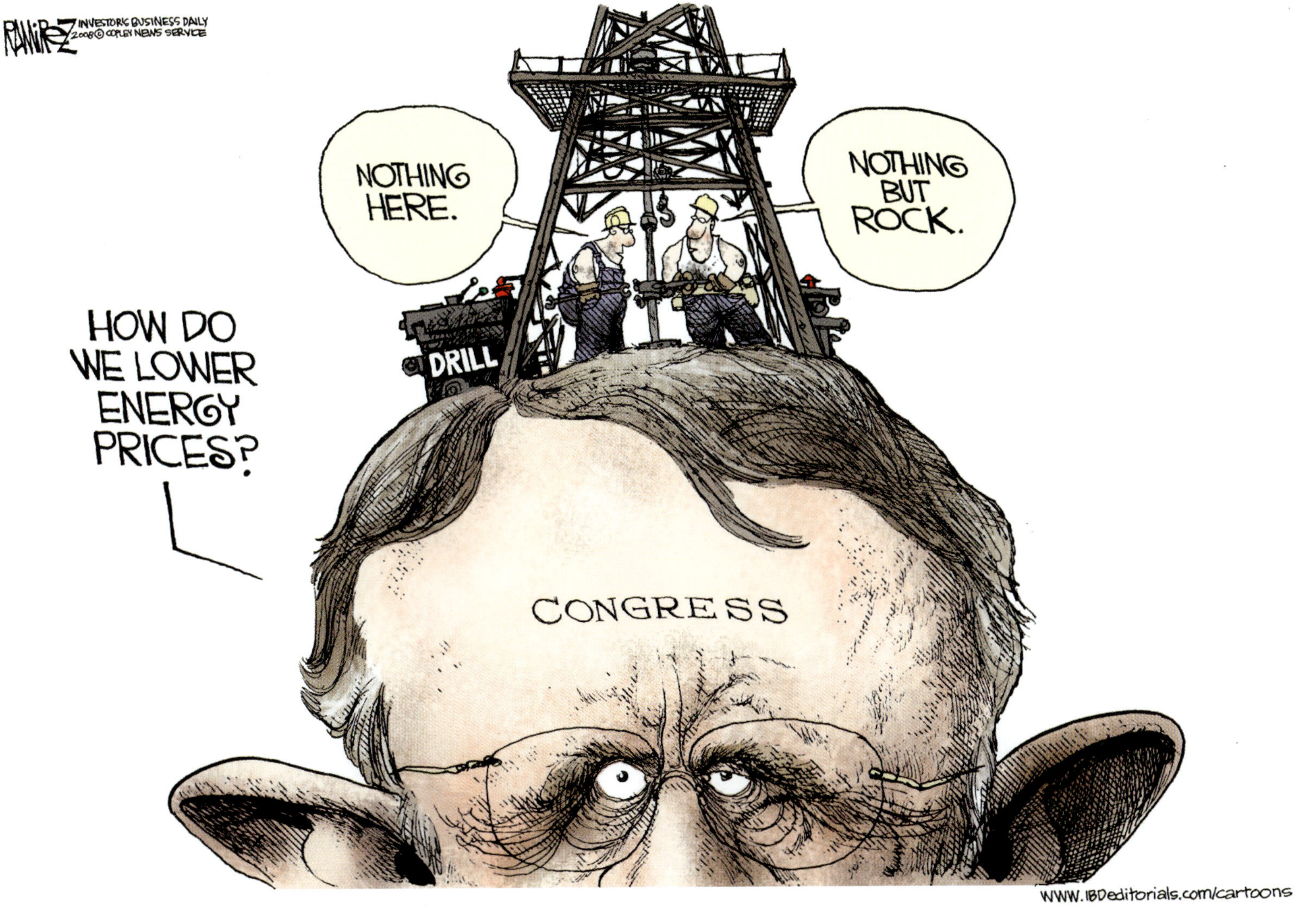
RAMIREZ INVESTOR'S BUSINESS DAILY 2008 © COPLEY NEWS SERVICE
NOTHING HERE.
NOTHING BUT ROCK.
HOW DO WE LOWER ENERGY PRICES?
DRILL
CONGRESS
WWW.IBDeditorials.com/cartoons

RAMIREZ
INVESTOR'S BUSINESS DAILY
2008© COPLEY NEWS SERVICE
THE FIRST BLACK PRESIDENT.
THE FIRST WOMAN PRESIDENT.
OH NOOO. NOT A MORMON.
1
WWW.IBDeditorials.com/cartoons

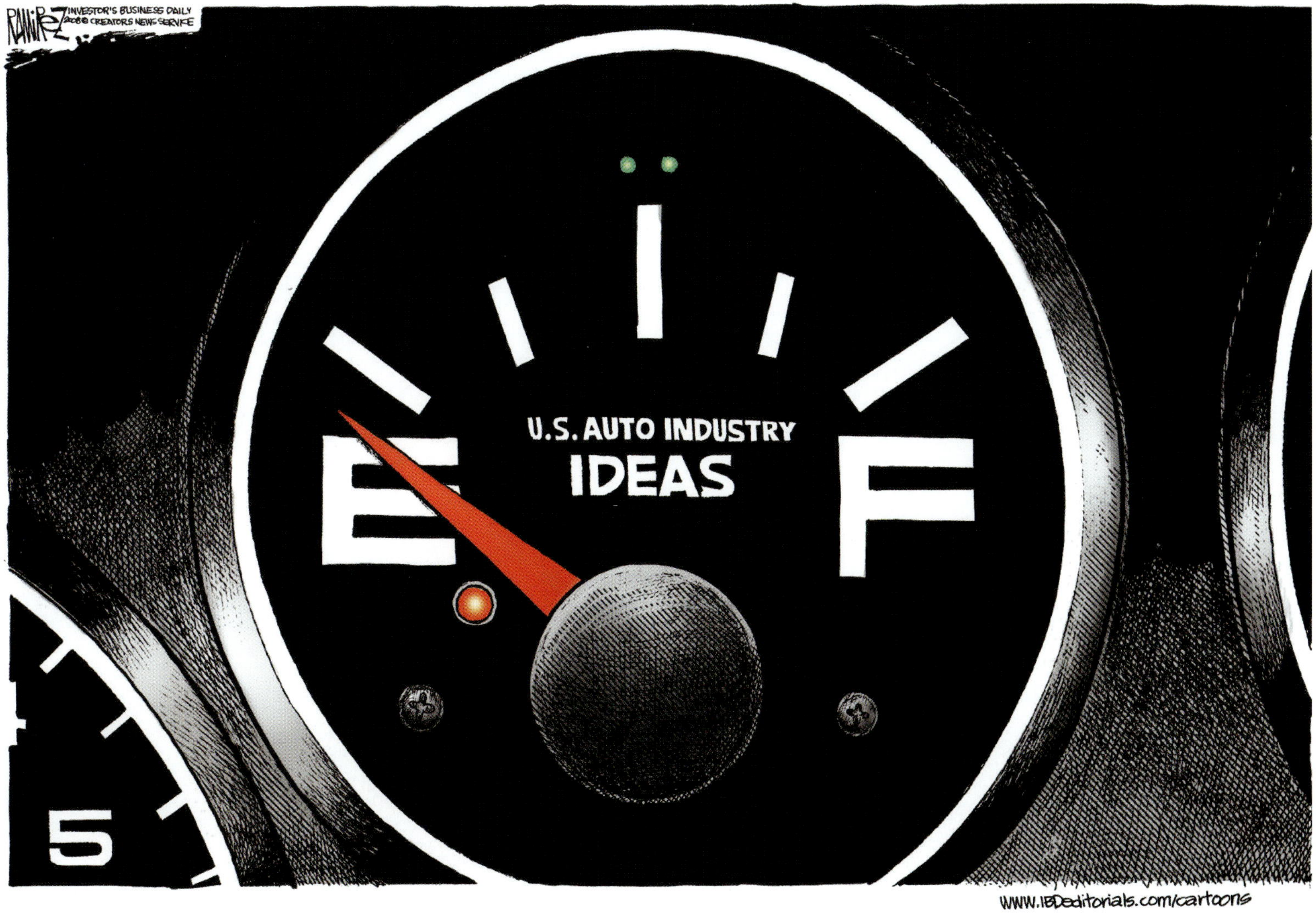
RAMIREZ
INVESTOR'S BUSINESS DAILY
2008 © CREATORS NEWS SERVICE
U.S. AUTO INDUSTRY
IDEAS
E
F
5
WWW.IBDeditorials.com/cartoons

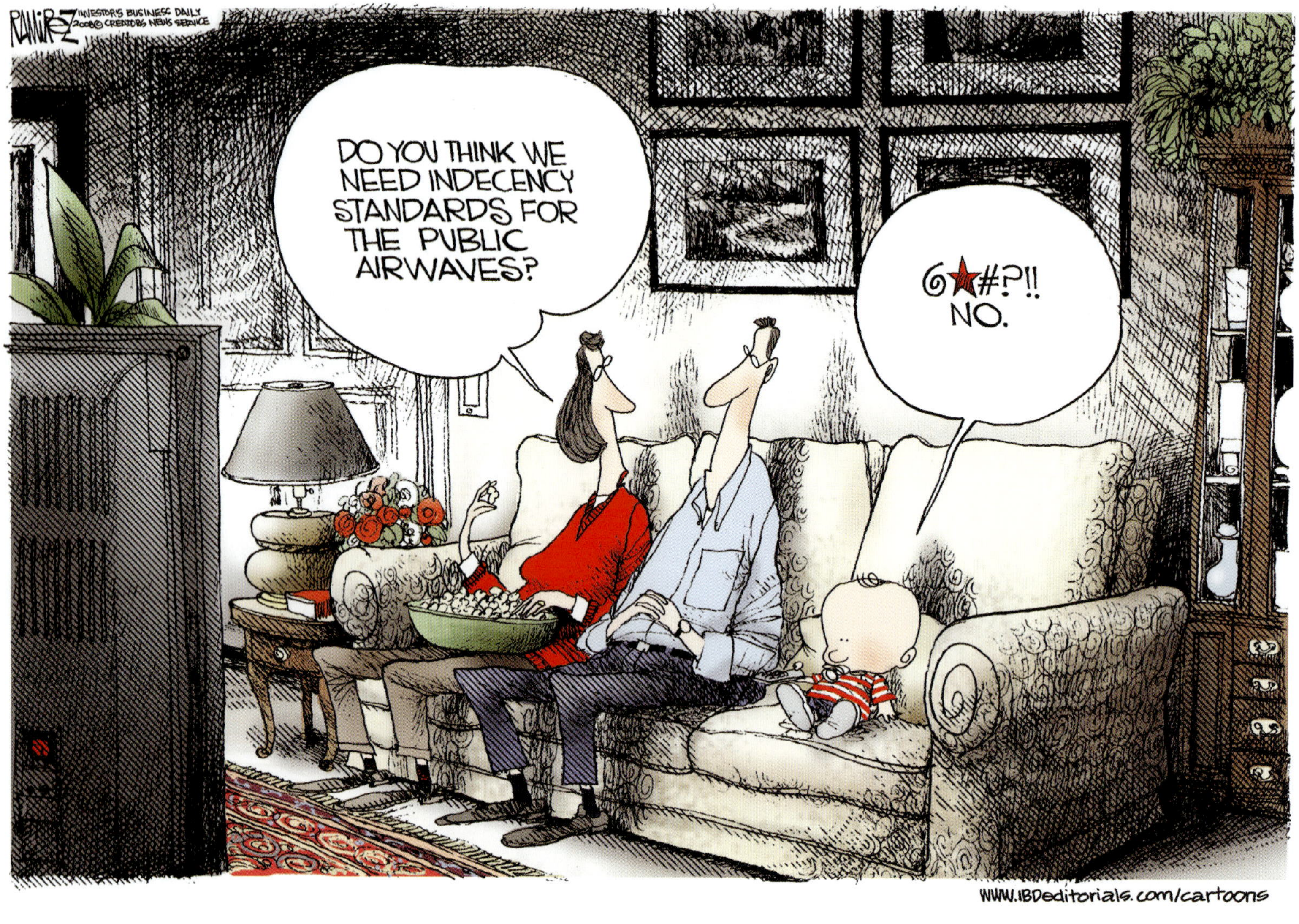
RAMIREZ INVESTOR'S BUSINESS DAILY 2008© CREATORS NEWS SERVICE
DO YOU THINK WE NEED INDECENCY STANDARDS FOR THE PUBLIC AIRWAVES?
#?!! NO.
WWW.IBDeditorials.com/cartoons

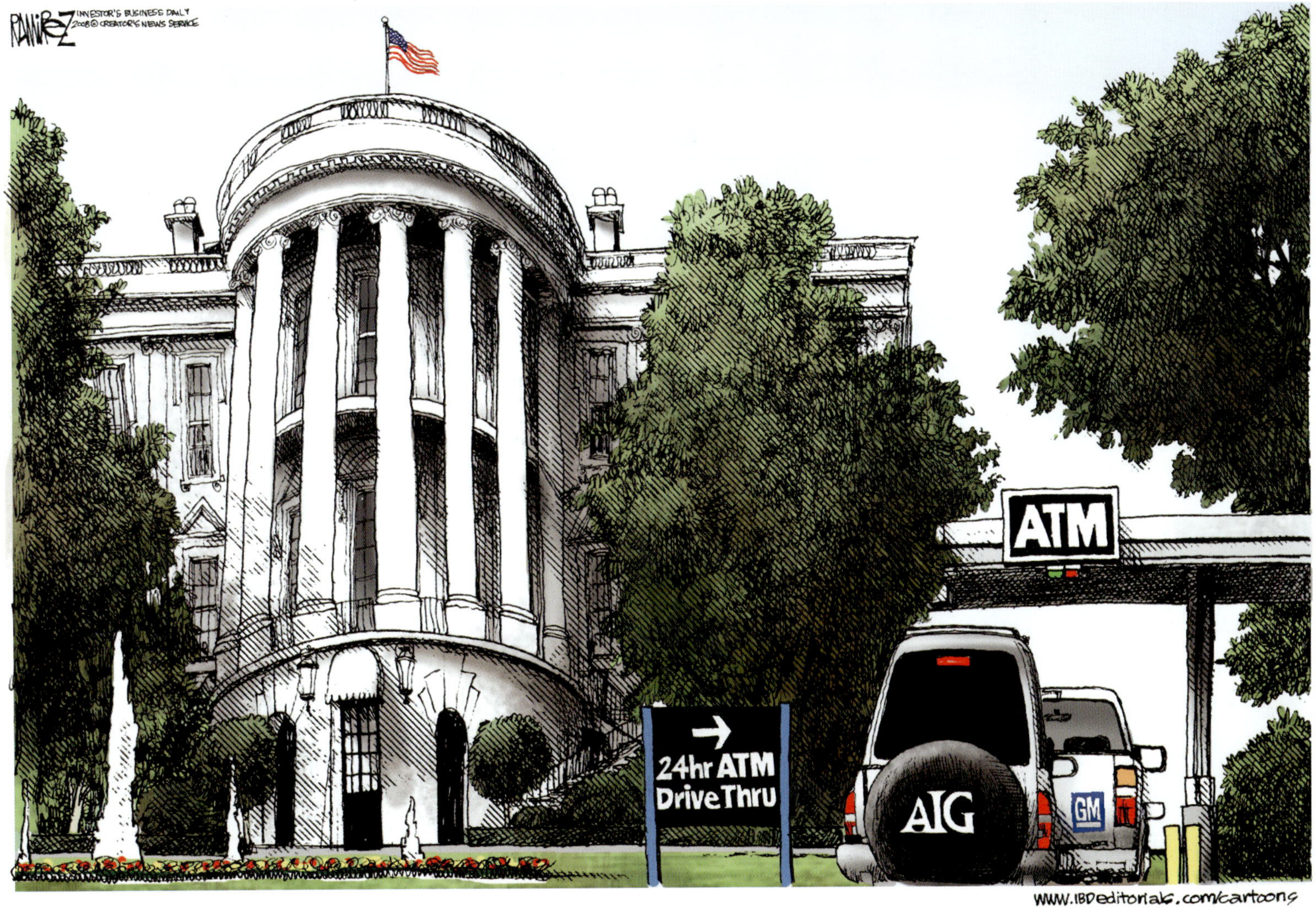
RAMIREZ
INVESTOR'S BUSINESS DAILY
2008 © CREATORS NEWS SERVICE
ATM
24hr ATM
Drive Thru
AIG
GM
WWW.IBDeditorials.com/cartoons

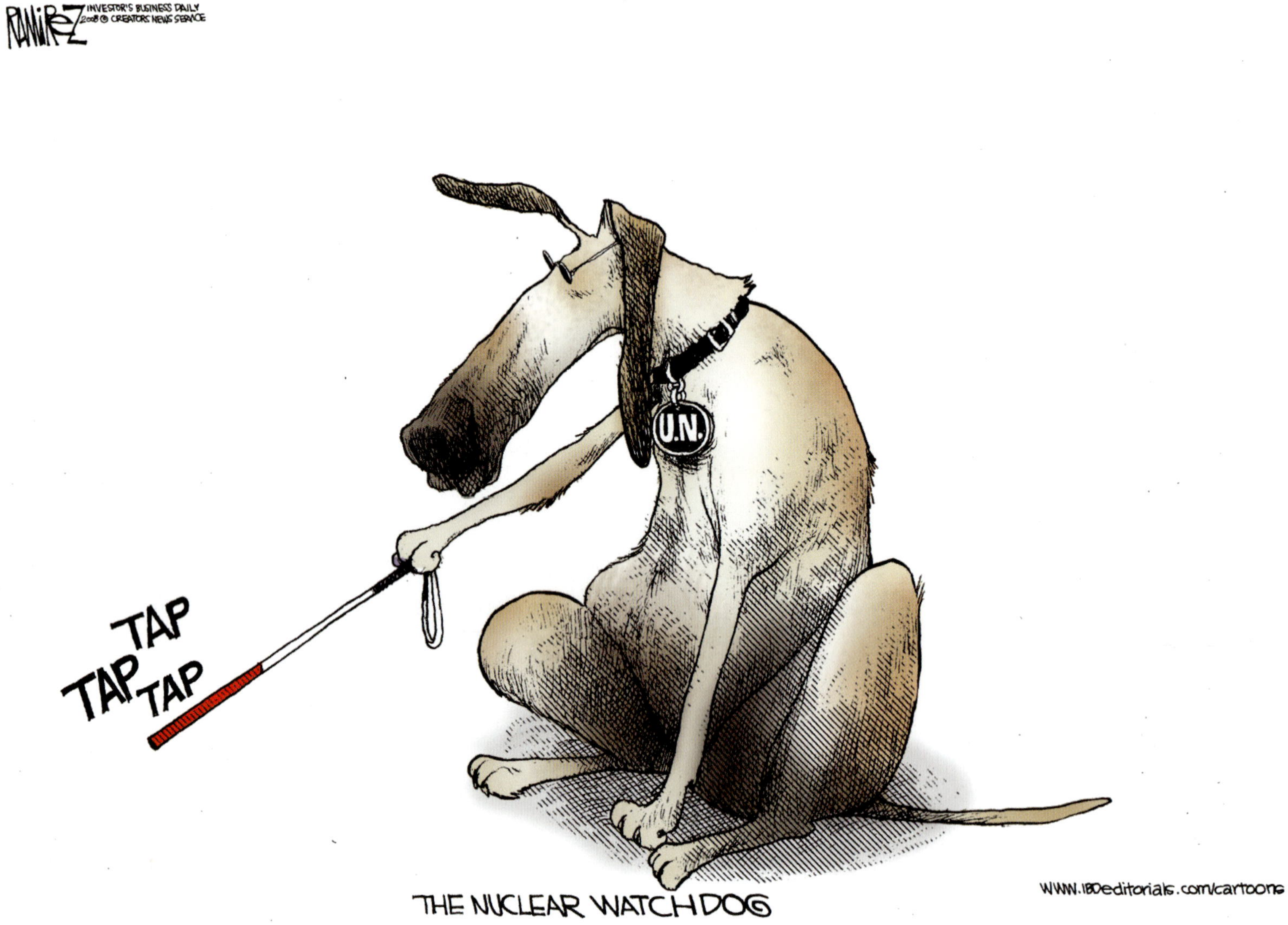
RAMIREZ
INVESTOR'S BUSINESS DAILY
2008 © CREATORS NEWS SERVICE
TAP
TAP
TAP
U.N.
THE NUCLEAR WATCHDOG
WWW.IBDeditorials.com/cartoons

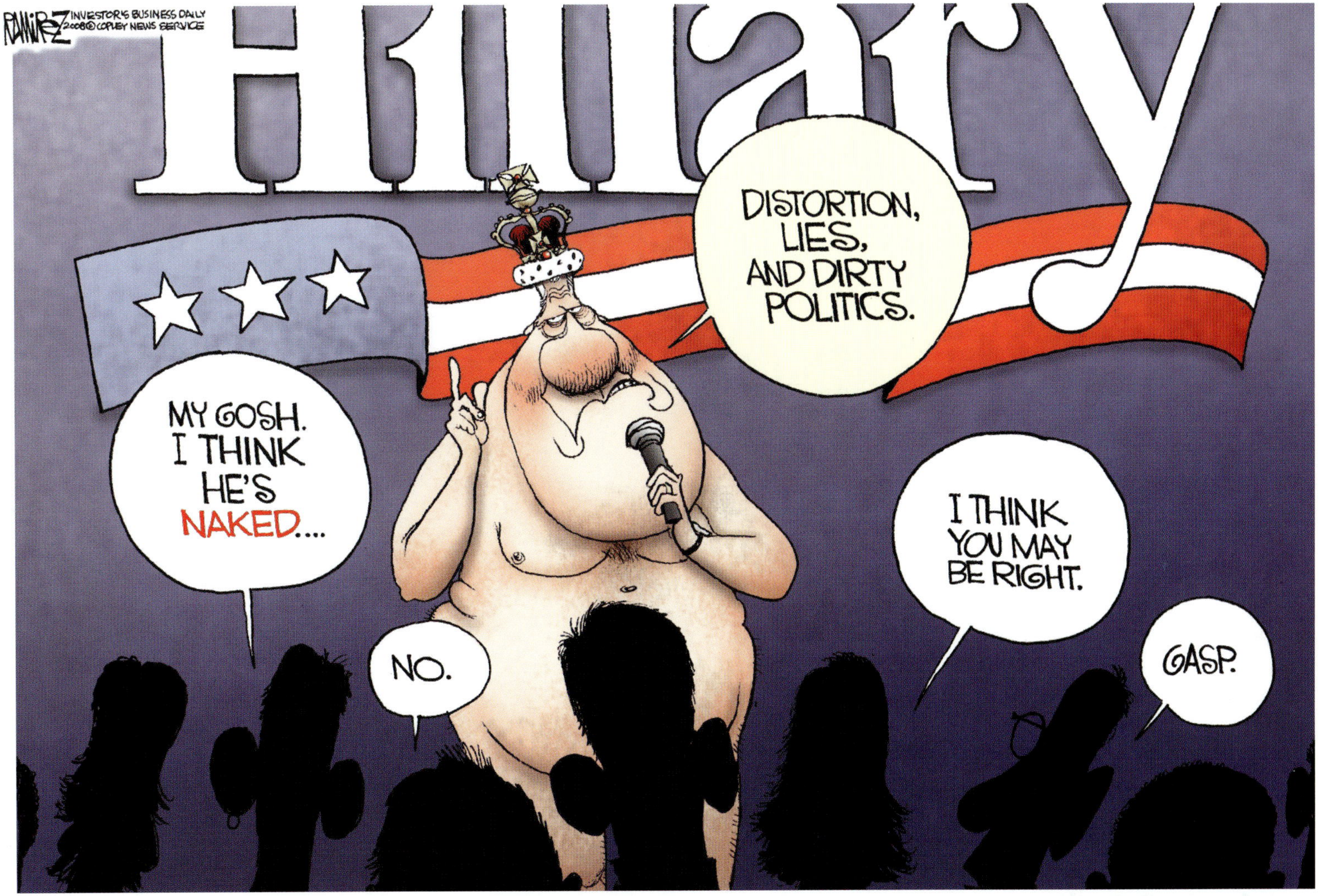

THE EMPEROR'S OLD CLOTHES

WWW.IBDeditorials.com/cartoons

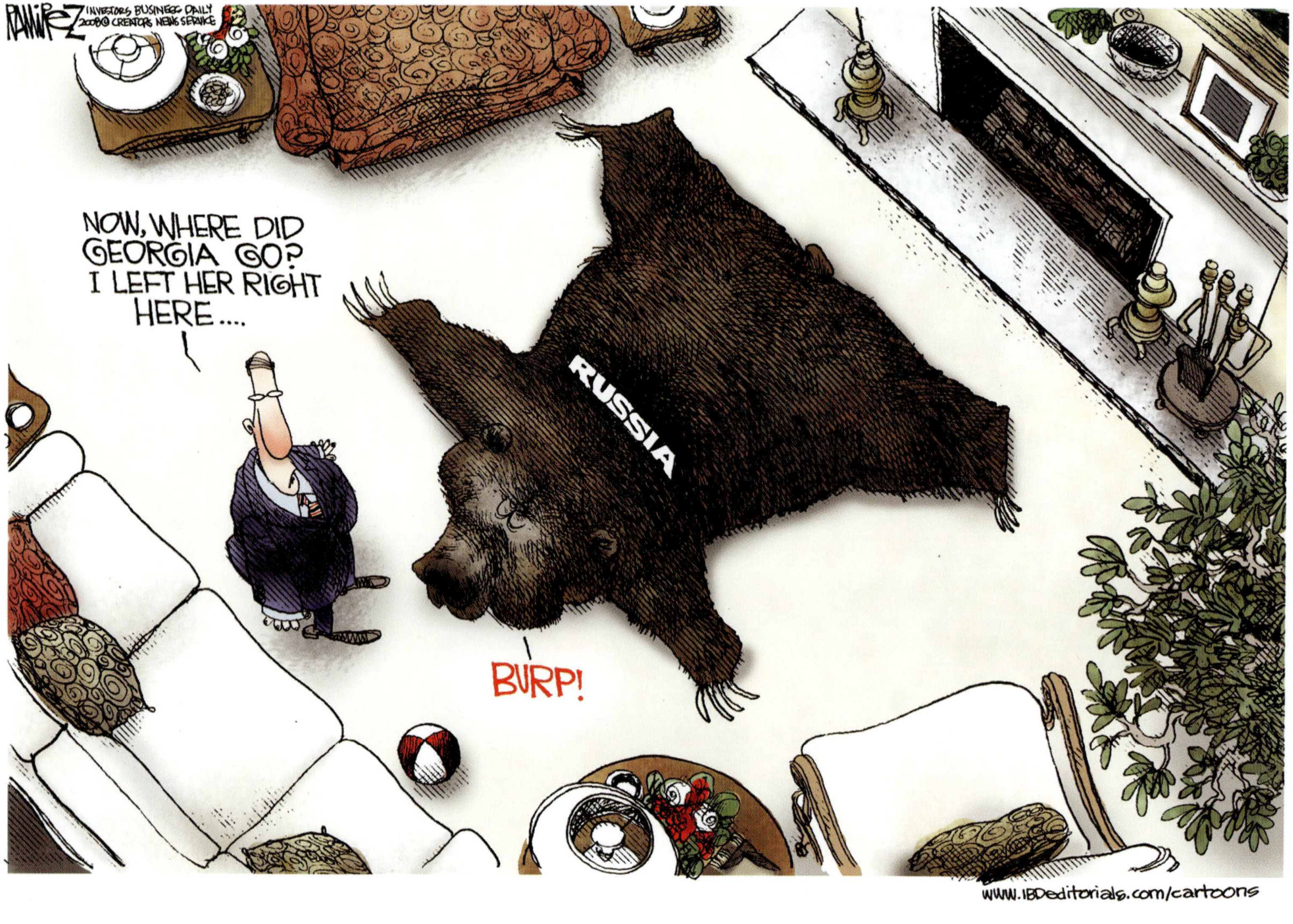
RAMIREZ
INVESTORS BUSINESS DAILY
2008© CREATORS NEWS SERVICE
NOW, WHERE DID GEORGIA GO? I LEFT HER RIGHT HERE....
RUSSIA
BURP!
www.IBDeditorials.com/cartoons

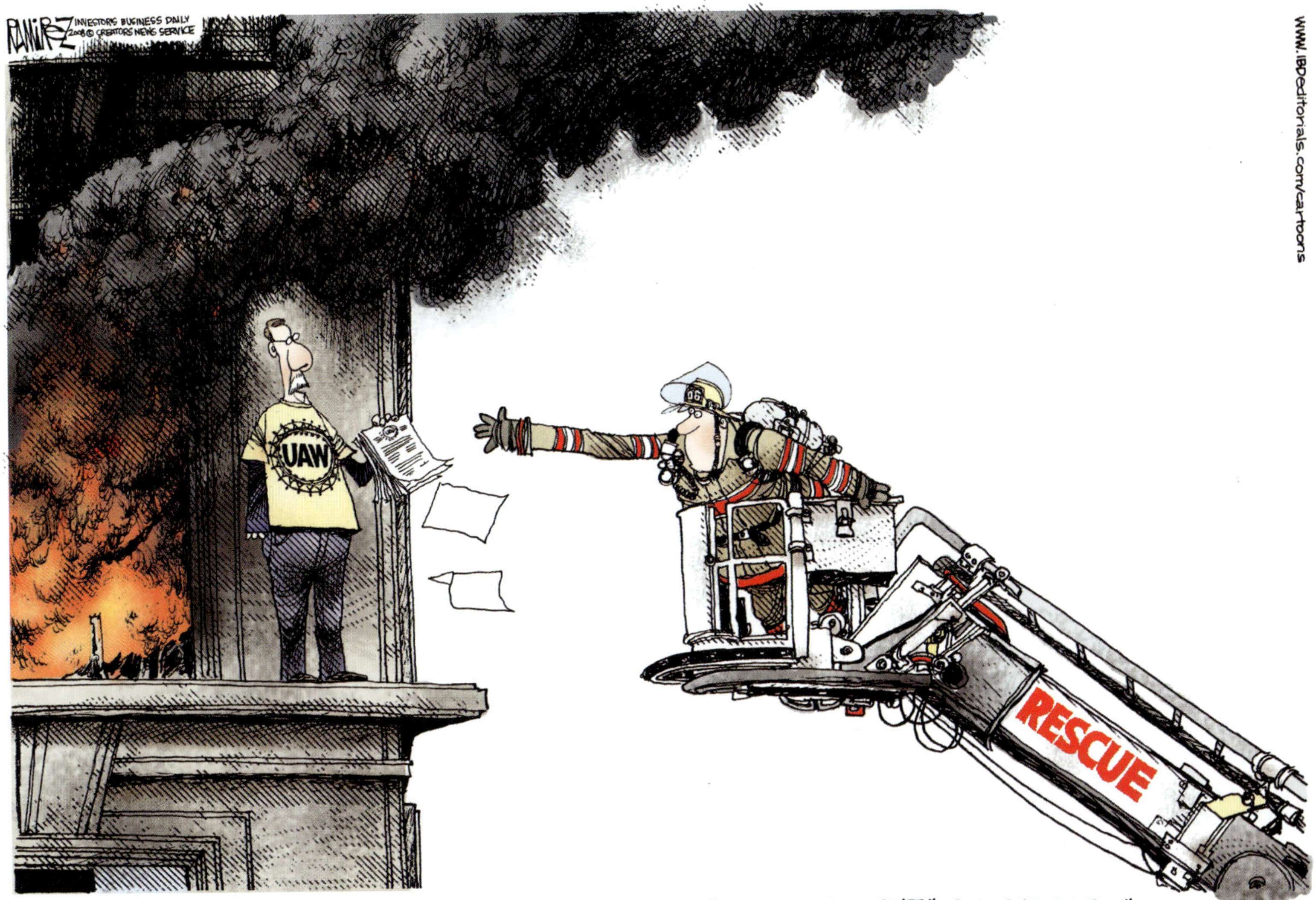
RAMIREZ
INVESTOR'S BUSINESS DAILY 2008 © CREATORS NEWS SERVICE
www.IBDeditorials.com/cartoons
UAW
RESCUE

"OUR CONTRACT CLEARLY STIPULATES NO "REACHING OUT" ON OUR PART."

RAMIREZ INVESTOR'S BUSINESS DAILY 2008 © COPLEY NEWS SERVICE
Fred Thompson 2008
I ANNOUNCE MY CANDIDACY FOR PRESIDENT OF THE UNITED STATES
Fred Thompson 2008
I QUIT.
WWW.IBDeditorials.com/cartoons

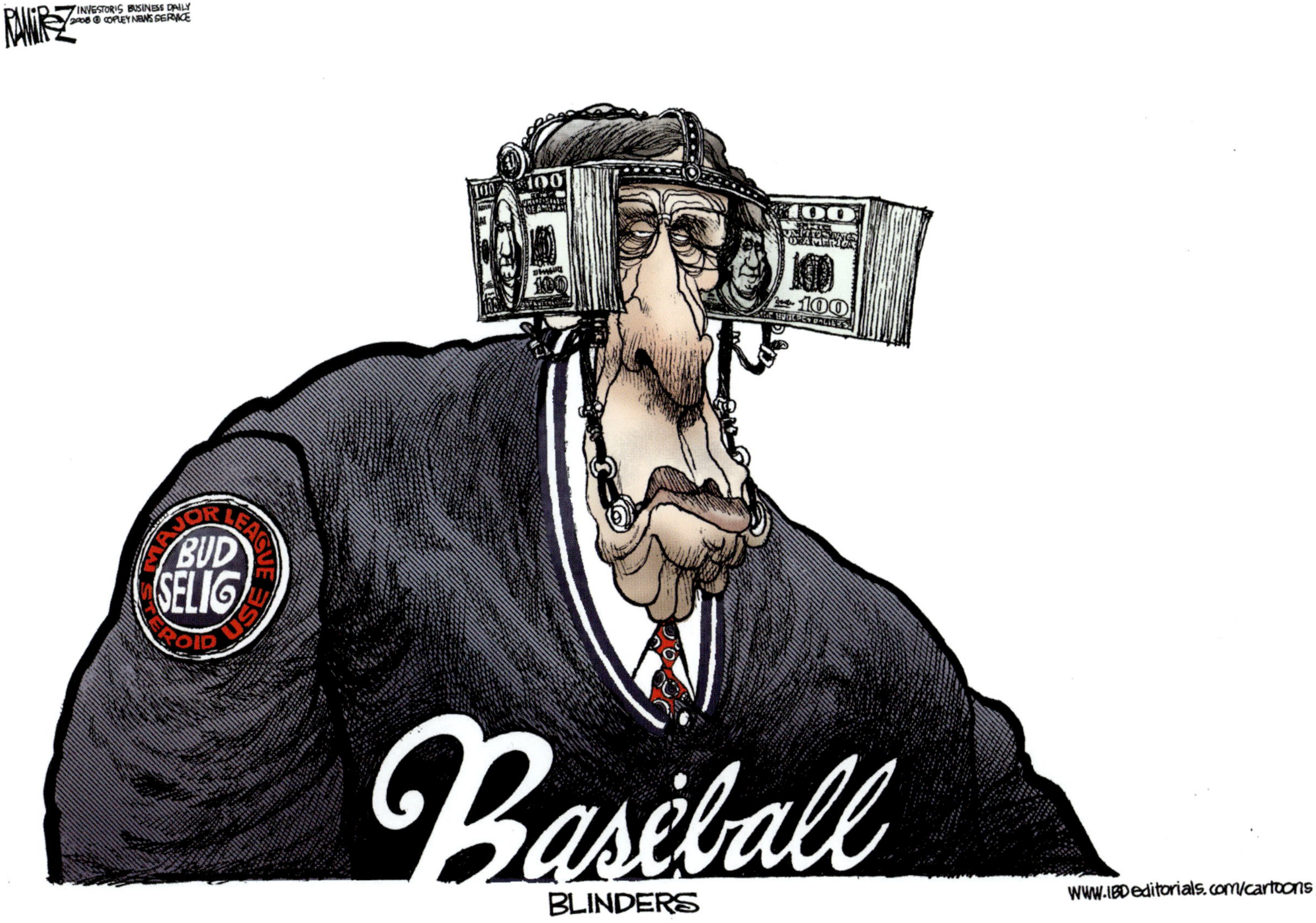
RAMIREZ
INVESTOR'S BUSINESS DAILY
2008 © COPLEY NEWS SERVICE
MAJOR LEAGUE STEROID USE
BUD SELIG
Baseball
BLINDERS
WWW.IBDeditorials.com/cartoons

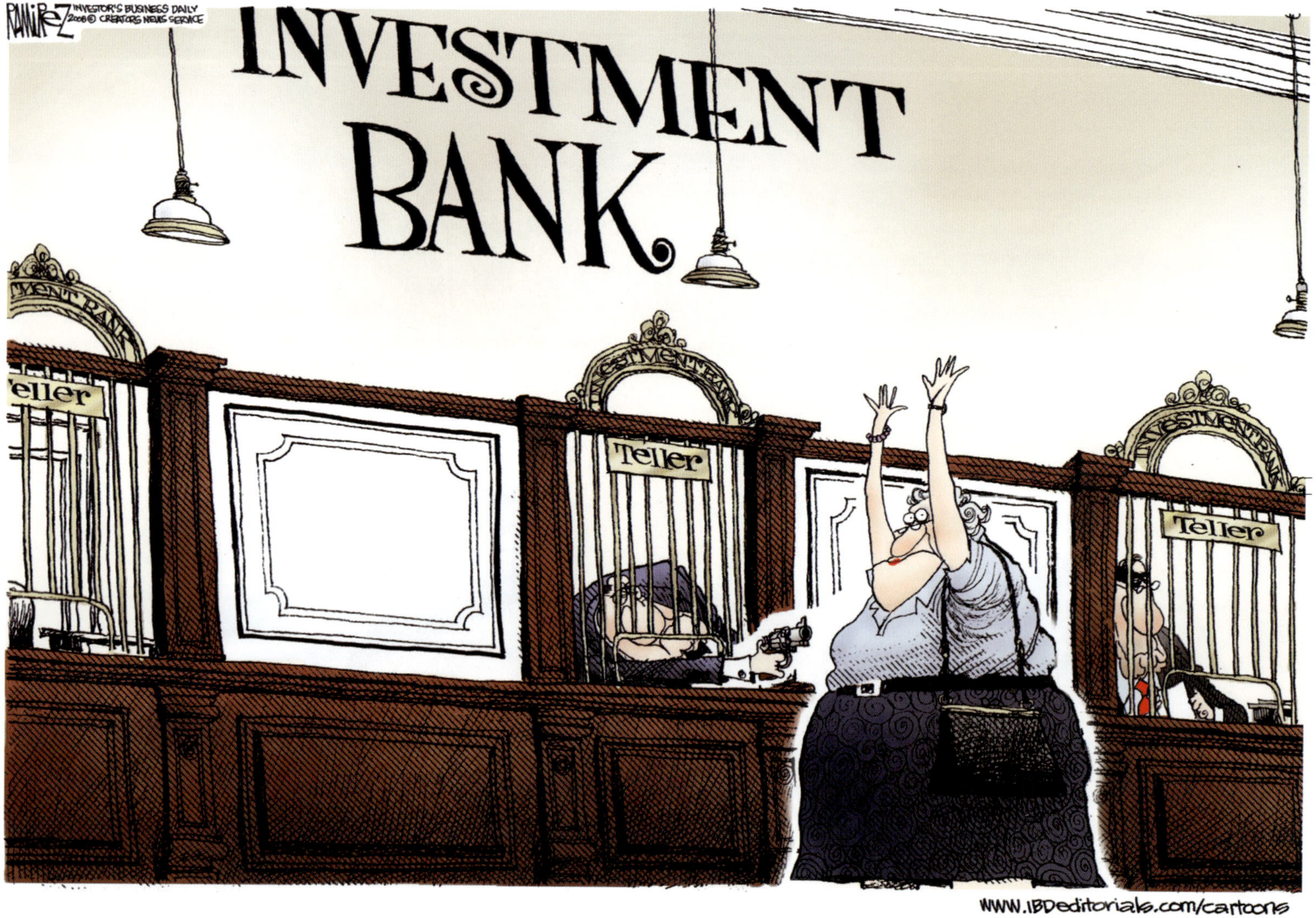
RAMIREZ INVESTOR'S BUSINESS DAILY 2008 © CREATORS NEWS SERVICE
INVESTMENT BANK
Teller
Teller
Teller
WWW.IBDeditorials.com/cartoons

RAMIREZ
INVESTOR'S BUSINESS DAILY
2008 © CREATORS NEWS SERVICE
GO AWAY.
WELL MY FRIENDS, AT LEAST WE STILL HAVE EACHOTHER.
McCAIN
www.IBDeditorials.com/cartoons

RAMIREZ INVESTOR'S BUSINESS DAILY 2008 © CREATORS NEWS SERVICE
BANK
CEO
I'M OKAY. I LANDED ON A TAXPAYER.
WWW.IBDeditorials.com/cartoons

Robert F. Kennedy Journalism Award

The Robert F. Kennedy Journalism Award was founded in December of 1968 and has far exceeded the expectations of its founders. The awards are judged by more than fifty journalists each year. It has become the largest program of its kind and one of few in which the winners are determined solely by their peers.

Known as the "Poor People's Pulitzers" within the press arena, the Robert F. Kennedy Journalism Award, in keeping with the life and legacy of the man for which it is named, honors those who report on issues that reflect Robert F. Kennedy's concerns, including human rights, social justice, and the power of individual action in the United States and around the world.

This living memorial to Kennedy has created programs in three areas, books, journalism, and human rights, which annually award prizes for work that is in keeping with the ideals espoused by RFK. Recipients of these awards receive international recognition and prizes for their inspiring work. These honorees have brought to light issues spanning from child abuse and juvenile crime to discriminatory banking practices and prejudice against AIDS victims. The program is led by a committee of six independent journalists.

In 1983, editorial cartoons became a category, and Don Wright of the *Miami News* won the first award.

2008 Robert F. Kennedy Journalism Award Winner

Jack Ohman—*Oregonian*

Born on September 1, 1960, in St. Paul, Minnesota, Jack Ohman has been the editorial cartoonist for the *Oregonian* since 1983.

Previously, he worked as the editorial cartoonist for the *Detroit Free Press* and the *Columbus Dispatch*. His cartoons are syndicated by Tribune Media Services to 329 newspapers in the United States and abroad. His work regularly appears in the *Washington Post*, the *Philadelphia Inquirer*, the *Boston Globe*, the *Chicago Tribune*, the *Baltimore Sun*, and hundreds of other publications.

Ohman has written or illustrated nine books. He drew the comic strip *Mixed Media* from 1994 to 1999. He has won the Overseas Press Club Award for best editorial cartoon on foreign affairs, the National Headliners Award for best editorial cartoons, as well as numerous other awards, both nationally and regionally. His latest book, *An Inconvenient Trout*, was published in September 2008. He is working on his next book, *Angler Management*.

Ohman is a former member of the alumni board at Portland State. He has three teenaged children.

Jack Ohman Interview

Dean: Turn-of-the-century journalist Finley Peter Dunne is quoted as saying, "The job of the newspaper is to comfort the afflicted and afflict the comfortable." What do you see as the role of the editorial cartoonists?

Jack: Well, I see the role of a political cartoonist as a conversation-starter and a provocateur. I am not happy when I am ambivalent in cartooning; nor am I happy when I feel constrained by the medium, which has increasingly been defined as a single panel gag or pun. If I feel passion, the reader feels passion. The voice of the cartoonist can be a shrill scream or a low tenor musing. I tend toward the latter. I think good cartoonists are proficient at conveying mood and voice. I try to have a variety of pitches and notes that I can play; I don't do the same thing all the time.

Dean: With the continuing decline of newspaper readership, what do you believe the future holds for the fate of the editorial cartoonist?

Jack: I suspect the editorial cartoonist and the newspaper will survive; it's the scope of the newspaper that troubles me. If our coverage shrinks, the range of subjects we can comment upon shrinks as well. There are far fewer journalists covering the Obama Administration than the Bush Administration, and this is bad for democracy. I see no sign of expansion. I think we'll be down to a thirty full-time cartoonists model in the United States very soon. Still, we're not going away, and neither are newspapers.

Dean: What do you feel distinguishes your work from that of your peers?

Jack: I think my work is pretty versatile. I can do a number of different things, from a single panel to a longer form narrative, which I prefer. My favorite cartoon is to take a subject and do three or four takes on a theme off of a premise. Editors seem only to want to run single panels now, so I have had to adjust accordingly. I have been going out in the community and doing what I call an investigative cartoon. I spend a half day or a day observing an event or subject, taking notes and photographs, and then distilling it down to a 250- to 300-word multipanel statement. I enjoy terse writing, and this is a good exercise for me. I think the best cartoonists are really more writers than artists.

OHMAN THE OREGONIAN ©2008 · 2/25
IT'S OK, HONEY... WE SENT THAT TEACHER TO ANOTHER SCHOOL AND THREW AWAY THE KEY...
NO CHILD MOLESTER LEFT BEHIND...
OREGON SEX ABUSE VICTIMS

OHMAN THE OREGONIAN · © 2008 · 10/22 · TMS
...I'LL BET YOU'RE REALLY SCARED BECAUSE OBAMA WANTS TO SPREAD WEALTH.
YOUR BANK FAILED
Pink Slip
401k
US
FORECLOSURE
For Sale
CREDIT CARD BILL

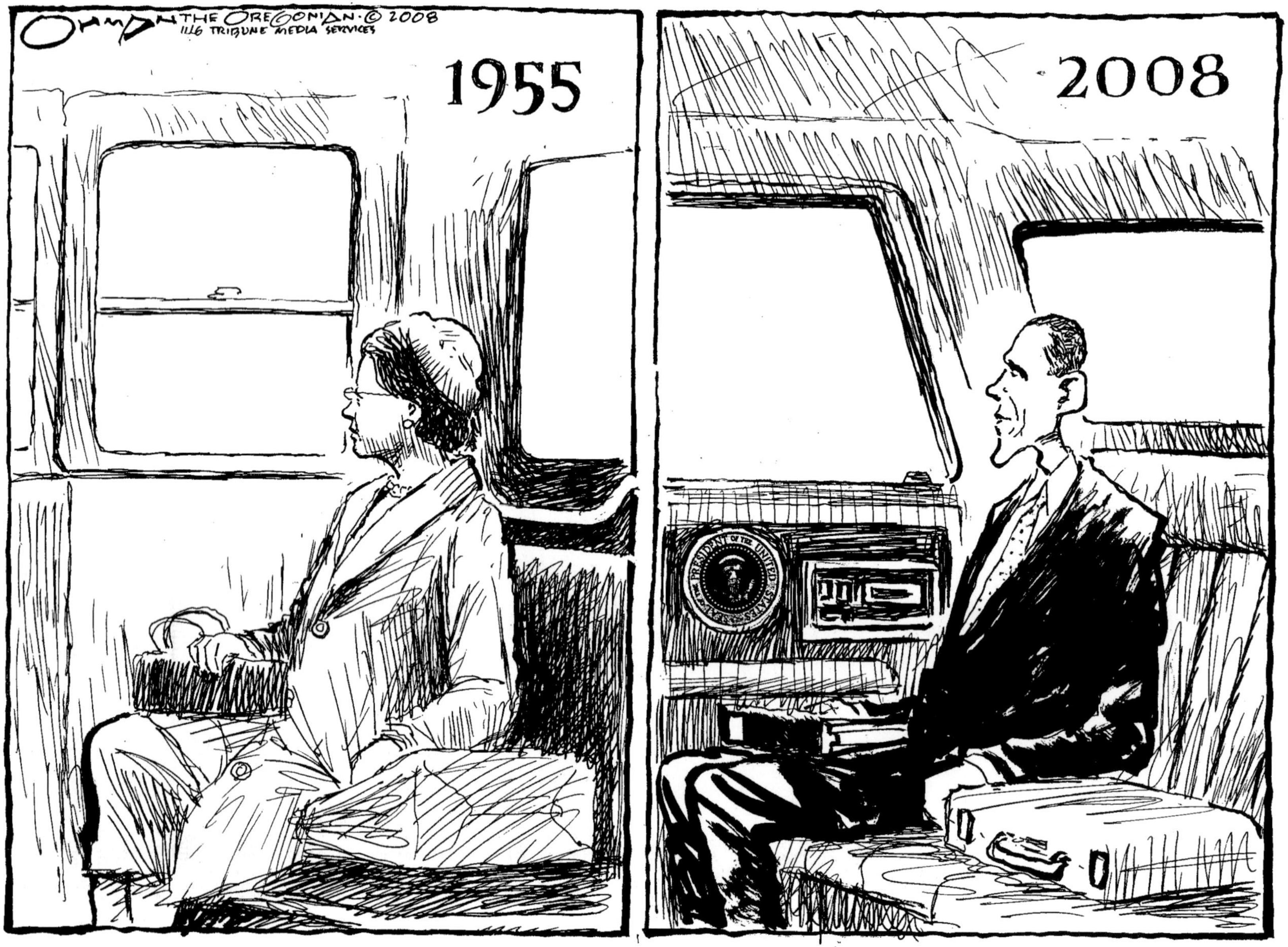
OHMAN THE OREGONIAN © 2008
TRIBUNE MEDIA SERVICES
1955
2008

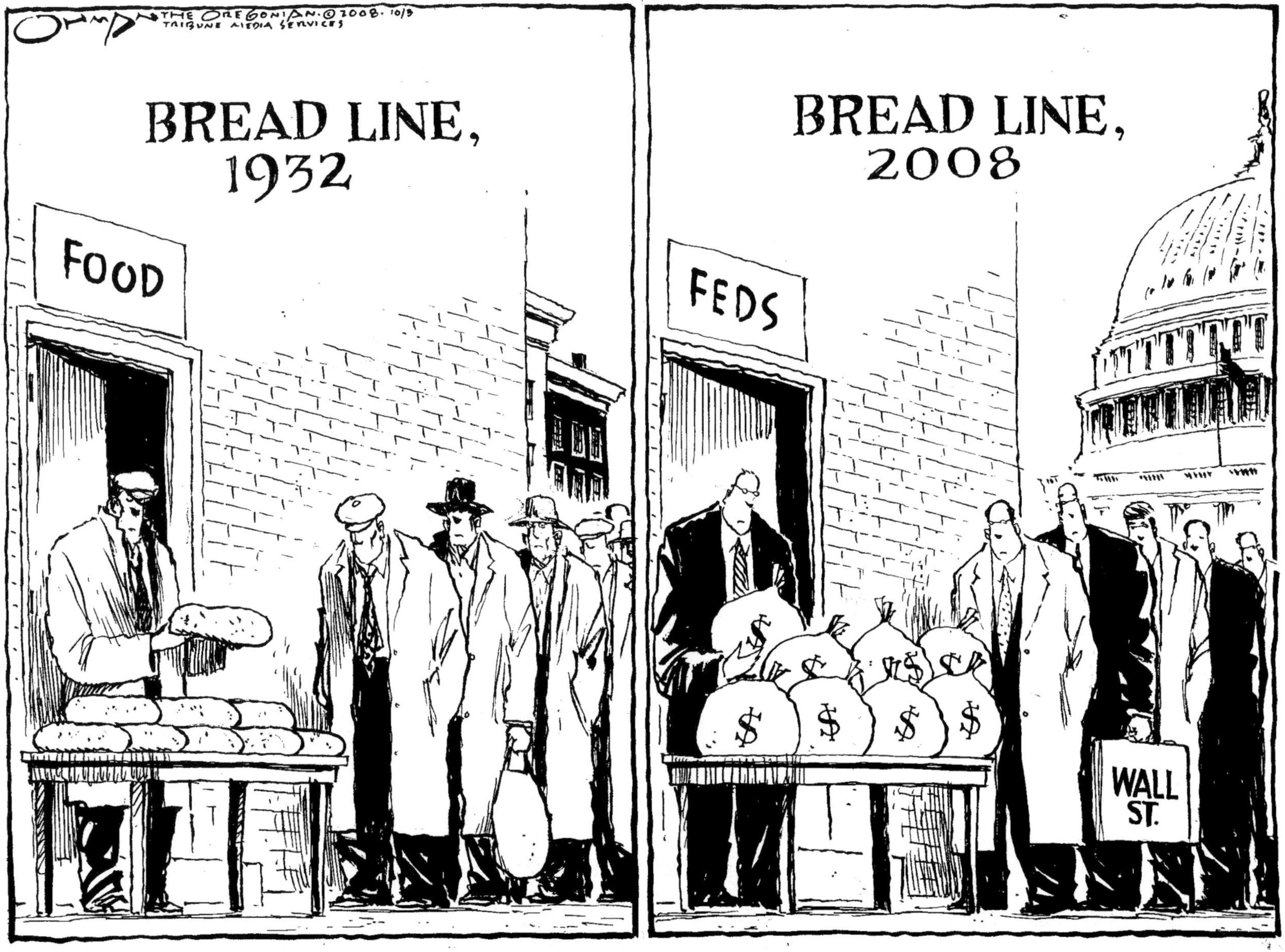
OHMAN THE OREGONIAN © 2008. 10/3
TRIBUNE MEDIA SERVICES
BREAD LINE, 1932
FOOD
BREAD LINE, 2008
FEDS
$
$
$
$
$
WALL ST.

OHMAN THE OREGONIAN · ©2008 · 4/16
TRIBUNE MEDIA SERVICES
...KNEE·HIGH BY THE FOURTH OF JULY!!!
ETHANOL!

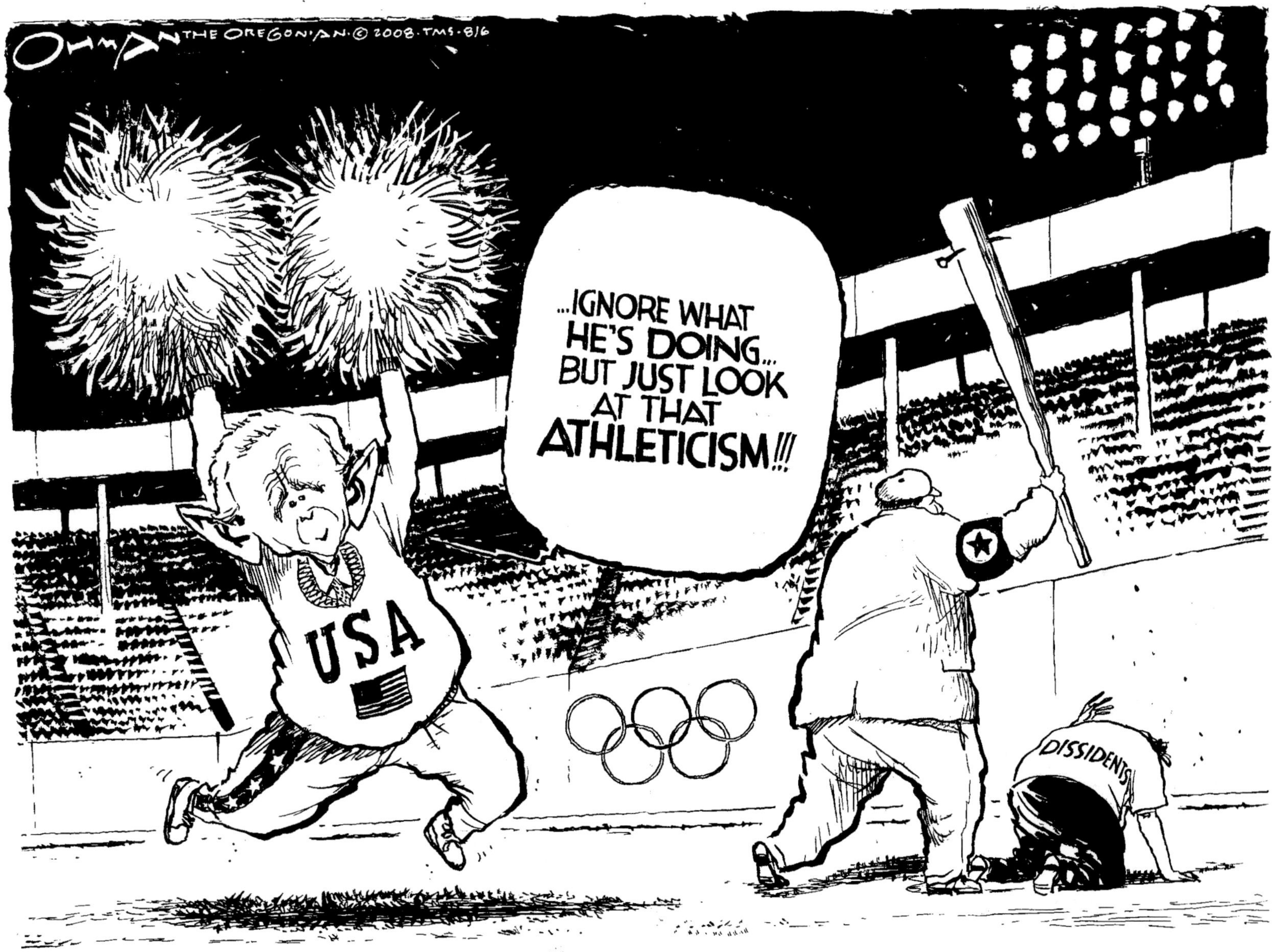
OHMAN THE OREGONIAN © 2008 TMS 8/6
...IGNORE WHAT HE'S DOING... BUT JUST LOOK AT THAT ATHLETICISM!!!
USA
DISSIDENTS

OHMAN THE OREGONIAN ©2008 4/14 TMS
...ANY PROGRESS TOWARD EQUALITY?
...YEP. WE BOTH JUST GOT LAID OFF AND FORECLOSED ON...
MLK

RECESSION SESSION

The nation's unemployment rate is now 6.7%; Oregon's is 7.3%. This led me to go to the Hillsboro office of the Oregon Employment Department to observe.

...the parking lot was jammed.

The staff there seemed cheerful and polite. It's a very orderly atmosphere, but there was palpable tension on the faces of the applicants. Some seemed more resigned, others exhausted.

"You're not getting laid-off until the 19th?"

Another woman leaves abruptly, apparently unhappy with some information she was given...

"They're so high-strung anymore..."

Job loss will do that.

One sign, placed on a table, advertised a PCC "College Survival and Success" course for "Veteran's Only."

Presumably they'll cover apostrophe use.

Ironically, across the street from the office was a pawn shop. I decide to go over there. I had never been in one in my life. It was very poignant.

There were good carpenter's tools everywhere. The manager said there was a lot more traffic in the store these days.

A woman says to a man who hugged her...

"You smell like alcohol..."

...She's not amused. It's 10:30 in the morning...

John Lennon was playing in the shop on one of the many stereos...

"And so this is Christmas..."

Robert F. Kennedy Journalism Award

Cast thy bread upon the waters...

I visited **Loaves and Fishes** the other day. They run the **Meals-on-Wheels** program for **low-income seniors**, and have 35 locations in Multnomah, Washington, and Clark counties. I went to the one on MLK...

It seemed alternately **cheery** and **poignant**. There was a lot of animated conversation, but also some **sad vignettes**. An old television blared.

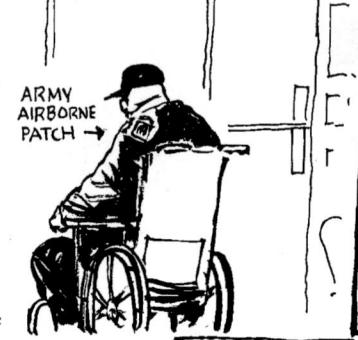

[TV screen: LOAN MODIFICATION!]
[ARMY AIRBORNE PATCH]

On TV, an infomercial called "The **Mortgage Relief Hour**" showed two well-fed looking men. It told viewers that they "have compassion for what you're going through." Uh huh.

[ACT NOW!]

"...When do you know when it's too late?"

"They'll put your furniture in the street and on the lawn!"

[STAFF WEARING SANTA HATS →]

A man in the corner played piano well!

Listening to the TV, a woman said...
"Boy, am I glad I got my house paid off..."
Her friend nodded.

They have two big metal racks for donated bread. Most seniors only took one or two loaves...

One woman, clearly not a senior, took about 12 loaves in a big bag...
I hope she was actually poor.

I asked a staffer if that was OK.
"Anyone can take as much as they want... ...do you want some bread?"

I said, no, thanks. Then her co-worker said...
"...Don't talk to that man! You don't know who he is!"
"She senses I am a cartoonist."

I think I will write them a **check**...

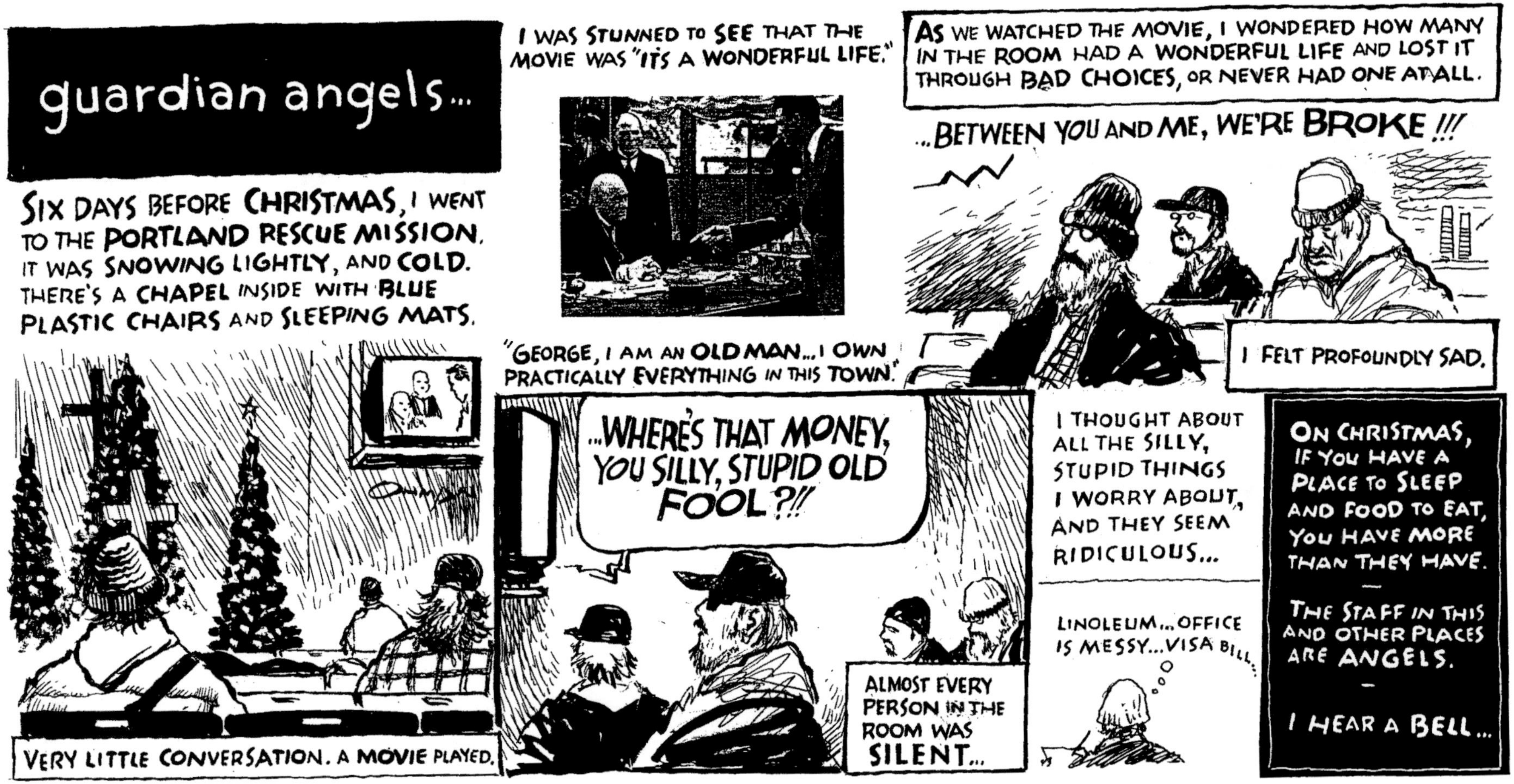
guardian angels...
SIX DAYS BEFORE CHRISTMAS, I WENT TO THE PORTLAND RESCUE MISSION. IT WAS SNOWING LIGHTLY, AND COLD. THERE'S A CHAPEL INSIDE WITH BLUE PLASTIC CHAIRS AND SLEEPING MATS.
VERY LITTLE CONVERSATION. A MOVIE PLAYED.
I WAS STUNNED TO SEE THAT THE MOVIE WAS "IT'S A WONDERFUL LIFE."
"GEORGE, I AM AN OLD MAN... I OWN PRACTICALLY EVERYTHING IN THIS TOWN."
...WHERE'S THAT MONEY, YOU SILLY, STUPID OLD FOOL?!
ALMOST EVERY PERSON IN THE ROOM WAS SILENT...
AS WE WATCHED THE MOVIE, I WONDERED HOW MANY IN THE ROOM HAD A WONDERFUL LIFE AND LOST IT THROUGH BAD CHOICES, OR NEVER HAD ONE AT ALL.
...BETWEEN YOU AND ME, WE'RE BROKE!!!
I FELT PROFOUNDLY SAD.
I THOUGHT ABOUT ALL THE SILLY, STUPID THINGS I WORRY ABOUT, AND THEY SEEM RIDICULOUS...
LINOLEUM... OFFICE IS MESSY... VISA BILL...
ON CHRISTMAS, IF YOU HAVE A PLACE TO SLEEP AND FOOD TO EAT, YOU HAVE MORE THAN THEY HAVE.
THE STAFF IN THIS AND OTHER PLACES ARE ANGELS.
I HEAR A BELL...

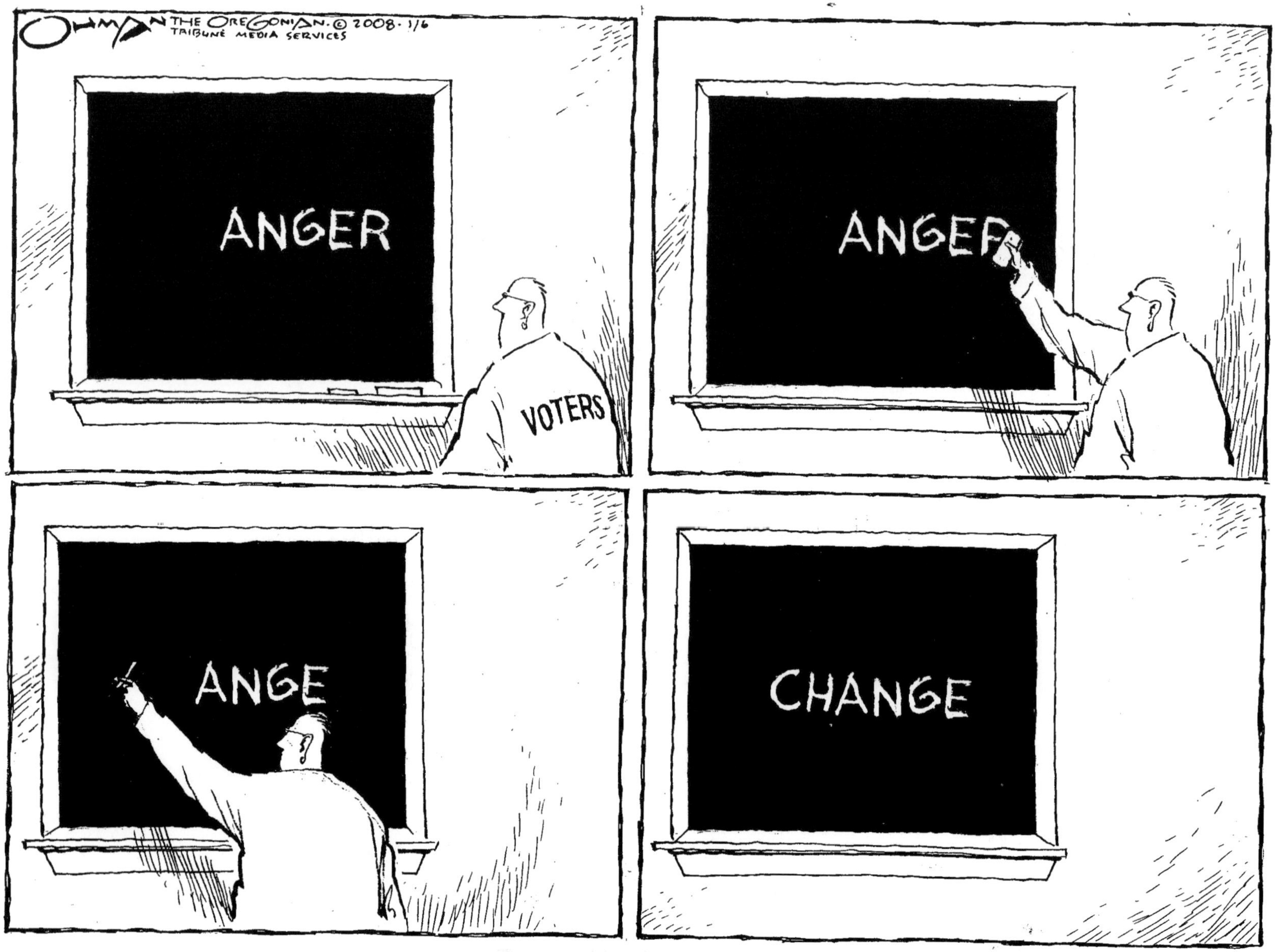
OHMAN THE OREGONIAN © 2008 · 1/6
TRIBUNE MEDIA SERVICES
ANGER
VOTERS
ANGE
CHANGE

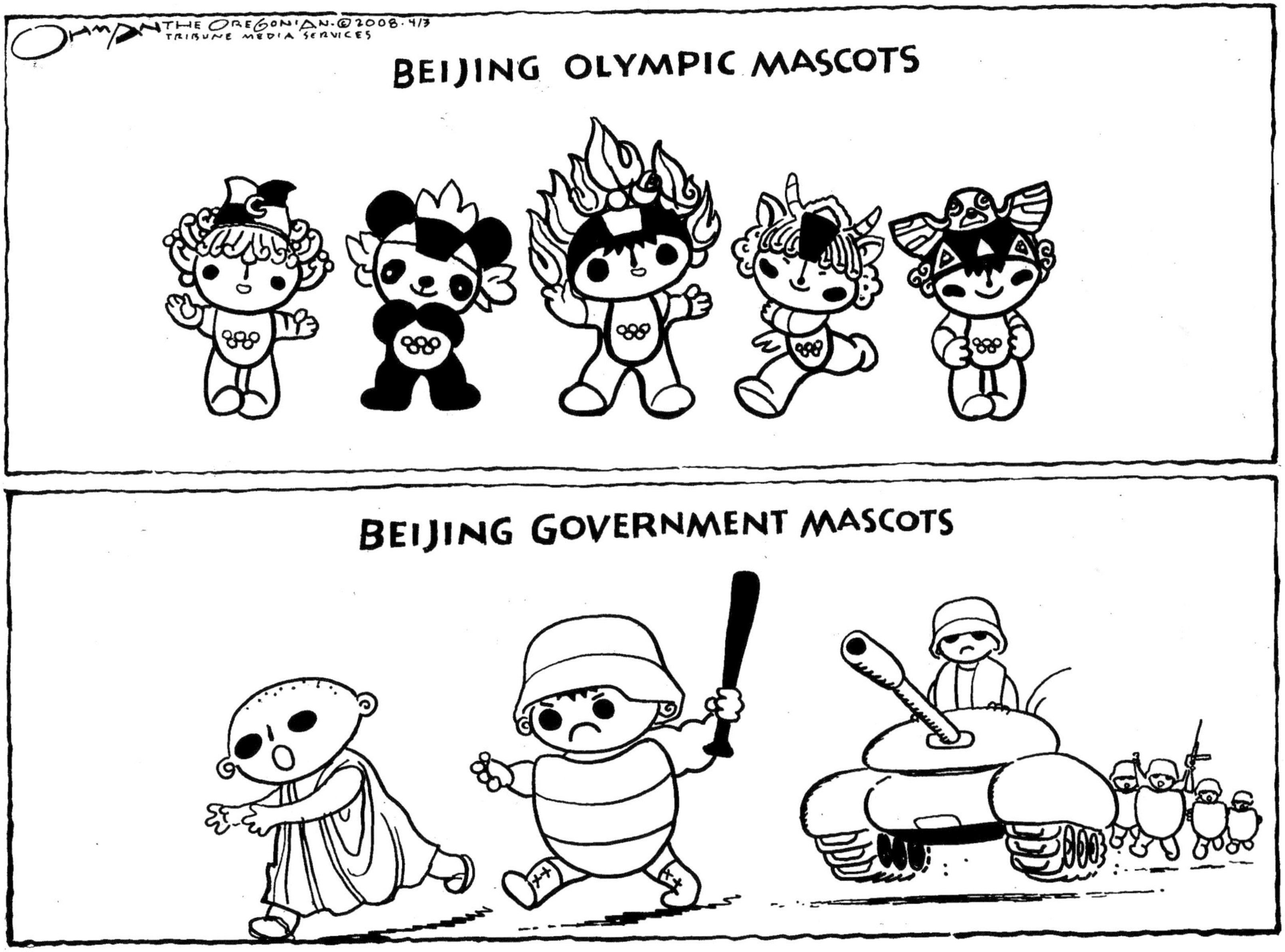
OHMAN THE OREGONIAN ©2008 4/3
TRIBUNE MEDIA SERVICES
BEIJING OLYMPIC MASCOTS
BEIJING GOVERNMENT MASCOTS

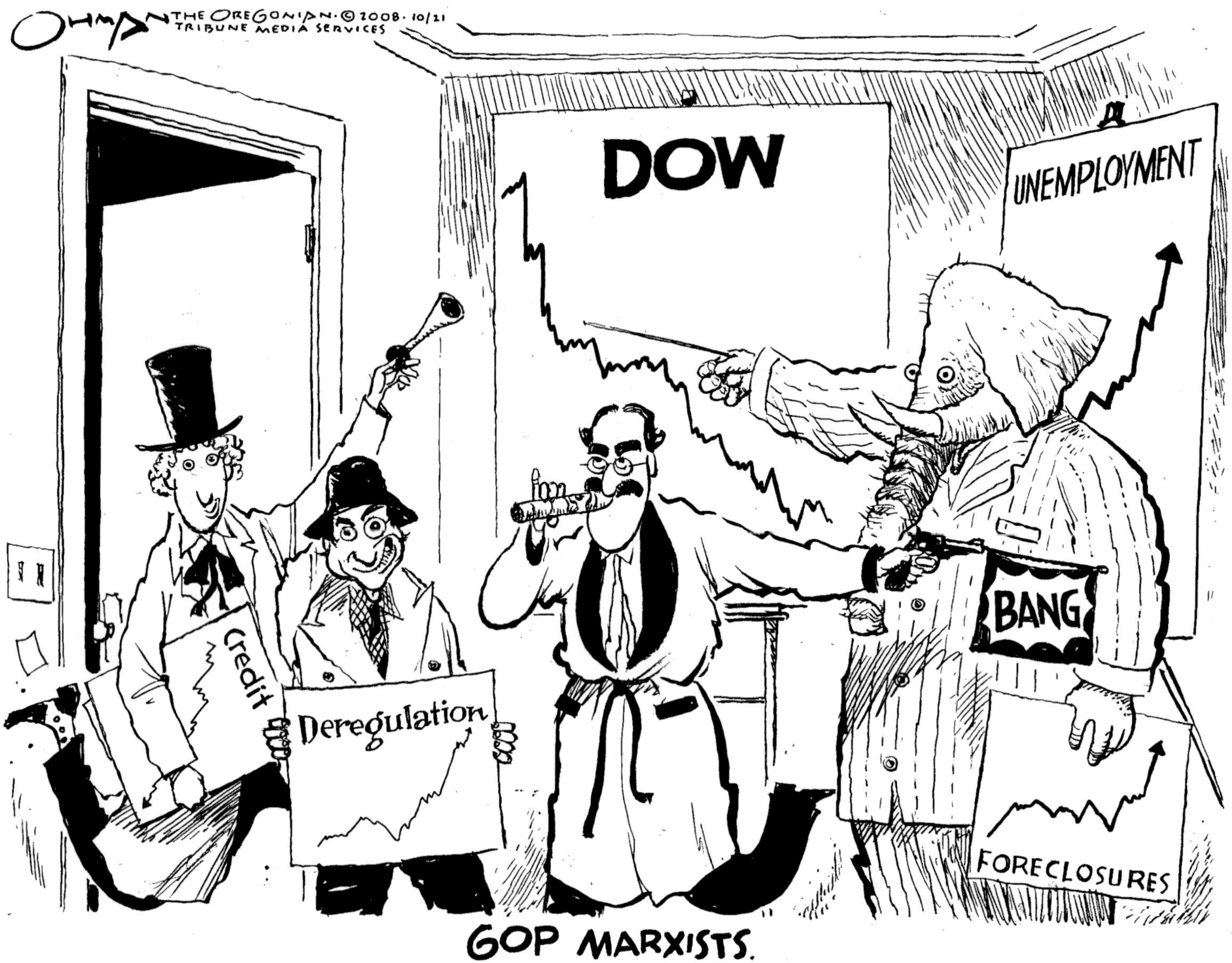
OHMAN THE OREGONIAN · © 2008 · 10/21
TRIBUNE MEDIA SERVICES
DOW
UNEMPLOYMENT
Credit
Deregulation
BANG
FORECLOSURES
GOP MARXISTS.

The John Fischetti Editorial Cartoon Competition Award

The youngest of four children, John Fischetti was born in Brooklyn, New York, on September 27, 1916. He studied at the Pratt Institute in Brooklyn and from there took a job at the Walt Disney Studios. When forced by eye strain to give up animation, he began freelancing for various newspapers and magazines, first in California, then in Chicago, where he soon started drawing political cartoons for the *Chicago Sun*.

During World War II, Fischetti drew cartoons for the *Stars and Stripes* as well as doing courtroom drawings for some of the war crimes trials. After the war, he freelanced in New York, much of it for the *New York Herald*. When it folded in 1966, he moved back to Chicago and worked for the *Chicago Daily News*, where he won a Pulitzer Prize in 1968. John Fischetti died on November 18, 1980, while working for the *Chicago Sun-Times*.

An endowment, created in Fischetti name in 1980, sustains the Fischetti Award for editorial cartoons as well as several scholarships at Columbia College in Chicago.

The first Fischetti was awarded in 1981 to Lee Judge of the *Kansas City Times*.

2009 John Fischetti Editorial Cartoon Competition Award Winner
Lee Judge—*Kansas City Star*

This must be a special award for Lee Judge, who was the first recipient of the Fischetti Award in 1981. Now, history repeats itself.

Judge was born in Roseville, California, May 3, 1953. He started drawing political cartoons for the *Sacramento Union* in 1976. He began working as the staff editorial cartoonist for the *San Diego Union* in 1979 and in 1981 was hired by the *Kansas City Star*, where he has worked ever since.

His political cartoons have appeared in hundreds of newspapers and magazines including the *New York Times*, the *Washington Post*, the *Chicago Sun-Times*, the *Boston Globe*, *Playboy*, *Washington Monthly*, and *National Review*. His work has also been featured on *Good Morning America*, *The MacNeil/Lehrer News Hour* and *C-SPAN*.

He has sold thousands of original cartoons, donating the proceeds to Project Warmth, a Kansas City charity. Judge is a past president of the AAEC.

Lee Judge Interview

Dean: Turn-of-the-century journalist Finley Peter Dunne is quoted as saying, "The job of the newspaper is to comfort the afflicted and afflict the comfortable." What do you see as the role of the editorial cartoonist?

Lee: Reminding people to laugh at the ridiculous.

Dean: With the continuing decline of newspaper readership, what do you believe the future holds for the fate of the editorial cartoonist?

Lee: Probably funny Taco Bell night manager.

Dean: What do you feel distinguishes your work from that of your peers?

Lee: Lack of artistic ability? There's only so much time in the day and you're going to spend it working on the art or the idea. I prefer to spend it on the idea. I hope it shows.

Dean: It has been said that how a person entertains him/herself speaks volumes of their character. Please name your favorite three books, three movies, three actors/actresses, and three musical performers.

Lee: If how I entertain myself speaks volumes about my character, I'm screwed.

Dean: Although the bulk of this book is dedicated to editorial contests in the U.S., the final section of this book deals with international Lurie Award. How do you think U.S. cartoons differ from those of other countries?

Lee: I've got no expertise in this area, so for the first time in my career as an editorial cartoonist, I'm going to let that stop me from commenting.

Judge ©2008 KANSAS CITY STAR / ljudge@kcstar.com
2/17
THE PRICE OF GAS.

2009 John Fischetti Editorial Cartoon Competition Award Honorable Mention

Mike Luckovich—Atlanta Journal-Constitution

One of two Honorable Mentions for this year's Fischetti is Mike Luckovich, editorial cartoonist for the *Atlanta Journal-Constitution*. He has won the 1995 and 2006 Pulitzer Prize; the 1989, 1993, and 2006 Overseas Press Club's Thomas Nast Award; the 1994 Robert F. Kennedy Journalism Award; the 2005 Society of Professional Journalist's Sigma Delta Chi Award; and the 1992, 2006, and 2007 National Headliner Award.

A Seattle native, Luckovich earned a bachelor's degree in political science from the University of Washington. He freelanced for a while with local papers in Washington while working as a traveling salesman to pay his bills. He joined the *Atlanta Journal-Constitution* in 1989 after working for the *New Orleans Times-Picayune* from 1984 to 1989. Creators Syndicate distributes his cartoons nationally.

(Editor's note: Mr. Luckovich was unavailable for an interview)

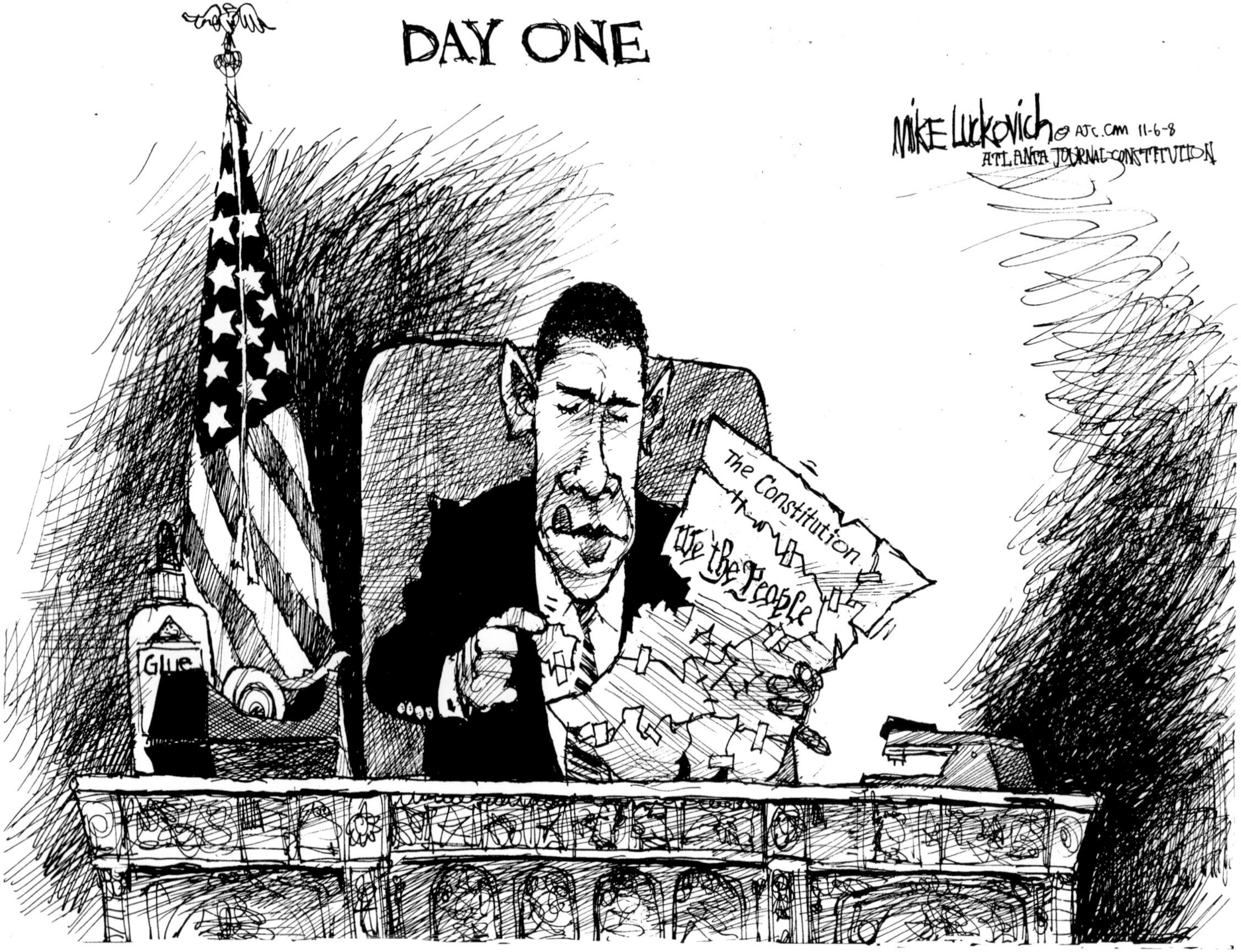
DAY ONE
MIKE LUCKOVICH © AJC.COM 11-6-8
ATLANTA JOURNAL-CONSTITUTION
The Constitution
We the People
GLUE

By permission of Mike Luckovich and Creators Syndicate, Inc.
(This cartoon was also entered as part of the Scripps Howard Award contest)

2009 John Fischetti Editorial Cartoon Competition Award Honorable Mention

Michael Ramirez—*Investor's Business Daily*

Michael Ramirez is a two-time winner of the prestigious Pulitzer Prize and a three-time Sigma Delta Chi Award winner. He is a senior editor and the editorial cartoonist for *Investor's Business Daily*. Ramirez is a Lincoln Fellow, an honorary member of Pi Sigma Alpha National Political Science Honor Society, and has won almost every journalism award in addition to the prestigious UC Irvine Medal from the University of California, Irvine. Author of *Everyone Has the Right to My Opinion*, he is a regular contributor to *USA Today* and the *Weekly Standard Magazine*. Ramirez's work is seen worldwide with a distribution of more than four hundred newspapers and magazines through Creators Syndicate. The former editorial cartoonist for the *Los Angeles Times*, his cartoons have been featured on CNN, Fox News, *The O'Reilly Factor*, and "The Rush Limbaugh Show." His work can be seen in such publications as the *New York Times*, the *Washington Post*, the *New York Post*, *Time*, *National Review*, and *U. S. News and World Report*.

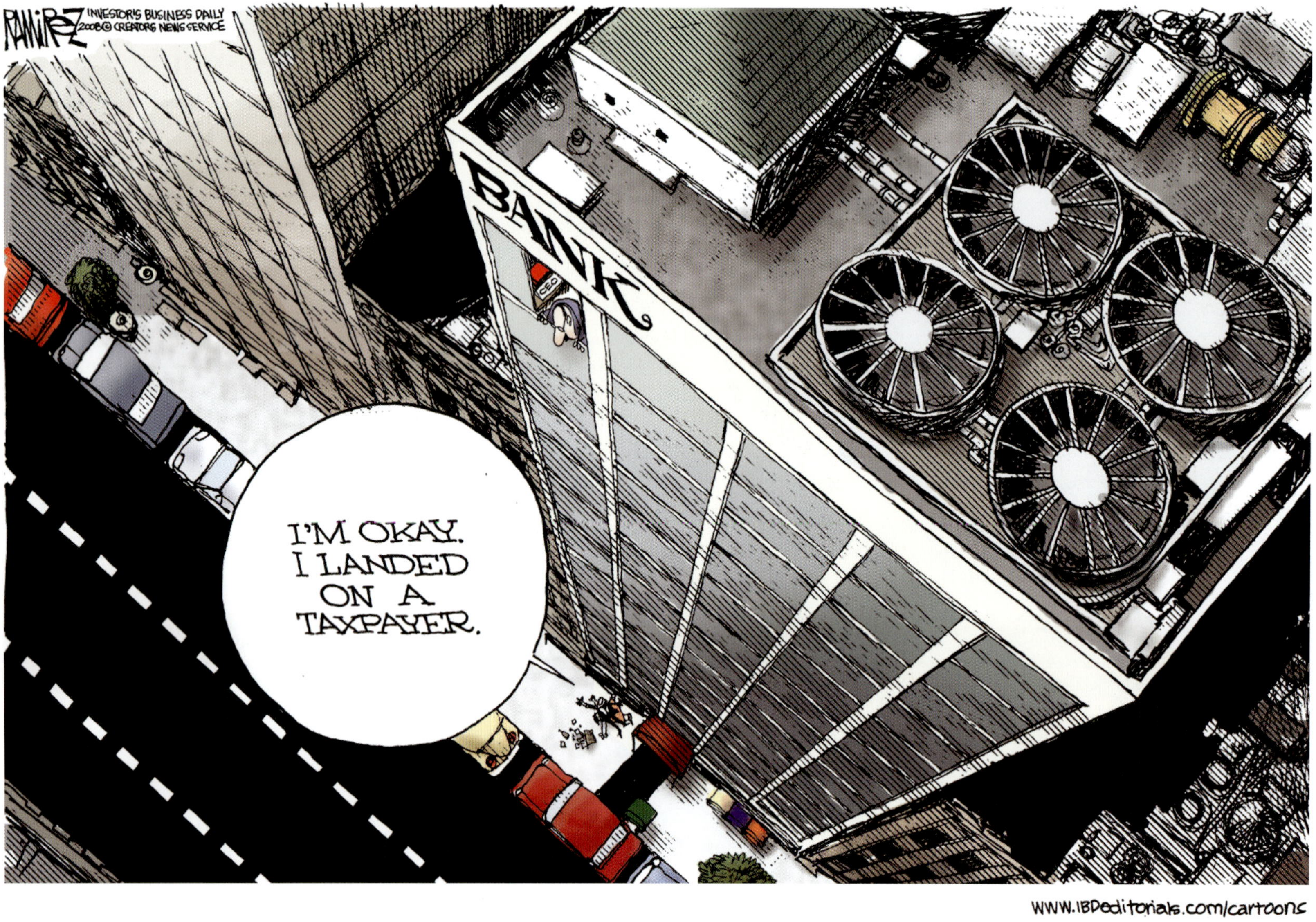

RAMIREZ INVESTOR'S BUSINESS DAILY 2008© CREATORS NEWS SERVICE
BANK
CEO
I'M OKAY. I LANDED ON A TAXPAYER.
WWW.IBDeditorials.com/cartoons

(This cartoon was also a part of the Reuben Award entry package)

The National Press Foundation's Clifford K. and James T. Berryman Award

In 1989, Florence Berryman, former art critic for the *Washington Star,* endowed an annual award in memory of her late father and brother, Clifford K. and James T. Berryman. Each year since, the National Press Foundation has sponsored the award. The first "Berryman" Award was given in 1990 to Signe Wilkinson of the *Philadelphia Daily News.*

Clifford K. and James T. Berryman were father and son editorial cartoonists who have both won the coveted Pulitzer Prize. Clifford Berryman won his Pulitzer for a cartoon depicting Pres. Franklin Roosevelt and various other government officials attempting to steer the USS *Manpower Mobilization* in different directions, but he is best known for a 1902 cartoon of another Roosevelt president, Theodore, and a small bear igniting a national phenomenon—"Teddy Bears."

Six years after Clifford K. Berryman won a Pulitzer for editorial cartooning, his son matched his achievement. James T. Berryman won his Pulitzer in 1950 for a McCarthy-era cartoon titled "All Ready for a Super-Secret Session," making the Berrymans the only father and son Pulitzer Prize for editorial cartoon winners.

2008 National Press Foundation's Clifford K. and James T. Berryman Award Winner

Nate Beeler—*San Francisco Examiner*

Since 2005, Nate Beeler's cartoons have appeared in both the *Washington Examiner* and in the *San Francisco Examiner*. His work has also appeared in *USA Today*, the *Los Angeles Times*, and the *Independent* (UK) and on CNN and Fox News. Beeler is syndicated internationally to more than eight hundred newspapers by Cagle Cartoons and to about three hundred college publications by MCT Campus.

Beeler's cartooning career began at his high school's student newspaper in Columbus, Ohio. Drafted into his school's newpaper while sitting in the principal's office for, what else, cartooning on school property, Beeler went on to earn a journalism degree at American University in 2002. While there, he won the three major college cartooning awards: the Charles M. Schulz Award, the John Locher Award, and first place in the SPJ Mark of Excellence Awards. In 2007, he won the Golden Spike Award, as voted upon by members of the Association of American Editorial Cartoonists at its fiftieth anniversary convention in Washington. Beeler lives just across the Potomac River in Alexandria, Virginia.

(Nate Beeler's cartoons are syndicated by Cagle Cartoons, Inc.; reprint permissions can be obtained online at Politicalcartoons.com)

Nate Beeler Interview

Dean: Turn-of-the-century journalist Finley Peter Dunne is quoted as saying, "The job of the newspaper is to comfort the afflicted and afflict the comfortable." What do you see as the role of the editorial cartoonist?
Nate: The goal of an editorial cartoonist should be that of any journalist: to be a check on power. I think journalism is part of the lifeblood of our nation, so its core duty is to be a check on government power.

Dean: With the continuing decline of newspaper readership, what do you believe the future holds for the fate of the editorial cartoonist?
Nate: Even though newspaper readership has declined, I don't believe there is too much cause for alarm in the long run. There will always be demand for news and accompanying commentary, though they may be delivered via new mediums, as we're seeing now with the Internet. Editorial cartooning has helped shape America in many subtle ways, and I think there will continue to be demand for the unique qualities of a cartoonist. We'll have to adapt to the changing landscape, of course, by learning new skills to fit new mediums. But it is the same situation with which all journalists are wrestling.

Dean: What do you feel distinguishes your work from that of your peers?
Nate: I try (usually in vain) to distinguish myself in two ways: through my artwork and my approach to politics. The power of an editorial is in the potency of its words, and the power of a cartoon is in the potency of its images. Because of this, I constantly push myself to draw dynamic, striking artwork. As for approaching politics, I think there are too many partisan editorial cartoonists drawing today. Republicans and Democrats are two sides of the same coin, and whichever one of them is in power at any moment deserves to see the business end of our crow quills. I've always chafed a bit under authority, so its no wonder I entered a profession that rewards that instinct. In America, government is the ultimate authority, so I'm suspicious of any party or person holding its reins.

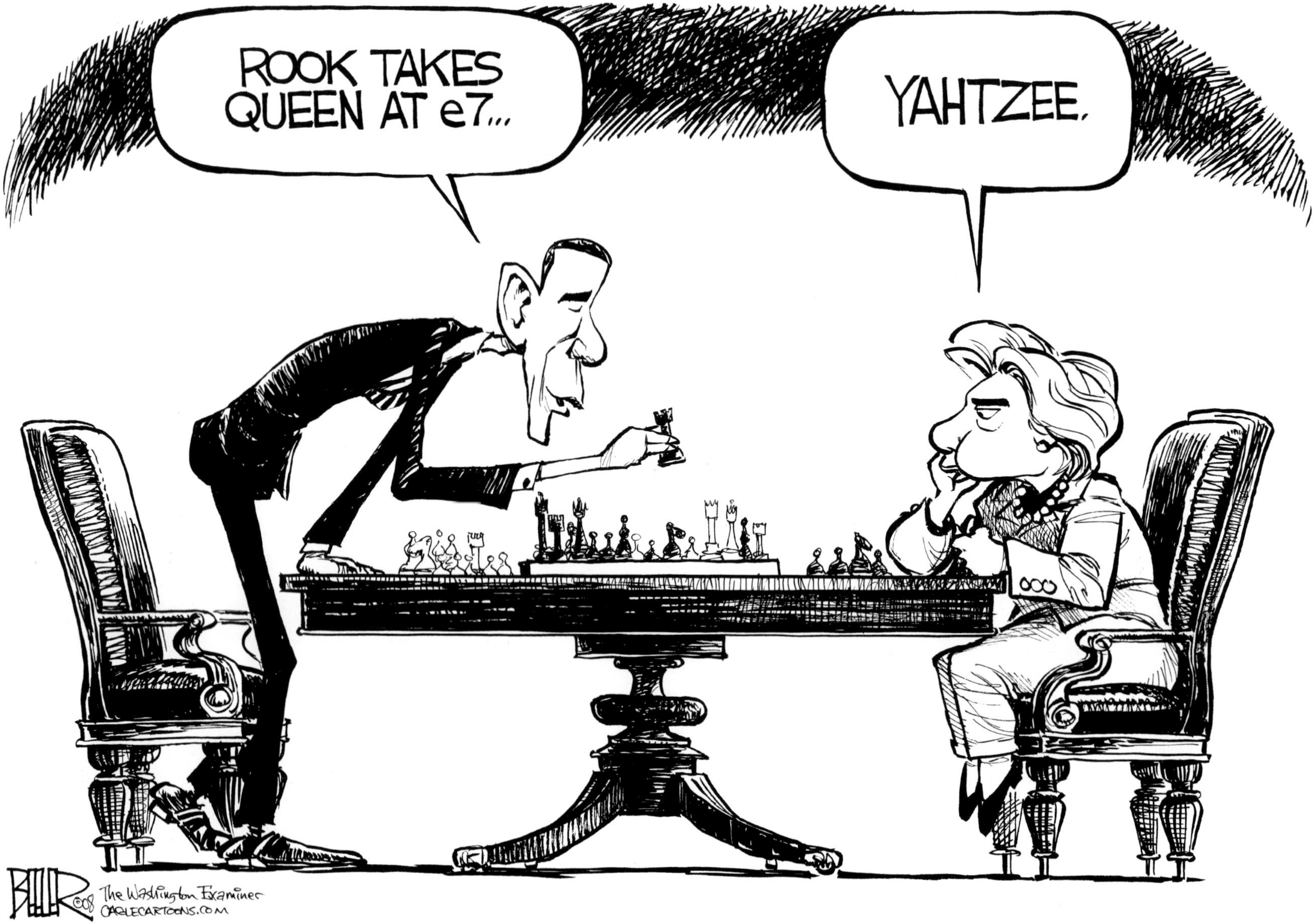
ROOK TAKES QUEEN AT e7...
YAHTZEE.
BEELER ©08 The Washington Examiner
CAGLECARTOONS.COM

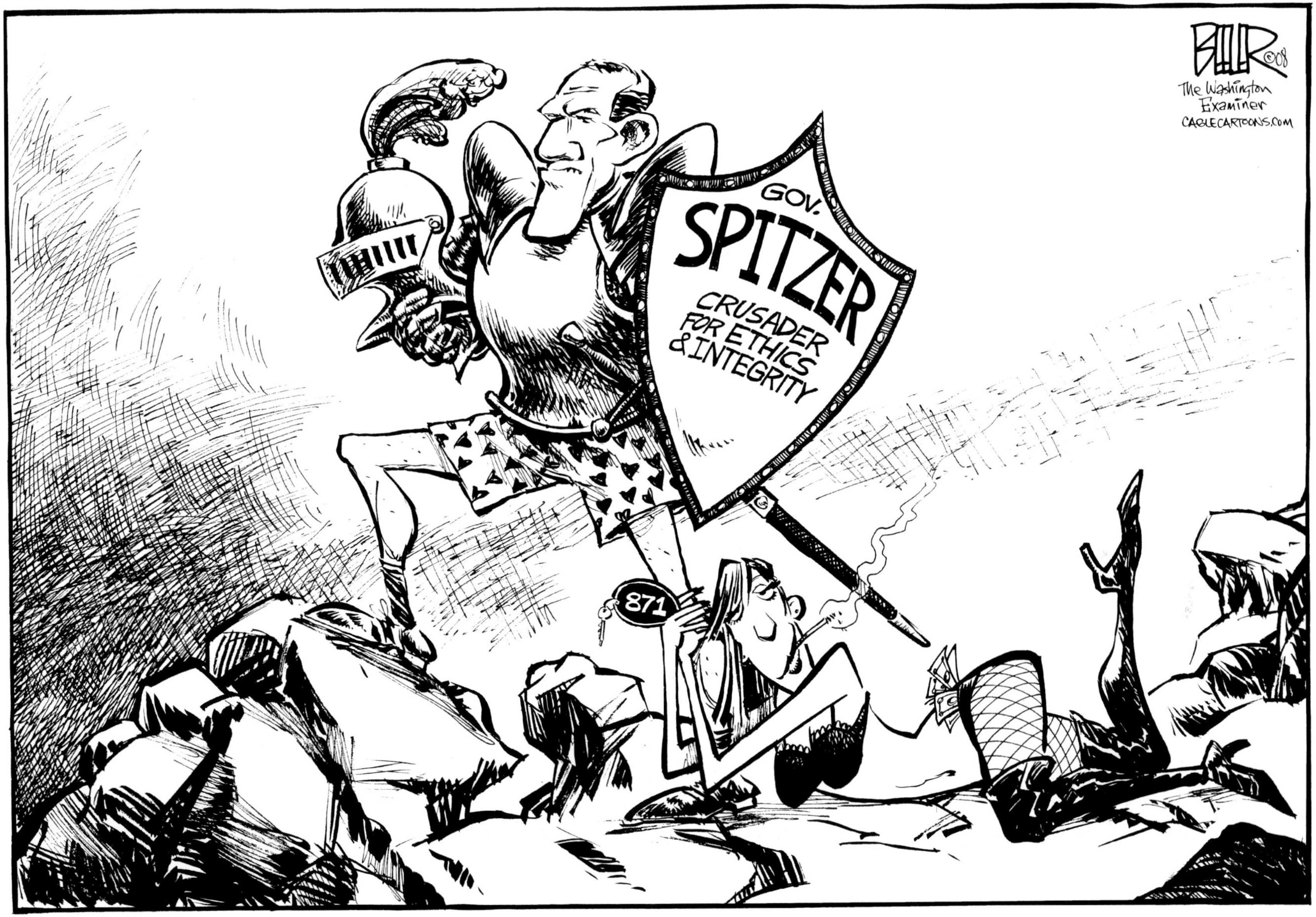
BEELER ©08
The Washington Examiner
CABLECARTOONS.COM
GOV. SPITZER
CRUSADER FOR ETHICS & INTEGRITY
871

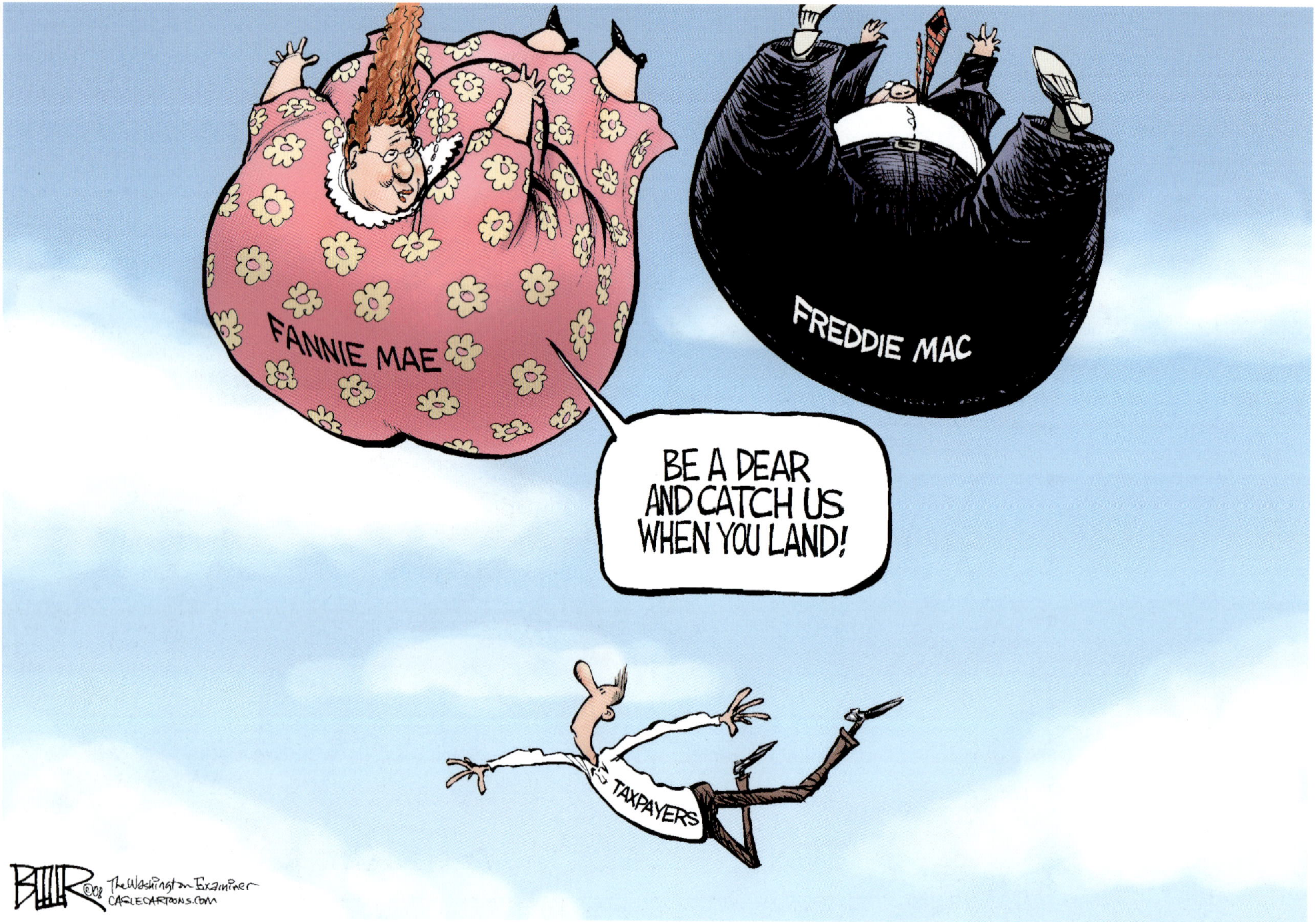
FANNIE MAE
FREDDIE MAC
BE A DEAR AND CATCH US WHEN YOU LAND!
TAXPAYERS
©08 The Washington Examiner
CAGLECARTOONS.COM

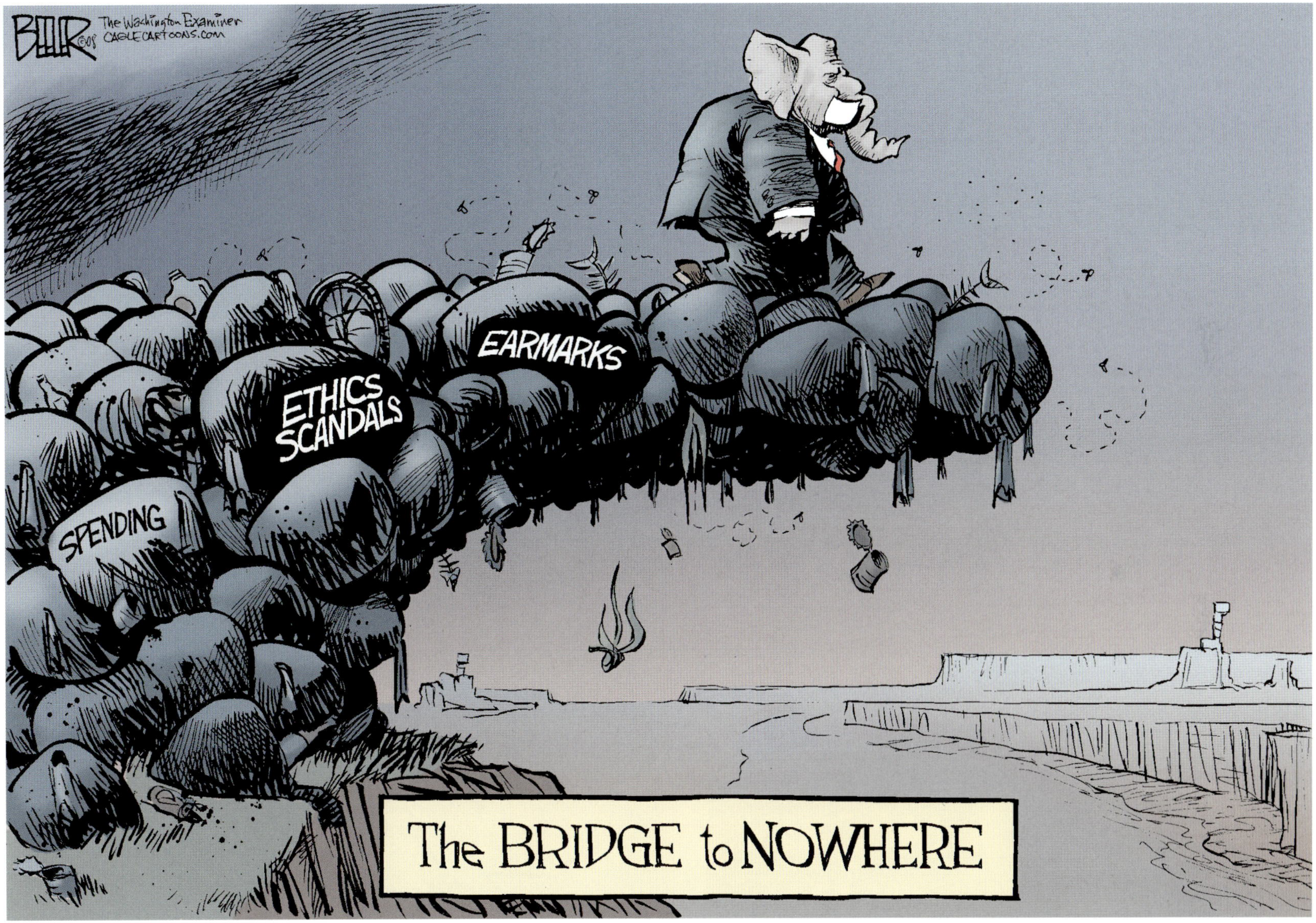
BEELER
The Washington Examiner
CAGLECARTOONS.COM
EARMARKS
ETHICS SCANDALS
SPENDING
The BRIDGE to NOWHERE

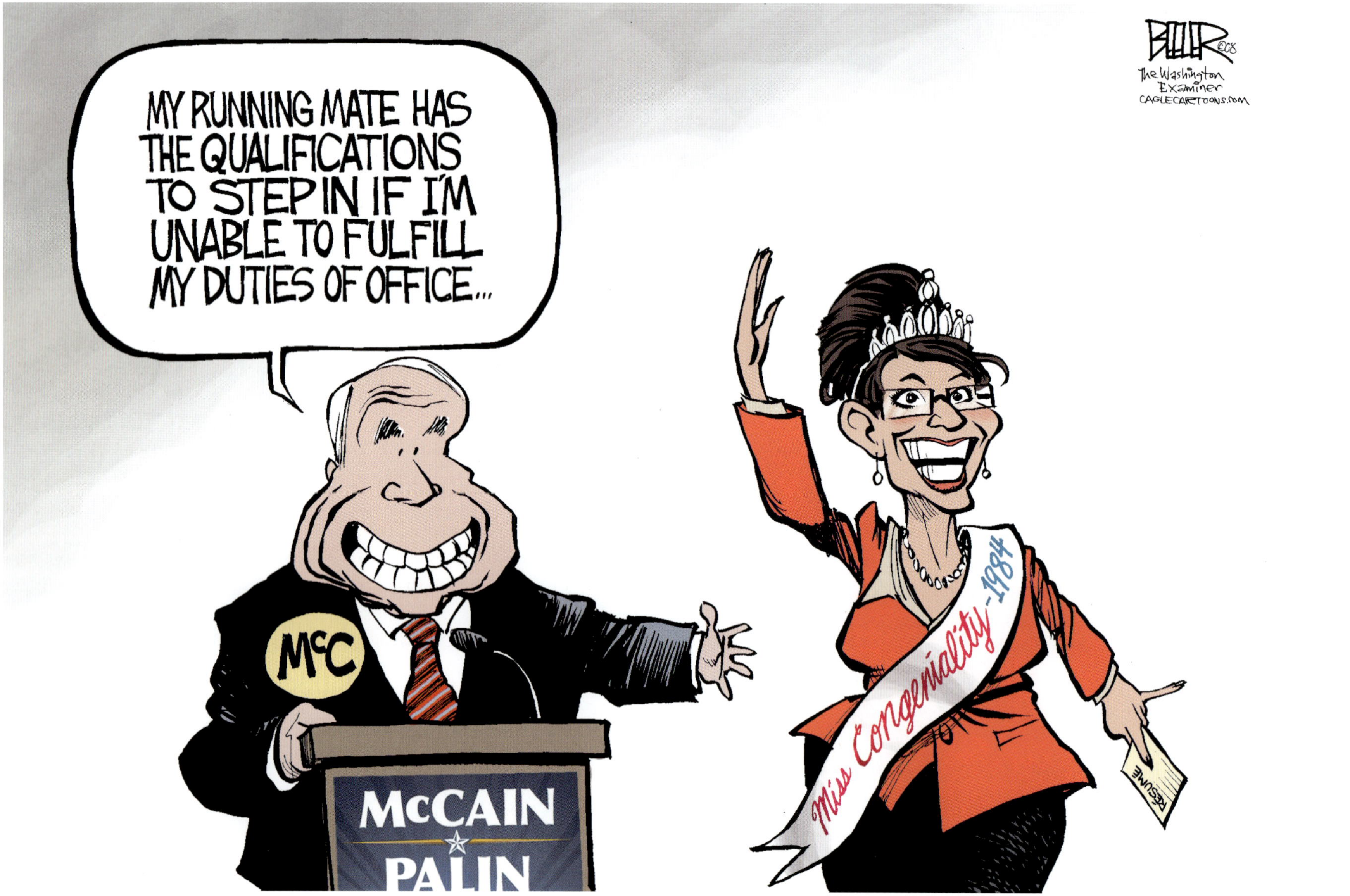
MY RUNNING MATE HAS THE QUALIFICATIONS TO STEP IN IF I'M UNABLE TO FULFILL MY DUTIES OF OFFICE...
BEELER ©08
The Washington Examiner
CAGLECARTOONS.COM
McC
McCAIN
PALIN
Miss Congeniality - 1984
RESUME

The Herblock Prize

The Herblock Prize was first awarded in 2004 to Matt Davies of the *Journal News* in Westchester County, New York. It is awarded annually for distinguished examples of original editorial cartooning that exemplify the courageous independent standard set by the late *Washington Post* cartoonist Herb Block.

Herbert Block was the beloved longtime editorial cartoonist for the *Washington Post*. Block was born on October 13, 1909. Born and educated in Chicago, he spent two years at Lake Forest College and took part-time classes at the Art Institute of Chicago. In 1929, he began work as the editorial page cartoonist for the *Chicago Daily News* and was syndicated through the NEA Service (Cleveland, Ohio) four years later. He served in the United States Army from 1943 to 1945 before joining the *Washington Post* in 1946.

The Herb Block Foundation, which funds the prize, was created in Herb Block's will as a grant-making organization with a mission of defending basic freedoms, combating all forms of discrimination and improving the conditions of the poor, and providing post-secondary educational opportunities to financially needy students.

Competition is especially keen for this award as it has for the past several years waived its entry fee, making it accessible to even struggling young would-be Herb Blocks.

2008 Herblock Prize Winner
Pat Bagley—*Salt Lake Tribune*

Pat Bagley, 48, was born in Salt Lake City, but grew up in southern California. Drawing was something he always had a knack for, but for his understanding of politics, he drew on his father's experience as mayor of Oceanside and an avid news junkie.

Bagley attended Brigham Young University, majoring in political science. His first cartoon for the school newspaper, the *Daily Universe*, wound up in *Time*, an auspicious start for this aspiring cartoonist.

Hired by the *Salt Lake Tribune* in 1979, Bagley has penned more than eight thousand cartoons in the last thirty years for the paper.

He has authored several books, including *Welcome to Utah*, a collection of original cartoons about the Beehive State; *This Is the Place*, a children's history of Utah; and *Dinosaurs of Utah*, a fun and factual compendium of Utah's past inhabitants.

(Pat Bagley's cartoons are syndicated by Cagle Cartoons, Inc.; reprint permissions can be obtained online at Politicalcartoons.com)

Pat Bagley Interview

Dean: Turn-of-the-century journalist Finley Peter Dunne is quoted as saying, "The job of the newspaper is to comfort the afflicted and afflict the comfortable." What do you see as the role of the editorial cartoonist?

Pat: Good cartoons do at least one of three things. They can inform, persuade, and/or entertain. It's not like juggling. You don't have to do all three at the same time. Or you can.

Dean: With the continuing decline of newspaper readership, what do you believe the future holds for the fate of the editorial cartoonist?

Pat: More people are seeing my cartoons than ever before. The Internet has opened my work up to anyone with a computer and a mouse. But like the rest of the industry, I have yet to find a way to make the increased exposure pay off. Folks are just too addicted to getting things free from the Internet. (Big sigh) It will all work out somehow.

Dean: What do you feel distinguishes your work from that of your peers?

Pat: My style is a bit breezier than most. I work very hard to make the cartoons look easy, but gesture, expression, and composition are important to me. But a good drawing will never save a bad cartoon idea. So I try to hone the idea sharp as broken glass before committing it to paper.

Dean: Although the bulk of this book is dedicated to editorial contests in the U.S., the final section of this book deals with international Lurie Award. How do you think U.S. cartoons differ from those of other countries?

Pat: Outside of the U.S., cartoonists are rock stars. I don't get it, but people in the rest of the world eat up cartoons that are obvious and polemical and, not infrequently, scatological. Missiles are a standard substitute for some world leader's penis. Funny, if it hadn't been done a thousand times before. Okay, I have to admit, it's never been done even one time in the *Salt Lake City Tribune*.

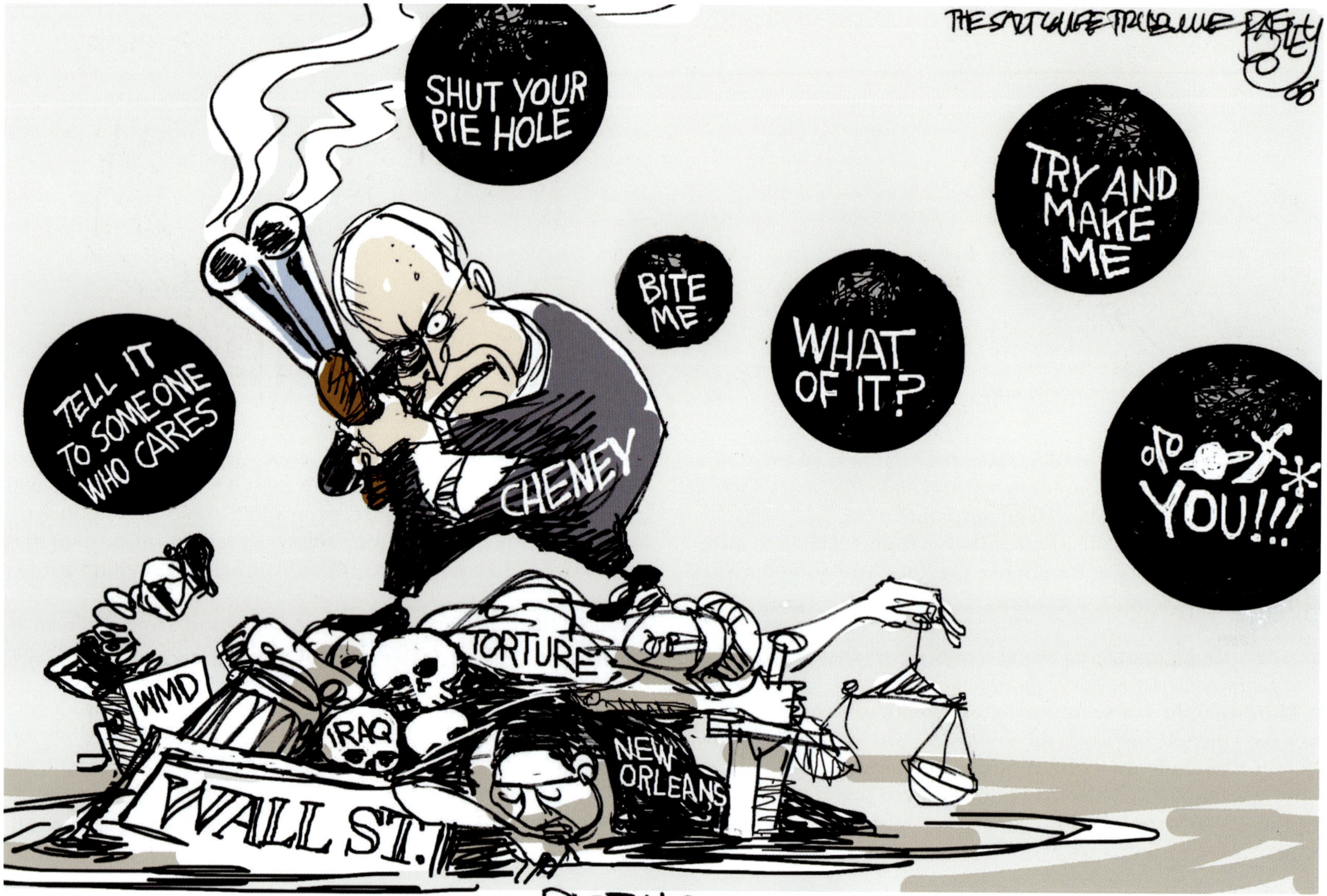
THE SALT LAKE TRIBUNE
'08
SHUT YOUR PIE HOLE
TRY AND MAKE ME
BITE ME
WHAT OF IT?
TELL IT TO SOMEONE WHO CARES
YOU!!!
CHENEY
TORTURE
WMD
IRAQ
NEW ORLEANS
WALL ST.

PARTING SHOTS

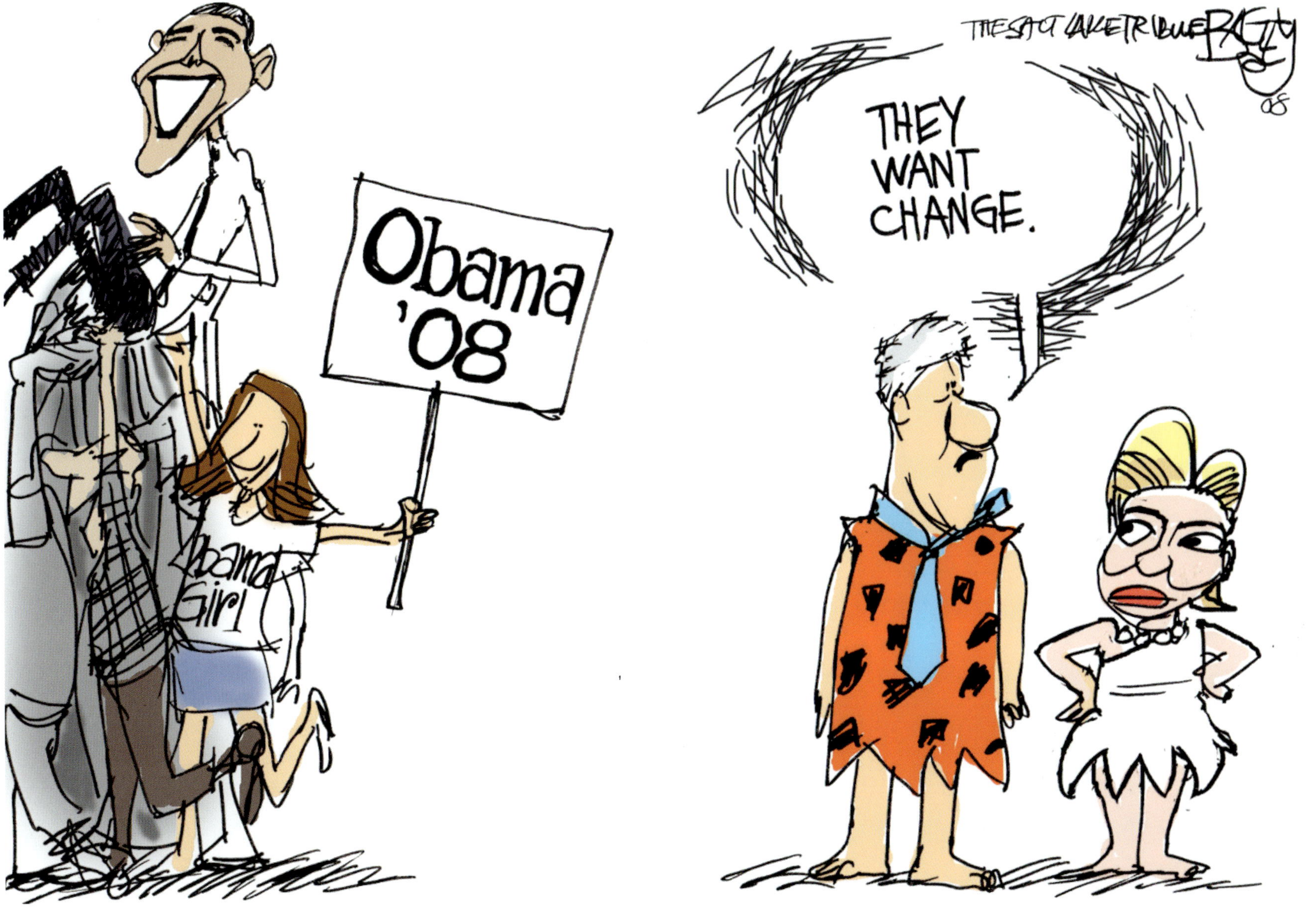
Obama
'08
Obama
Girl
THE SALT LAKE TRIBUNE
THEY WANT CHANGE.

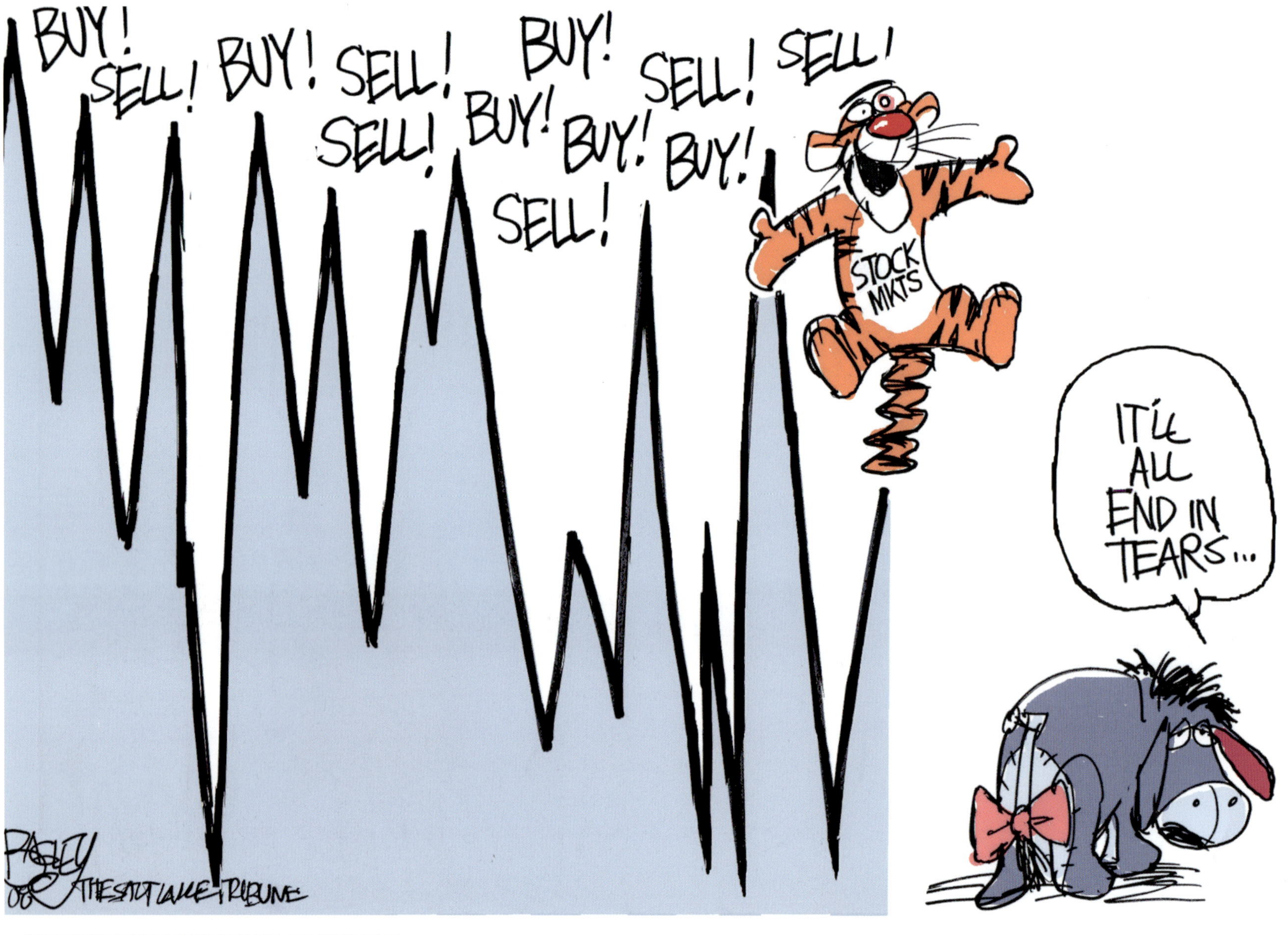
BUY!
SELL!
BUY!
SELL!
SELL!
BUY!
BUY!
SELL!
BUY!
SELL!
BUY!
SELL!
STOCK MKTS
IT'LL ALL END IN TEARS...
PASLEY 08 THE SALT LAKE TRIBUNE

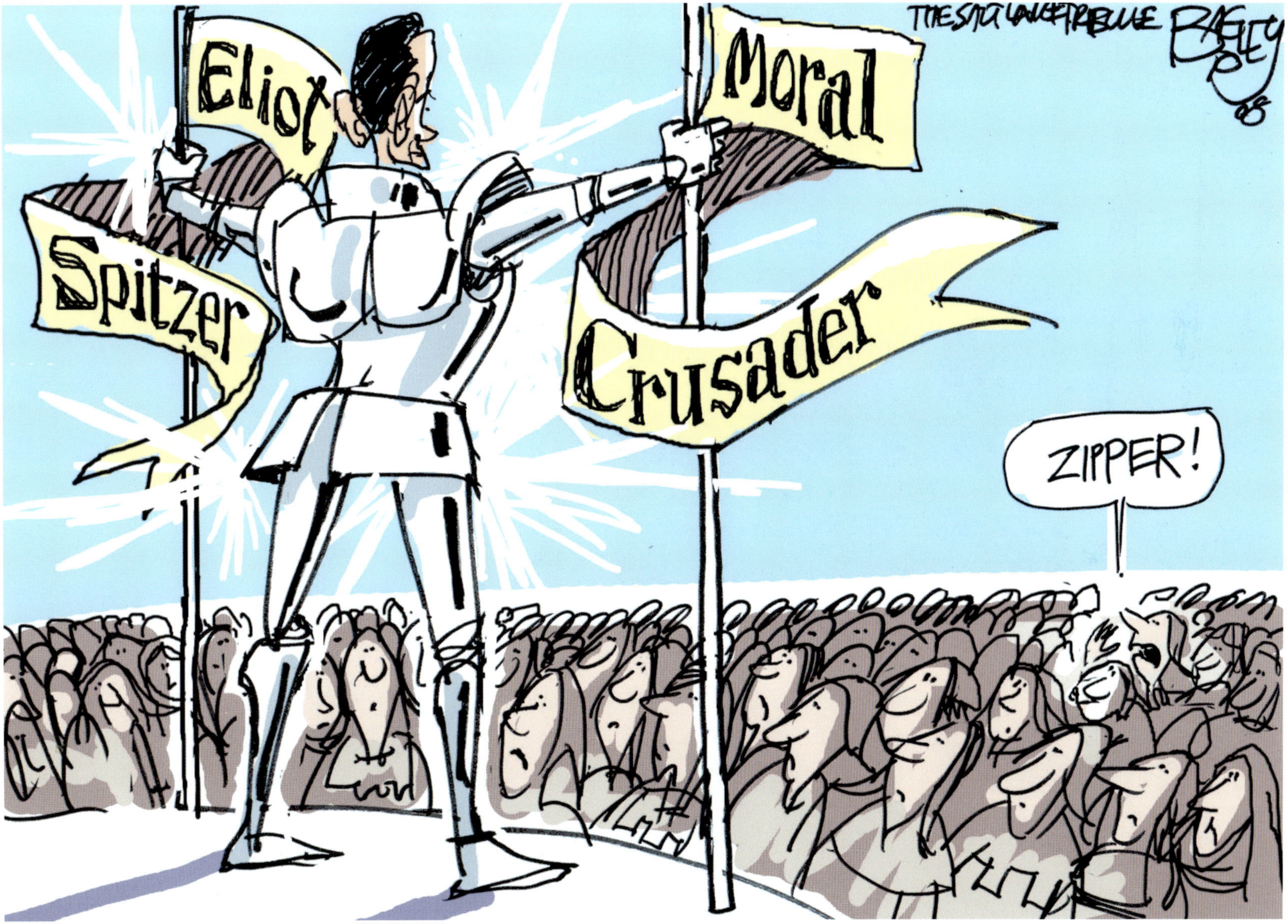
THE SALT LAKE TRIBUNE
BAGLEY
Eliot
Spitzer
Moral
Crusader
ZIPPER!

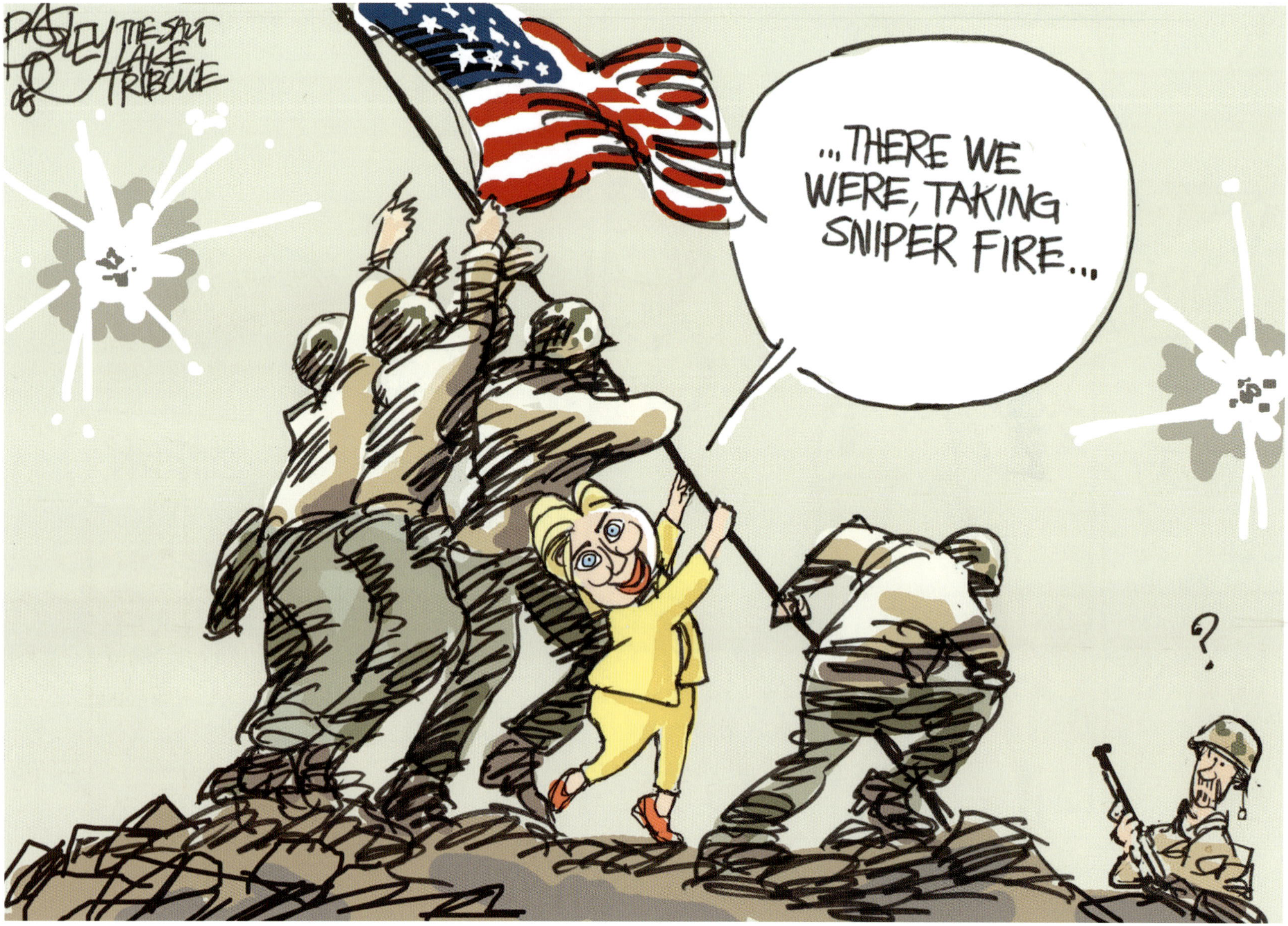
...THERE WE WERE, TAKING SNIPER FIRE...
?

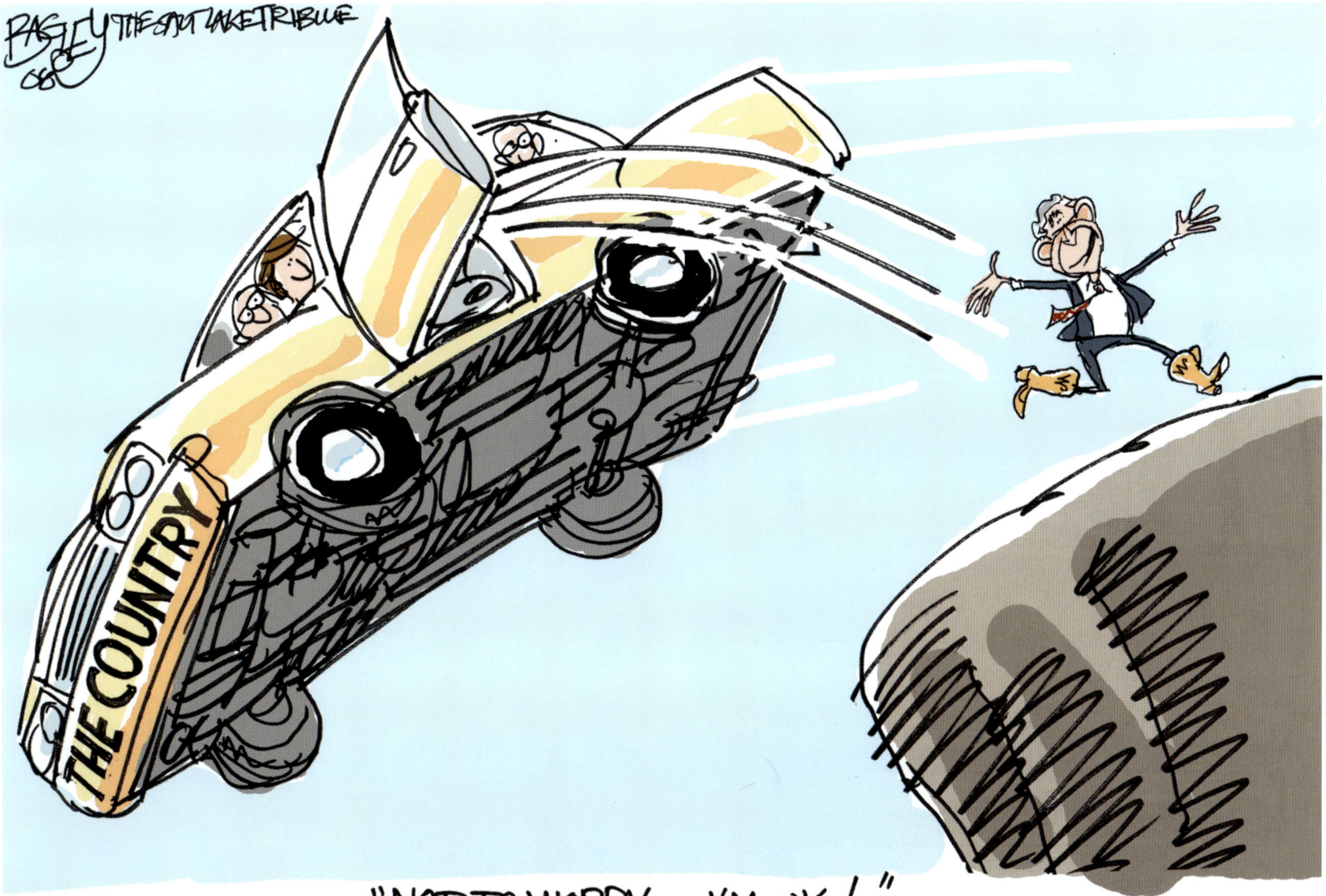
BAGLEY THE SALT LAKE TRIBUNE
08
THE COUNTRY

"NOT TO WORRY— I'M OK!"

THE SALT LAKE TRIBUNE
'08
STRAIGHT TALK EXPRESS
McCAIN '08
BUSH POLICIES

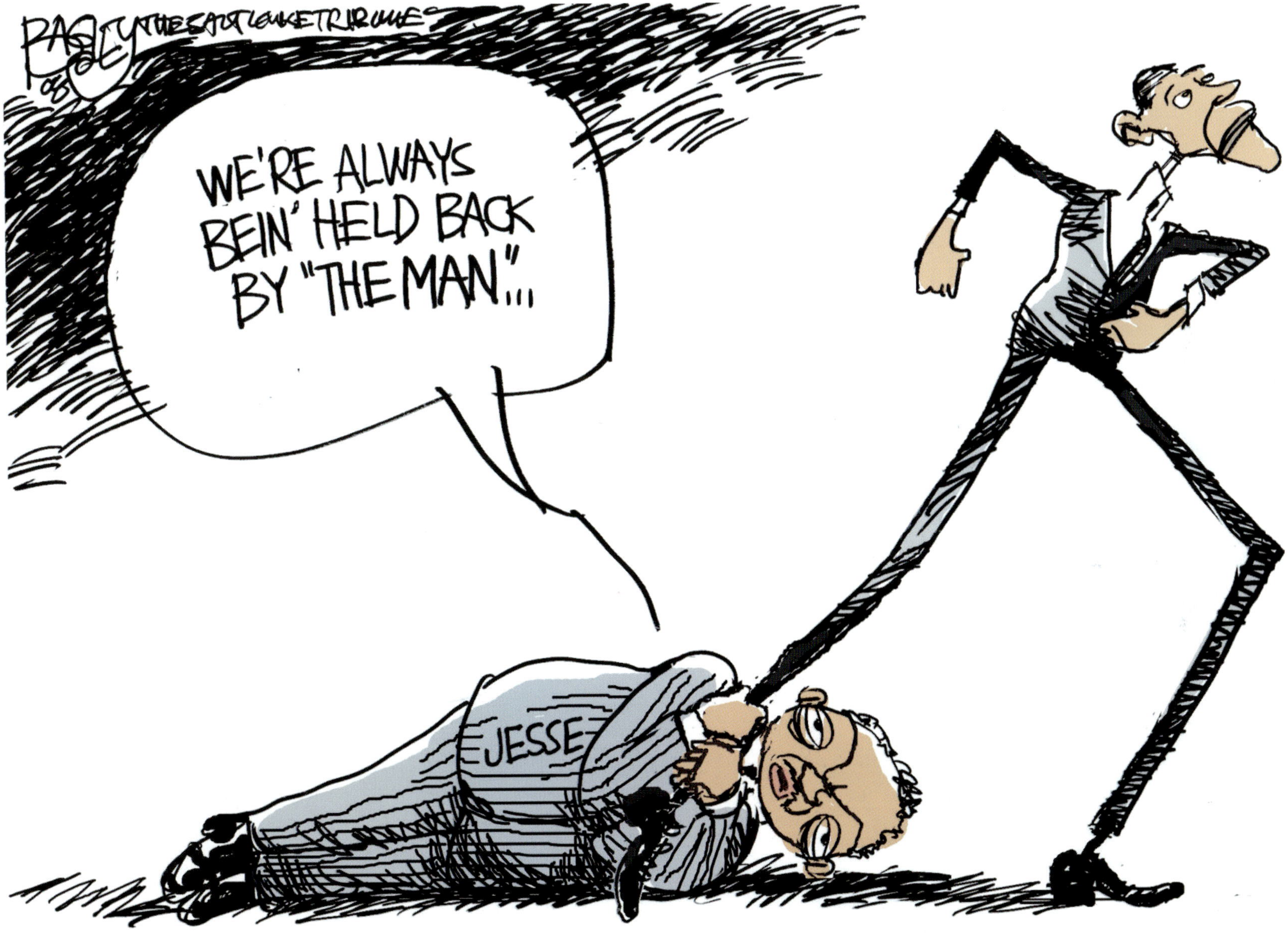
WE'RE ALWAYS BEIN' HELD BACK BY "THE MAN"...
JESSE

CRASH!
BOOM!!
$
RUMMMMBLE
THE ECONOMY IS BASICALLY SOUND.
SCREAM!
SMASH!

BAGLEY
THE SALT LAKE TRIBUNE
JUSTICE
DEPARTMENT OF JUSTICE
JOB APPLICATION
NAME FIRST MIDDLE LAST
SEX: HETERO HOMO
ADDRESS STREET CITY RED STATE
BORN MM DD YY
PARTY AFFILIATION REPUBLICAN TERRORIST
BORN AGAIN MM DD YY
TRUE/FALSE
GEORGE BUSH IS AWESOME T F
I AM UNWORTHY.......... T F
GOD .... T F
GUNS.................. T F
GAYS .... T F
WHICH BEST DESCRIBES YOU:
CONSERVATIVE
SOCIAL CONSERVATIVE
NEO CONSERVATIVE
DITTO HEAD
WORK EXPERIENCE
GOP CAMPAIGN WORKER
SON OF BIG DONOR
SWIFT BOATER FOR TRUTH
CORPORATE LOBBYIST
TALK RADIO HOST
GUATEMALAN DEATH SQUAD
EXTRA CREDIT: I AM CURRENTLY UNDER CONGRESSIONAL INVESTIGATION FOR CORRUPTION Y☺ N☹
EXPLAIN WHY FOX NEWS IS FAIR AND BALANCED
BONUS POINTS FOR EVERY TIME YOU SAY "THE LIBERAL MEDIA"
REFERENCES INCLUDE AT LEAST ONE (1) UNBORN FETUS
NAME
ADDRESS
DAYTIME PHONE

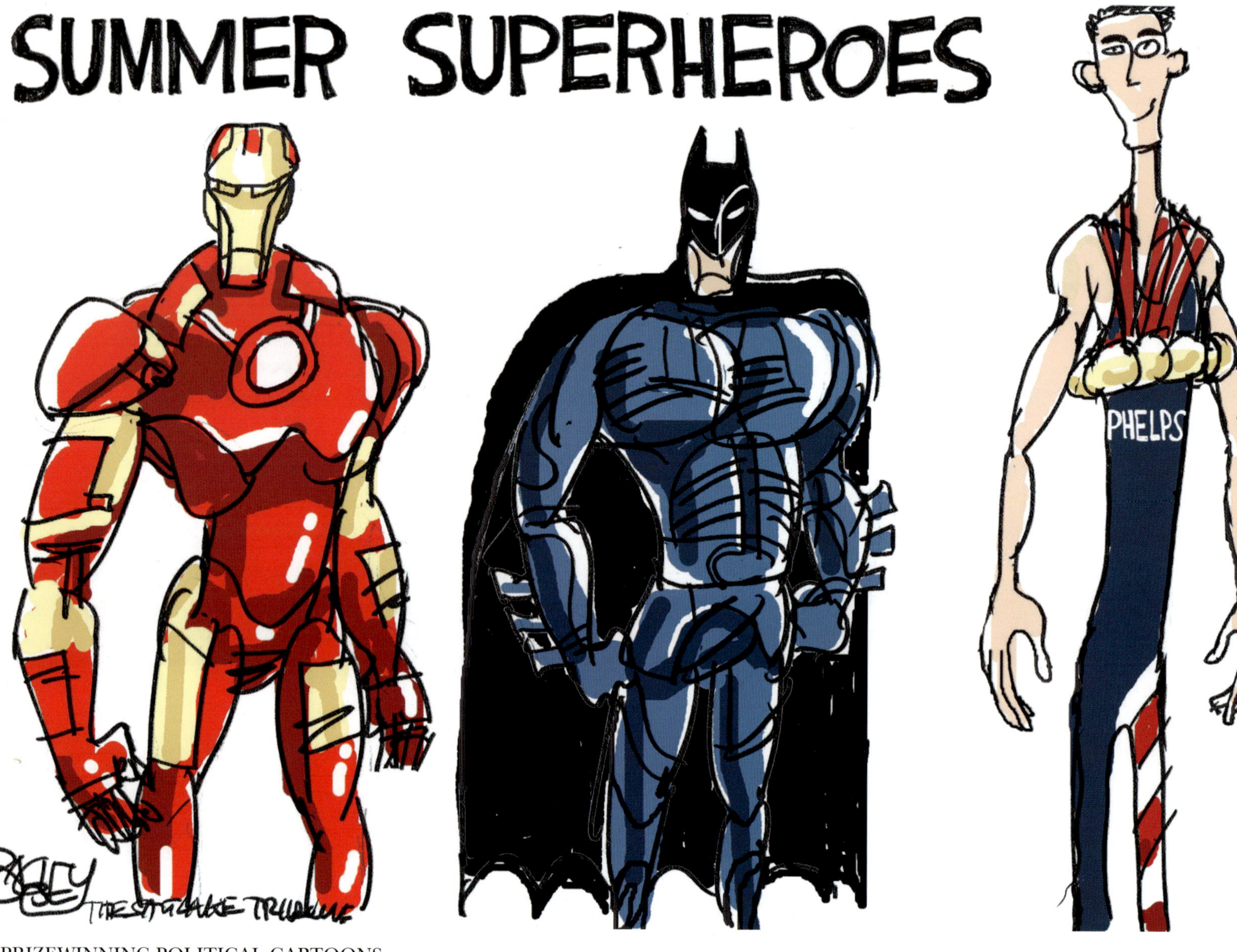
SUMMER SUPERHEROES
PHELPS

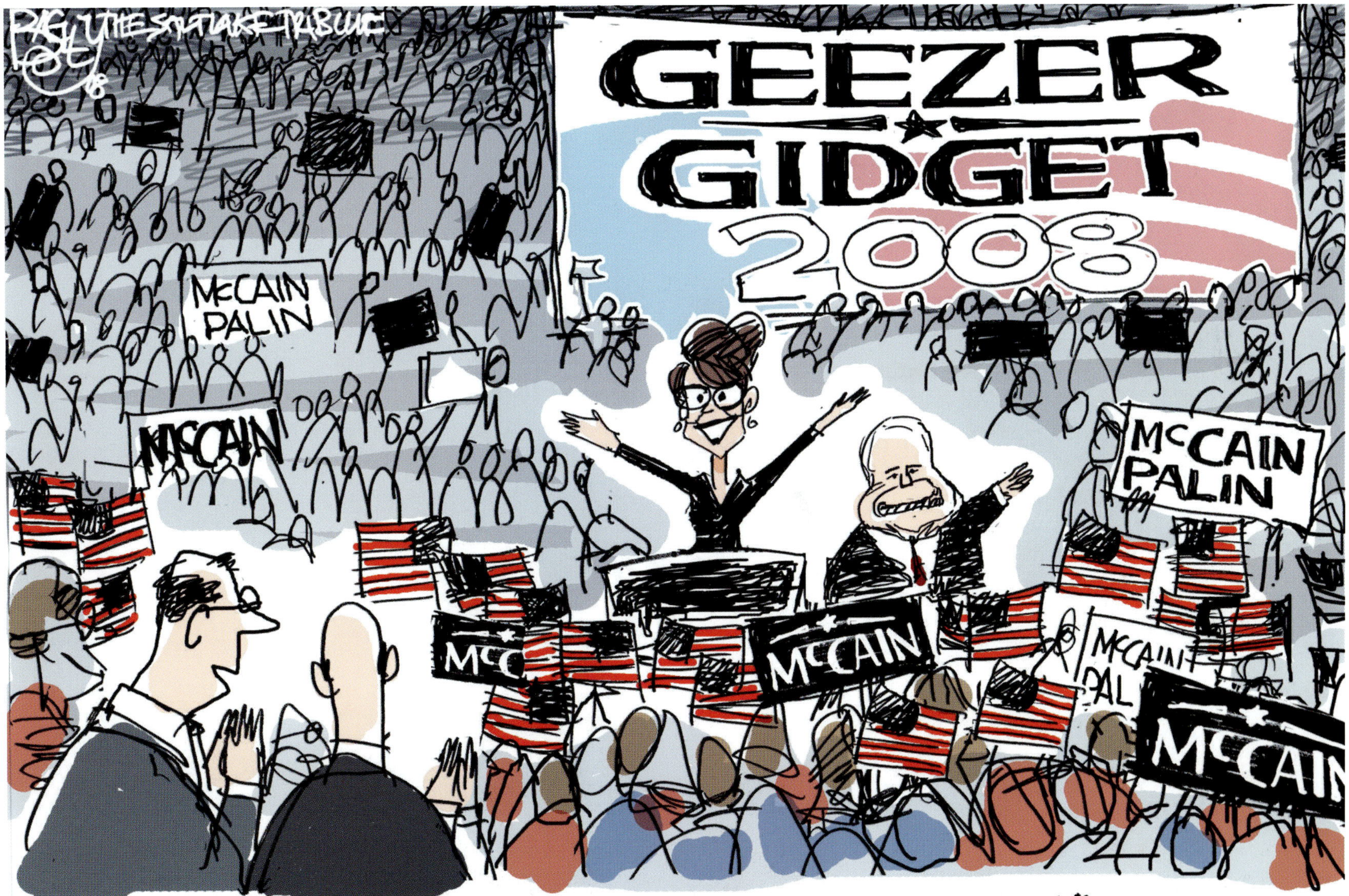

"SHE'S EVEN PRETTIER THAN ROMNEY."

GOV. PALIN, WOULD YOU MIND STEPPING OUT OF THE BOX TO ANSWER A FEW QUESTIONS?
NO PRESS BEYOND THIS POINT
PRESS
PRESS
NEXT ELITIST QUESTION.
Palin
V.P.
Palin
with her PITBULL
RUSH

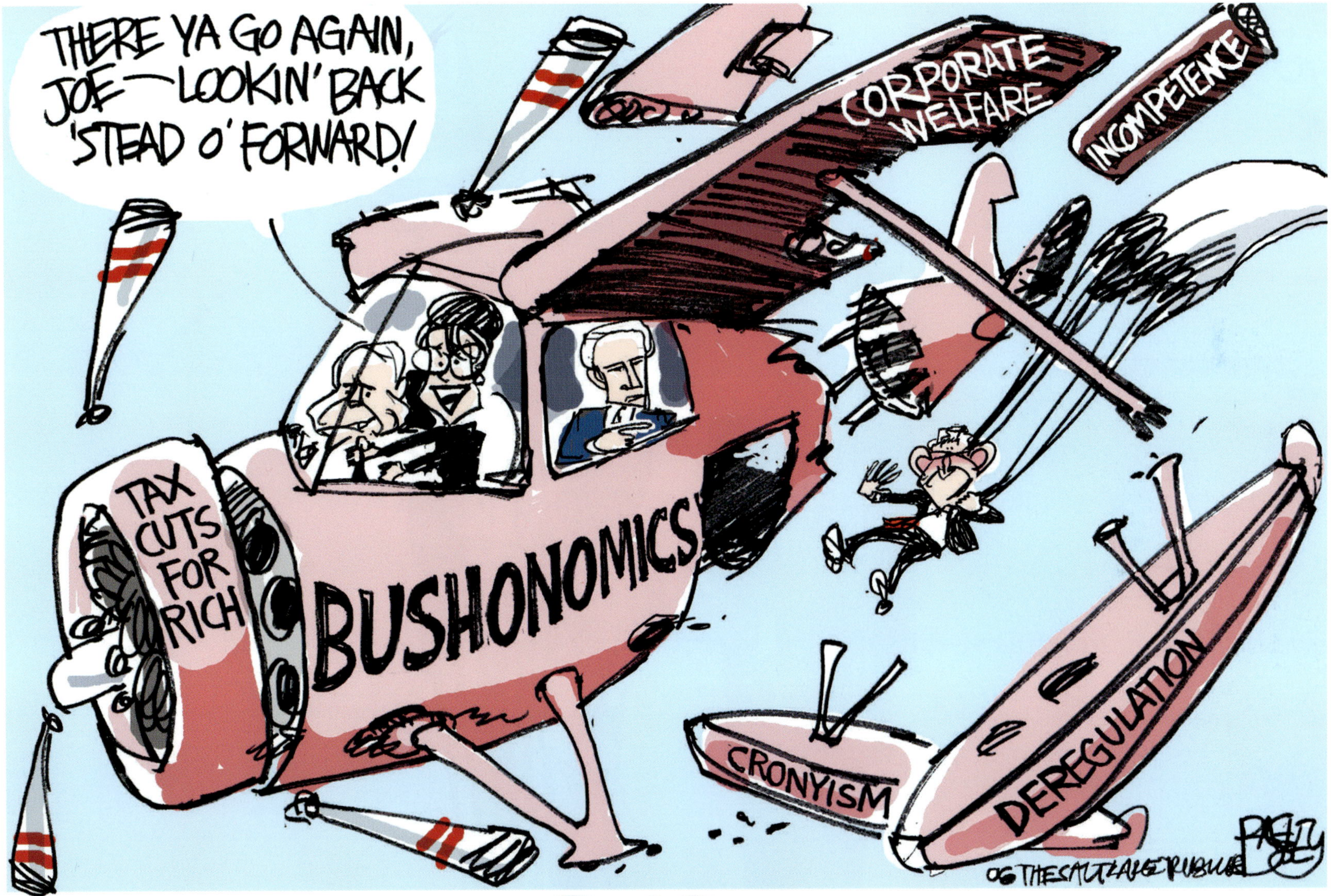
THERE YA GO AGAIN, JOE—LOOKIN' BACK 'STEAD O' FORWARD!
CORPORATE WELFARE
INCOMPETENCE
TAX CUTS FOR RICH
BUSHONOMICS
CRONYISM
DEREGULATION
'06 THE SALT LAKE TRIBUNE
BAGLEY

BUSH PILOT

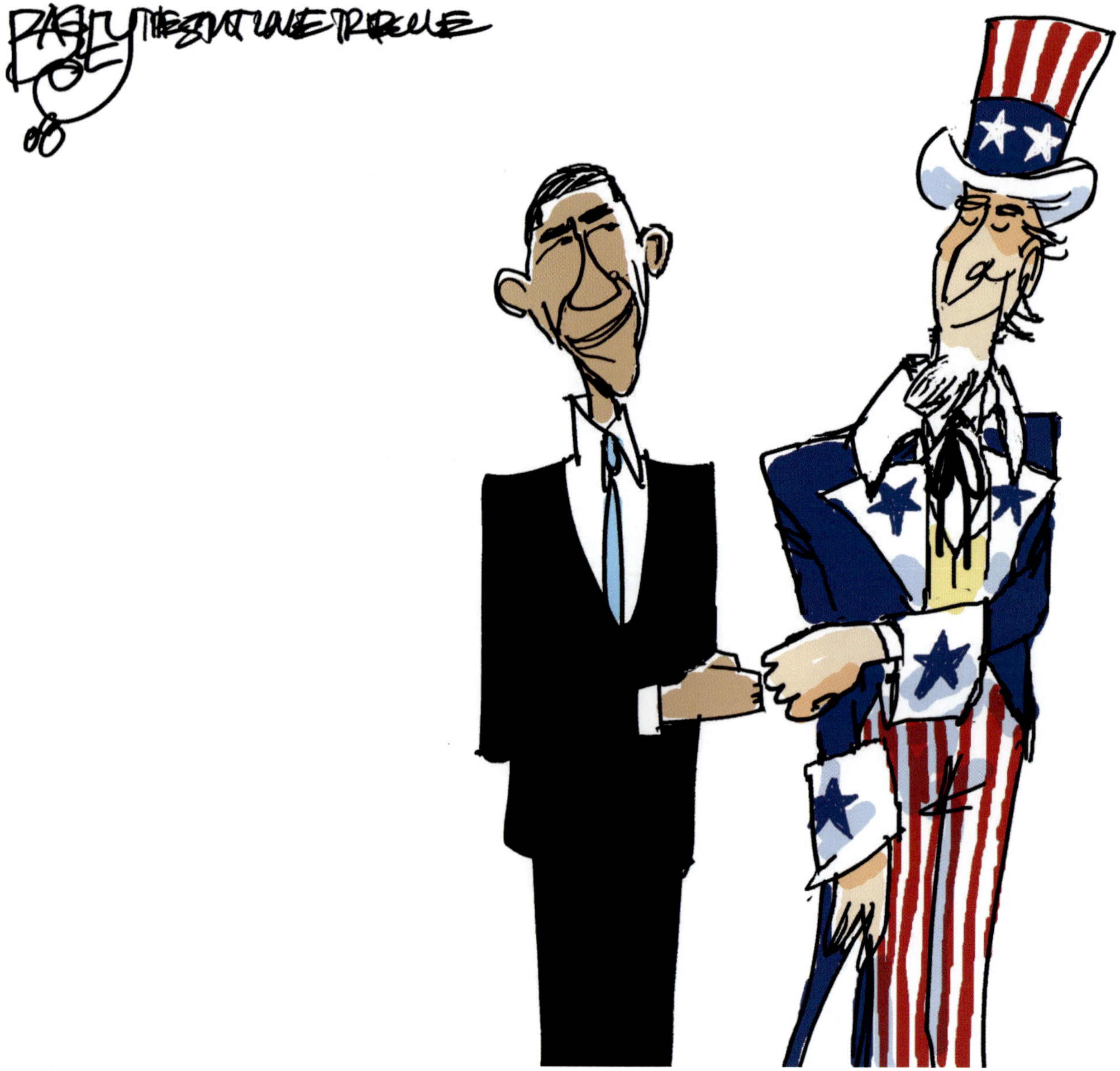

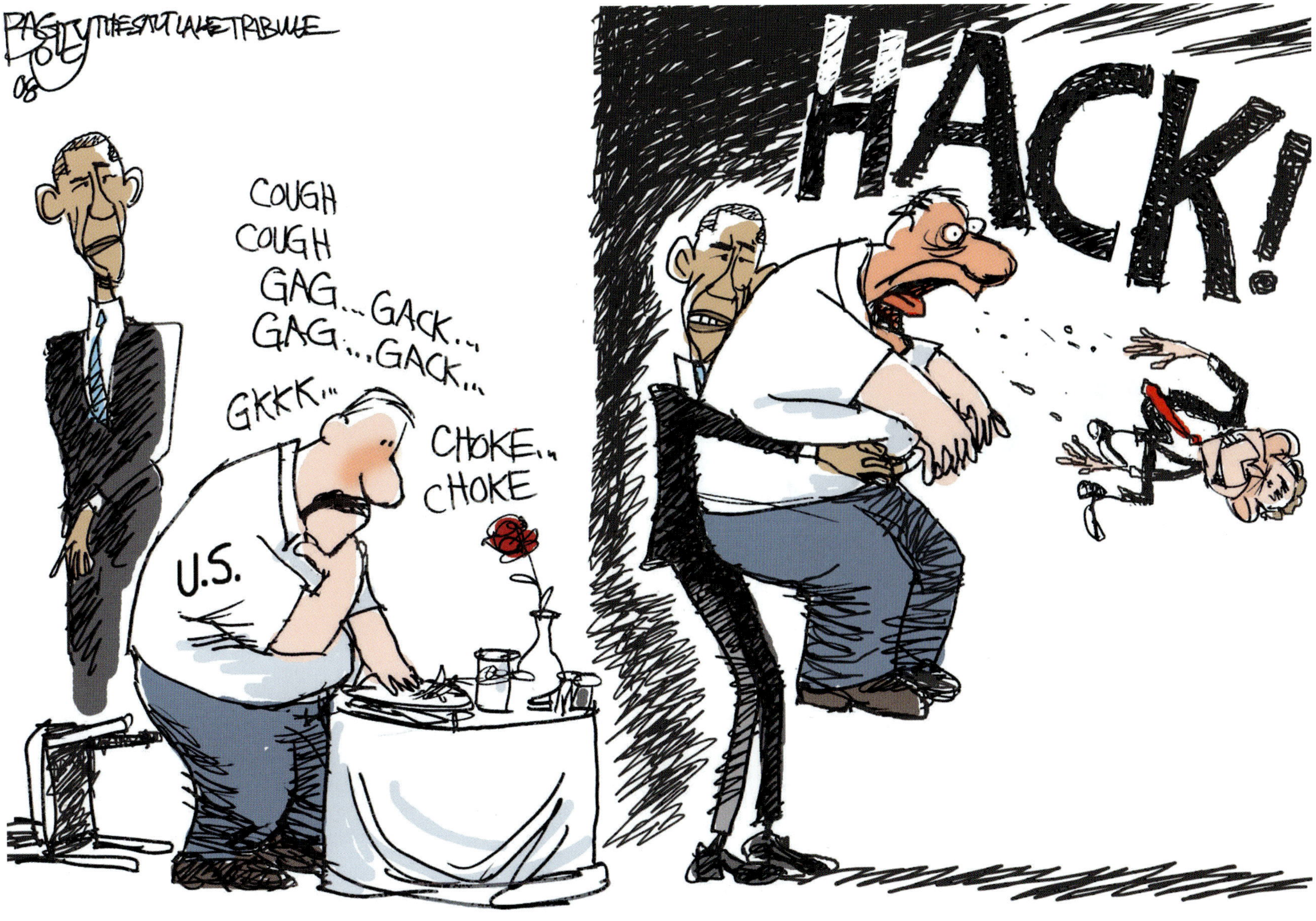
COUGH
COUGH
GAG...GACK...
GAG...GACK...
GKKK...
CHOKE..
CHOKE
U.S.
HACK!

IT WAS BUSH'S FAULT...
IT WAS McCAIN'S FAULT...
IT WAS PALIN'S FAULT...
SUCK
SUCK
SUCK
GUNS
GOD
GAYS
REAGAN-
OMICS

CLINGING

The Ranan Lurie Political Cartoon Award

Named after world-renowned political cartoonist Ranan Lurie, the Ranan Lurie Political Cartoon Award is sponsored by the United Nations Correspondent's Association as well as the United Nations Society of Writers and Artists.

Although this award is international in scope, it is of such prestige that it deserves to be included in this book.

In their desire to promote the highest standard of excellence in political cartoons depicting the spirit and principles of the United Nations, the UNCA, and the United Nations Society of Writers and Artists have established this annual political cartoon award given in the international field. The organizations named the award after political cartoonist Ranan Lurie as they find that his political cartoons epitomize the high standards they would like to see. The award was created in 2000 to recognize cartoons that "enhance, explain and help direct the spirit and principles of the UN."

2008 Ranan Lurie Political Cartoon Award Winner

Michael Kountouris—*Elephtheros Typos* (Athens)

Michael Kountouris was born in Rhodes, Greece, in 1960. He has worked as an editorial cartoonist since 1985, most recently with *Elephtheros Typos* in Athens, which unfortunately closed its doors this year.

A founding member and secretary of the Greek Cartoonists Association, Kountouris has been a regular member of the Athens Journalists Union since 1993.

He has an impressive lists of awards, including First Prize at the Eighth Biennial of Tehran (2007); Premio Internationale Scacchiera, Marostica, Italy (2005); Grand Prix CURUXA 2005, La Coruna, Spain; and First Prize Golden Hat, Knokke-Heist, Belgium (2003). As a children's book illustrator, Kountouris has also been awarded the Illustration Prize IBBY Greece 2002 and the First Design and Illustration Prize EBGE Greece 2006.

(Michael Kountouris's cartoons are syndicated in the U.S. by Cagle Cartoons, Inc. with reprints available at Politicalcartoons.com)

The Ranan Lurie Political Cartoon Award 221

2008 Ranan Lurie Political Cartoon Award—Second Place

Valeriu Kurtu

Valeriu Kurtu was born in 1956 in the town of Ungeny on the border of Moldova and Romania. He attended Kishinev Art College in Moscow before enrolling at the Gerasimov Institute of Cinematography's (VGIK) department of cartoons, from which he graduated in 1982. In 1986, Kurtu became a member of the Federation of Cartoonist Organisations (FECO), and in 1987, he graduated from Goskino as a script writer and film producer. He has since produced seven animated films.

During this time, Kurtu continued producing caricatures, publishing in leading satire magazines in Russia (*Krokodil*), Germany (*Eulenspiegel*), Romania (*Urzika*), and his homeland of Moldova (*Ciparusch*).

In 1994, he expanded his personal and artistic life and relocated to Berlin with his family, becoming the owner of an art gallery (Kurtu–Kunst) with his wife, who is also an accomplished artist in her own right. Kurtu continues to work successfully for a large number of newspapers and magazines. Throughout his career, he has been awarded more than a hundred prizes, medals, and diplomas from international exhibitions as well as caricaturist contests in many countries.

(GRATIS für alle WEB.DE-Nutzer: Die maxdome Movie-FLAT!
Jetzt freischalten unter http://movieflat.web.de)

The Ranan Lurie Political Cartoon Award 223

Index

Asmussen, Don, 73, 126
Bagley, Pat, 200
Beeler, Nate, 192
Bennett, Clay, 76
Breen, Steve, 12, 68, 96
Britt, Chris, 88
Hunter, Alexander, 133
Judge, Lee, 184

Kallaugher, Kevin, 105
Kountouris, Michael, 220
Kurtu, Valeriu, 222
Luckovich, Mike, 113, 187
Ohman, Jack, 168
Ramirez, Michael, 145, 189
Thompson, Mike, 54
Wuerker, Matt, 34